BOYS
BEHIND GLASS

JENNIFER SPERRY STEINORTH

PAINTINGS BY JENNY WALTON

Library of Congress Cataloging-in-Publication Data

Names: Steinorth, Jennifer Sperry, author. | Walton, Jenny, 1976-
  illustrator.
Title: Boys behind glass : poems / Jennifer Sperry Steinorth ; paintings by
  Jenny Walton.
Description: Huntsville : TRP: The University Press of SHSU, [2025] |
  Includes bibliographical references and index.
Identifiers: LCCN 2025023326 (print) | LCCN 2025023327 (ebook) | ISBN
  9781680034424 (trade paperback) | ISBN 9781680034431 (ebook)
Subjects: LCSH: Online dating--Poetry. | Men--Identity--Poetry. | Online
  identities--Pictorial works. | LCGFT: Poetry.
Classification: LCC PS3619.T476434 B69 2025 (print) | LCC PS3619.T476434
  (ebook) | DDC 811/.6--dc23/eng/20250519
LC record available at https://lccn.loc.gov/2025023326
LC ebook record available at https://lccn.loc.gov/2025023327

Printed and bound in the United States of America

First Edition Copyright: 2026

TRP: The University Press of SHSU
Huntsville, Texas 77341
texasreviewpress.org

BOYS
BEHIND GLASS

It's a really great story, Lois. But no one would ever believe it.

Clark Kent/Superman
The Underground World, 1943

What we see
                we see

        and seeing

                        is changing

Adrienne Rich, "Planetarium"

Will it last very long this way?
Till the end, my dear.

Sergei Diaghilev & Igor Stravinsky
on *Rite of Spring*

CONTENTS

I.

MIRROR MIRROR

LITTLE SONGS & LOOK BOOK

II.

THE SPECULUM

O

OKAY OKAY

[A FLOATING FRAME]

THE LOOK BOOK:

The images herein hail from *Match/Enemy*, a series of over 200 watercolor "portraits" of men matched to the artist via the online dating service **OKCupid** between 2014 & 2016. The numeric titles come from algorithmic calculations based on user response to questions in the app, the first number indicating percentage of compatibility (Match) & the second, incompatibility (Enemy). The Enemy **algorithm**, published to encourage oppositional attraction, has since been discontinued.

Match/Enemy focuses on a subset of men who have chosen to obscure, alter, or hide their facial features in their public facing profile picture, a liberty no longer allowed on many such apps. By choosing to replicate these **portraits** the artist explores the ideas of altered & adopted personas within social media and contemporary portraiture.

The works on paper are 9 x 12", approximately 4 times the size of the images as displayed on the artist's iPhone screen. On each painting the artist spent two to three hours, about the time one might take on a first date.

THE LITTLE SONGS:

Drawing from traditions of **sonnet portraiture**, these little songs **surveil** the mind of a single woman on a dating website looking for love via hetero**sexual romance**. While the 200+ paintings of *Match/Enemy* form a composite portrait of the artist, the 50 portraits herein, chosen by the poet, distort that reflection. The woman through whom we consider the men is a fiction, no relation to the artist. If anything the poems are informed by the poet's obsessions w/**gaze**, performance, intimacy & aversion & by the better & worser of 25 years of **marriage**.

THE SPECULUM:

Sticky notes & bank notes. Doctor's notes & whole notes. Notes of plum & honeysuckle. High, auxiliary, side notes. Personal drawn & quarter notes. Dissent decrees. **Hero** ancestries. A scrambled backward trajectory. Liner notes. Promissory notes. A travel log. Margin calls. Mortgage notes. A bulletin board. A murder board. Boogie board. Foot notes & toenails. Cheat **codes** & ransom notes. *The End* is Not the End notes. A patchwork map. A flash mob. Haystacks. Graveyard. Tales from the **crypto**grapher's diary. Crib notes. Jumping off a cliff notes. Wrong notes. Key notes. Blue notes. Death notes. A calculus of love notes tucked in a Converse™ shoebox of a **Gen X** poet w/50 half-smoked candles.

TABLE[1] OF IMPATIENCE

Reader, I see you. On the one hand, a Look Book is all well & good—& who can resist a Little Song (that takes almost no time at all) but what of the bit named for a medical instrument oft unpleasant…How do I read this you ask? Your author is not unsympathetic. Ever try a ***Choose Your Own Adventure***™? You can get w/ this or you can get w/ that.[2] It's your read, do what you wanna do. Still haven't found what you're looking for? I got you. You might…

One.   Begin at the beginning.[3] When you reach the end, stop.[4]

Two.   Begin at the beginning. When you hit the index, circle back, ad infinitum. It's a trap! Go for a walk. Phone a friend.

Three.   Find a picture on which you would swipe left/swipe right. Hang out. Read its companion. Locate its savory/unsavory associates in the Speculum. *See* artist's notes.[5] **Double** back to the **portraits. Repeat.**

Four.   Find a page in the Speculum that draws you. Let it draw you. Now you have your own **portrait!**

Five.   Begin at the end w/the Origin Story. Work backwards.

Six.   Hunt the index for your fav words, artists, **villains, kings,** subjects. Track them & their associates. Spar w/ their **portraits.** *See* note regarding satisfaction.

Seven.   Open at random. Let the wind take you.

Eight.   Stick it under your pillow. Sweet **dreams.**

---

1   *See also* turn tables*, banquet tables, table rapping,** bistro tables, picnic tables, tables stacked against, table salt, table talk, periodic table, flipping over tables, cards on the table, water table, ping pong table, coffee table book, dancing on tables, money under the table, drunk under the table, feet under the table, table manners, the tables have turned, table wine, table knife, time table, night table, tip the tables, bring to the table, seat at the table, drawing table, drafting table, operating table, dressing table, table it, table dance, set the table, pool table, actuarial table, **communion** table, knights of the round***, behold the **Lord's** table.

2   *See* Black Sheep, "The Choice is Yours," *A **Wolf** in Sheep's Clothing,* 1991.

3   Of the book. But also, every pairing is a beginning. Also, other beginnings occur at the end/late middle/part way in.

4   But what about the footnotes wormholing the endnotes? & the toenails snagging the footnotes? What order do I read them? Can I skip it? Can you kick it? Reader, there will not be a test. And while it is customary in the land & time of this author to read words on a page, left to right, top to bottom, the author knows some folks only eat the muffin tops.****

5   Notes to **sonnets** & **portraits** may not result in satisfaction. Check the internet. Check your head.

---

* E.g. Along w/**Black Sheep** here spins 1969 Isley Brothers, 1987 U2, 1992 Beasties & 1990 **Tribe Called Quest.**
** Communing w/the dead.
*** *See also* **Camelot**
**** But the author should probably mention: in a **king** cake, the prize always sinks to the bottom.

I.

MIRROR

MIRROR

LITTLE SONGS

& LOOK BOOK

A SPELL FOR ALGORHYTHMIX

O Cupid sweet bequeath to me some par
allel beauty   yield dopplegangs of mind
to infinity mirror mine   that we may harm
onize & (you take cream?) homogenize
(for mouthfeel) similarly prime behinds
let level be the mass & frequency
of take-home pay & cataclysmic lies
no question who be nanny   who be fam
Or! if incongruent Cupid let me
level up! let he who'd spare no glance
volte-face & wanton plunge...

                        is not (is knot)
the song she means to sing is not (is naught)
the ring she wants to belle is not the hell
she penny wished & backward cast

                     (& casting

                        starward
                  tripped
                    & fell)

                into the well

TORSO OF A MAN IN PLAID

the Queen of Hearts says *off with their heads* but guillotined

suitors make this lass lonely or worse   *aware*
has she shut herself in a room of one-way mirrors?

her mind observes her face her scowl troubles
her mind she clocks herself outside herself

even w/ closed eyes but can they? why not face
what she would face should they meet face-to-face

should either ever propose?   no one escapes
even in plaid sleeves rolled   buttons done up

save for the throat   the foe in the looking glass
though he's staged his play before an obscure hedge

she knows   she *knows!*   of what he is afraid
plain as the nonchalance of his bearded frame

if there were a face to face   would it turn away?

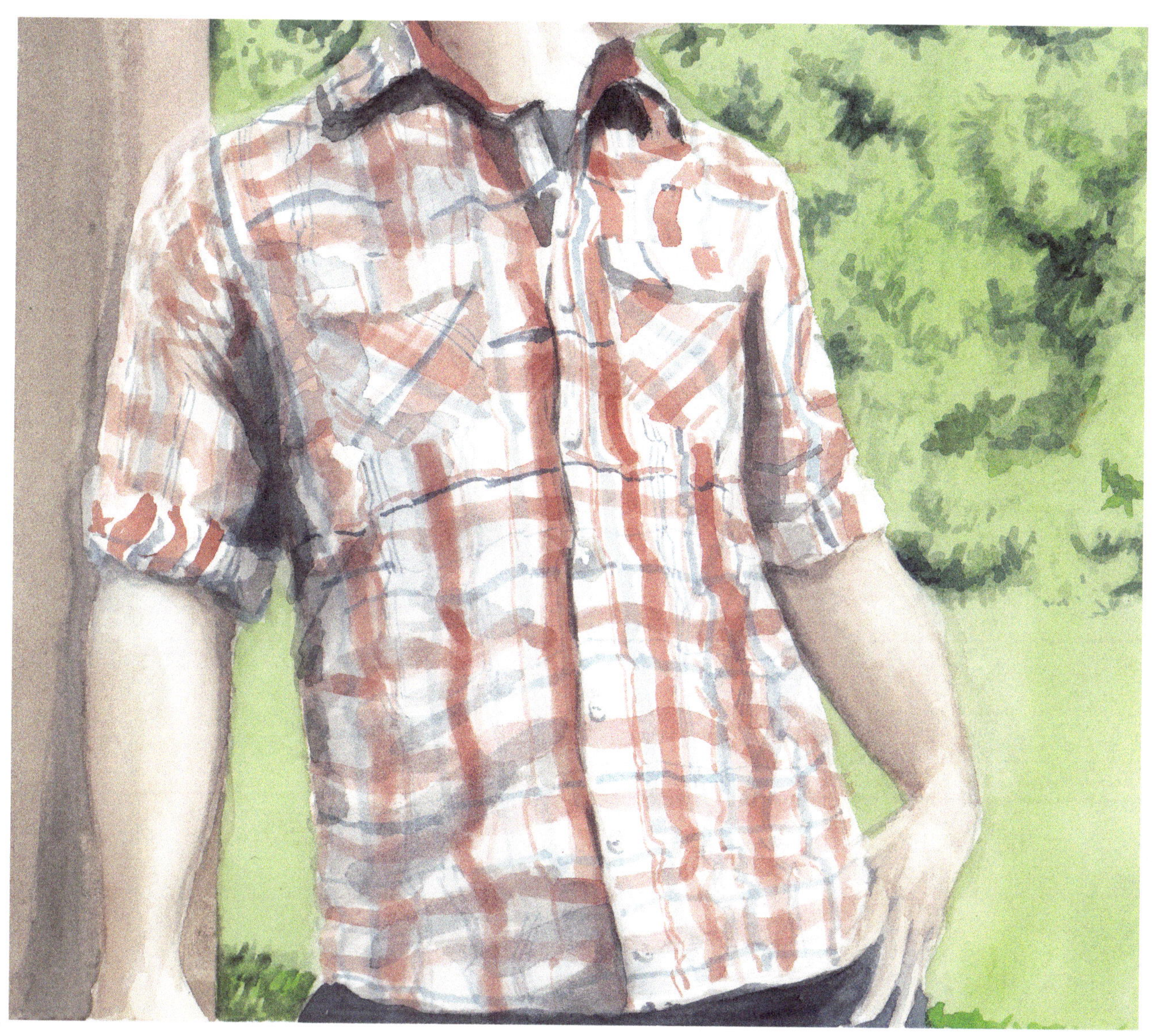

match/enemy   97/5

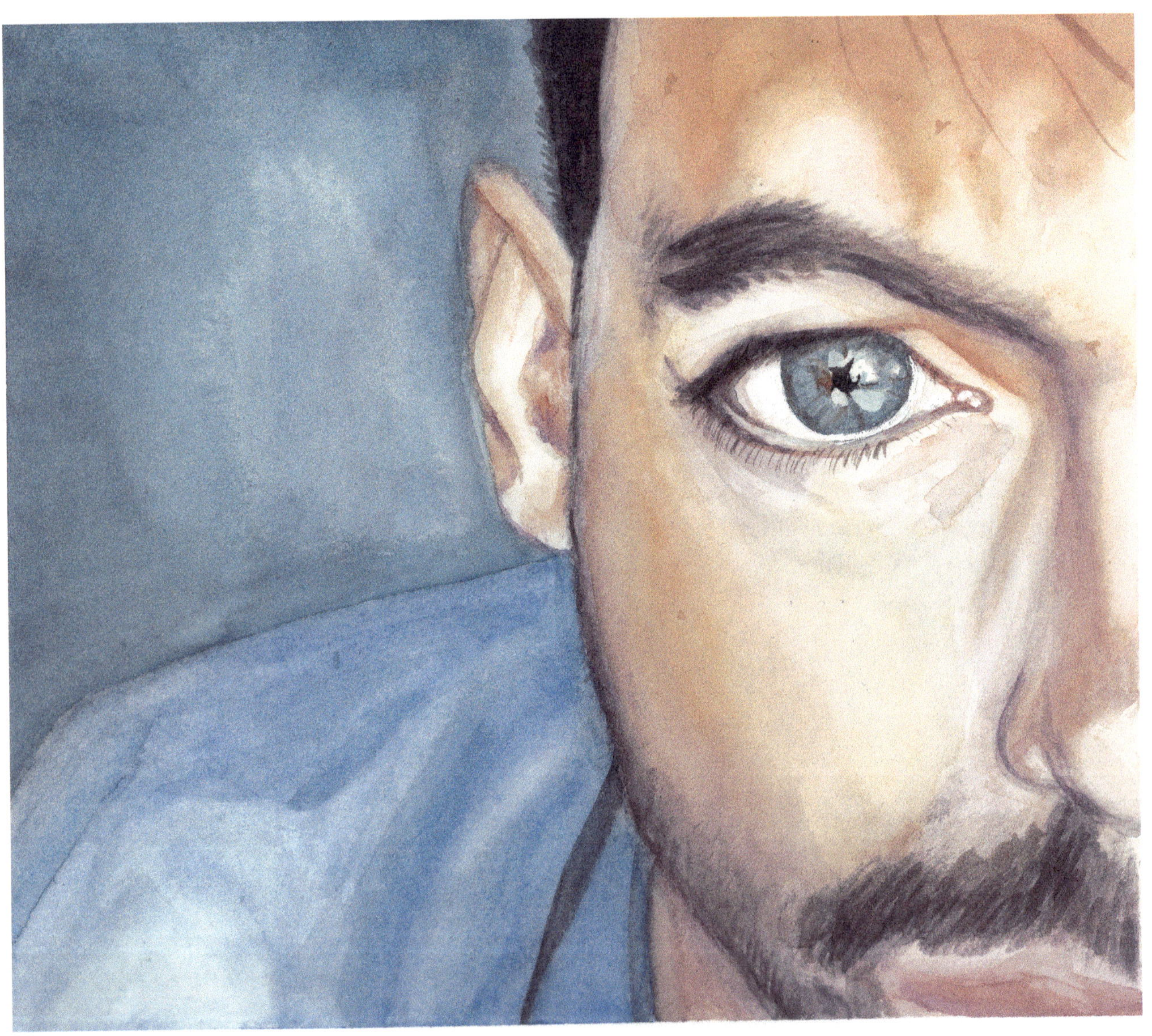

match/enemy

58/31

OK WOUNDED

half a face is better than no face
unless he's Two Face/d   & this side's beautiful

the star of a mind digesting too many shades
of blue   reduced to a scoreboard who

wouldn't occlude the burn sites   smite
of hydrochloric acid   cicatrix of the blast

from which he could not save his bae   what if
all love required was not turning away

she's practiced loving the broken for example herself
but kiss too close to wounds & someone leaves

she's seen it before   no stranger to sorrow
her mother left her a rent-controlled studio

in midtown   but who wants to coagulate
solo tomorrow & tomorrow & tomorrow...

DON'T LOOK DOWN

this one wears a mask to protect his eyes

some mountains are like scissors— that sharp

w/ proper protection anyone can face
a 35mm lens
anyone can fall in love w/ a double

black diamond   but maybe he wants more
than conquest   near death   the thin un
populated air

          so what if she won't ski?

or dive

          or surf
                    maybe what scares him most
is holding still   optic wells   being tethered
to a person in pain   germs   sure is pretty
up there where he chooses to stop & reflect
on what his goggles deflect   so much light
versus the dark knotty pine   of the lodge

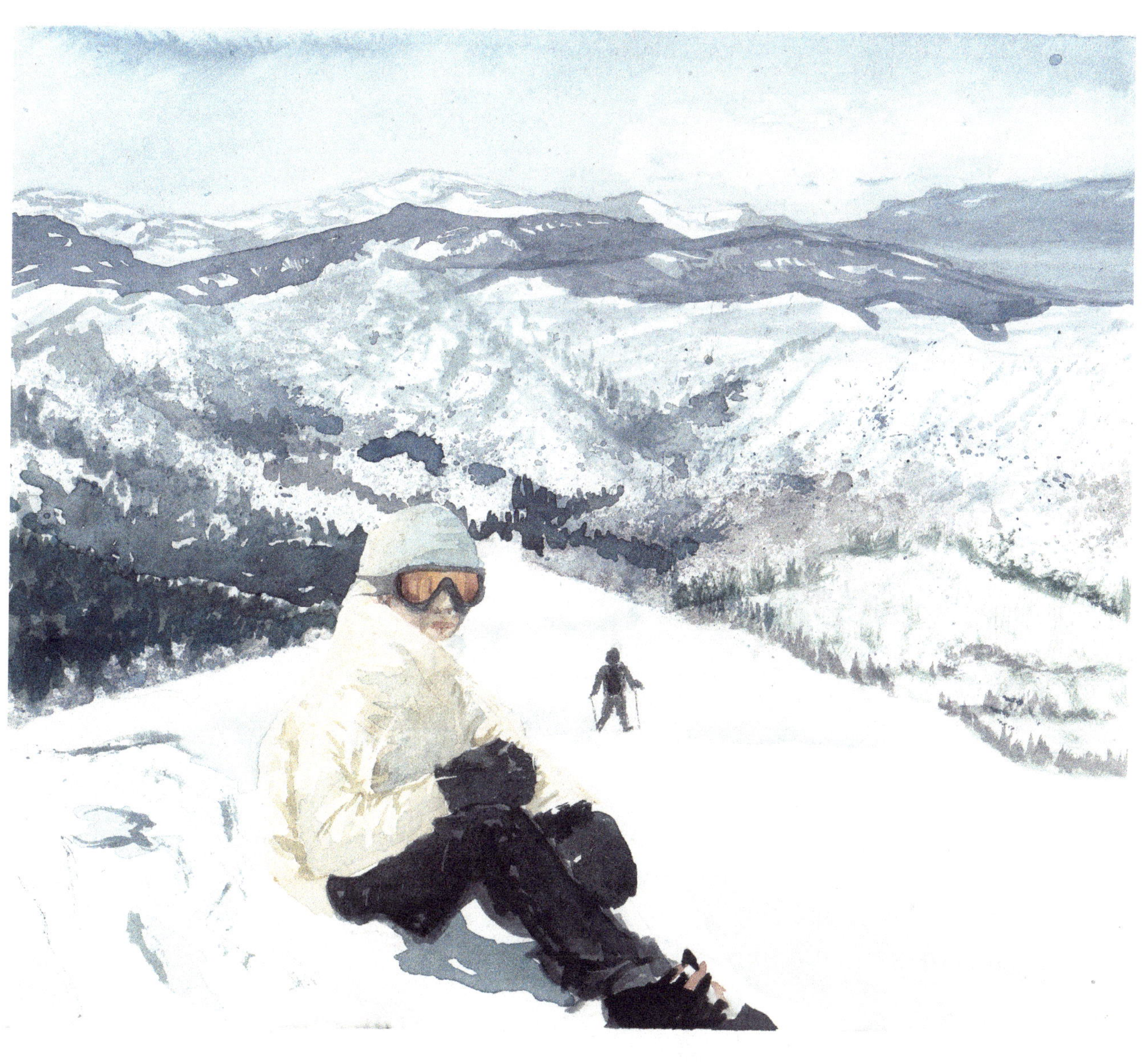

match/enemy

92/0

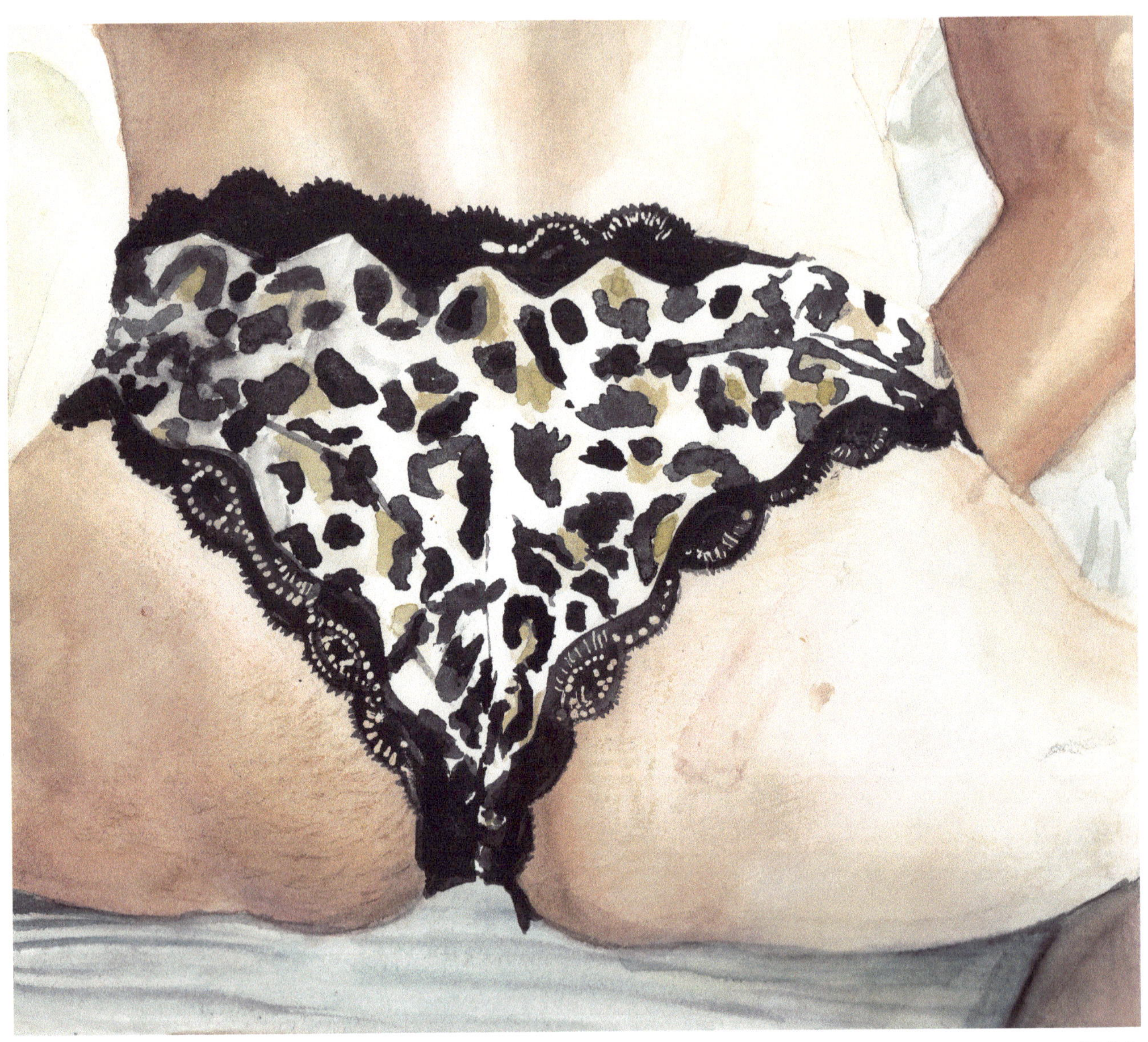

match/enemy   47/22

THERE THERE

now here's an ass   or perhaps a prix fixe meal
might as well offer a money back guarantee
but why define— by quartered thigh   poached
cheek   leopard lace— her O face?

she supposes from the backside focus
he wishes both to affront *and* oblige
wants her to believe he knows himself
she's not buying it   no appetizer   entrée   no

dessert   she's shuffling through half-drawn
drawers to get him dressed   fishing for socks
& shoes under the bed   kisses his forehead

asks after his mother   locates peanut butter
bread   reads him *White Fang* till he's snoring
in her lap   slips out the door between breaths

OK POKER FACE

what kind of player shows their cards? the kind
that knows nobody wins? (at cards) aces
to ashes luck to dust   broadcasting *what?*
he's hot stuff? out of luck? got money to burn?
that gambling's a sin? what begins in diamonds ends
in spades? perhaps he prefers craps   wants
to stop drop & roll   according to Hoyle
nothing beats four of a kind   a deadbeat dad

taught her that   taught her to read the room
faces palms ran one hell of a con   like all
these portraits   a house of cards   a house on fire
still   way back in the non-digital age
childhood in flames   after the cat it was their crap
photographs she'd have run back in to save

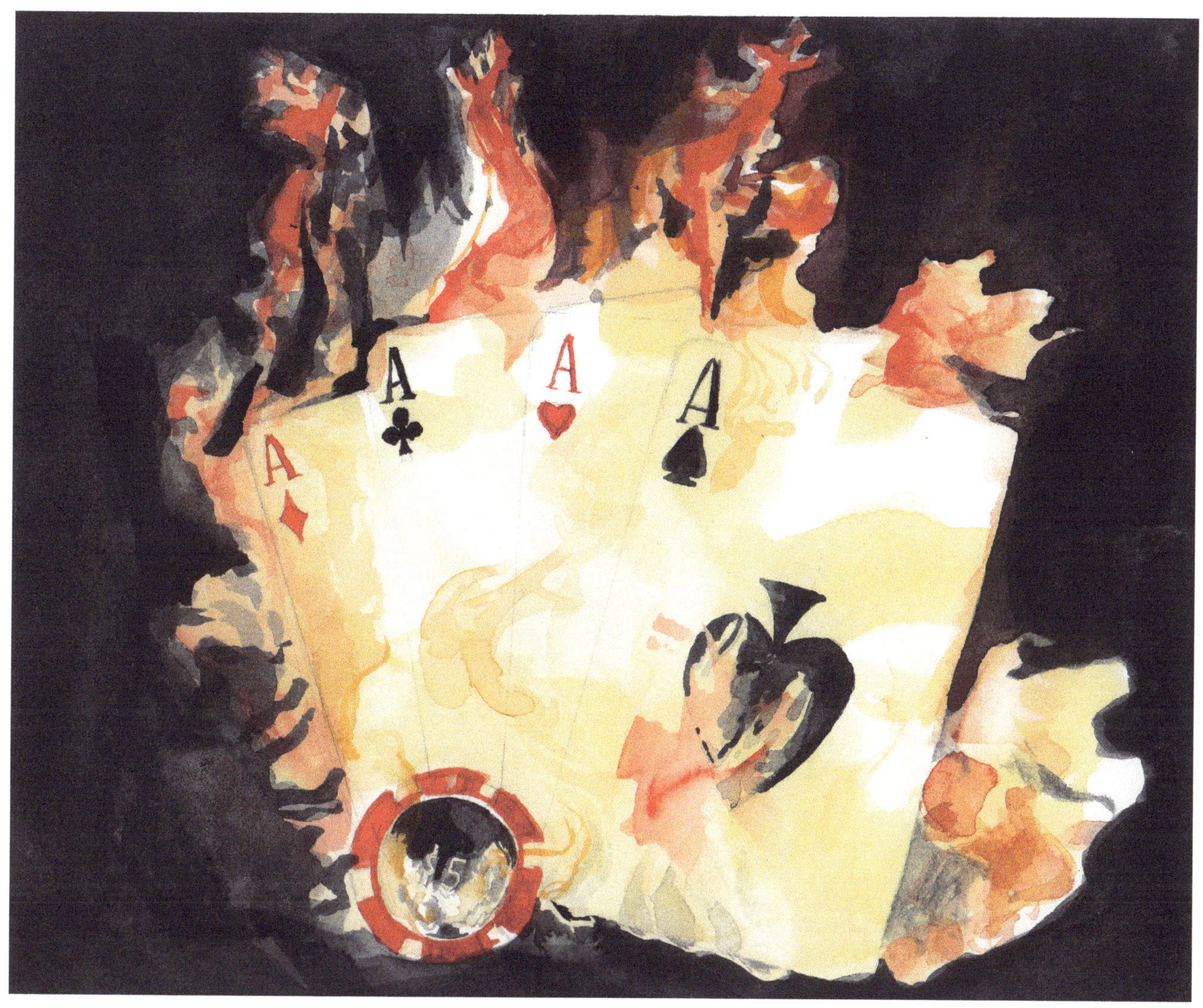

match/enemy

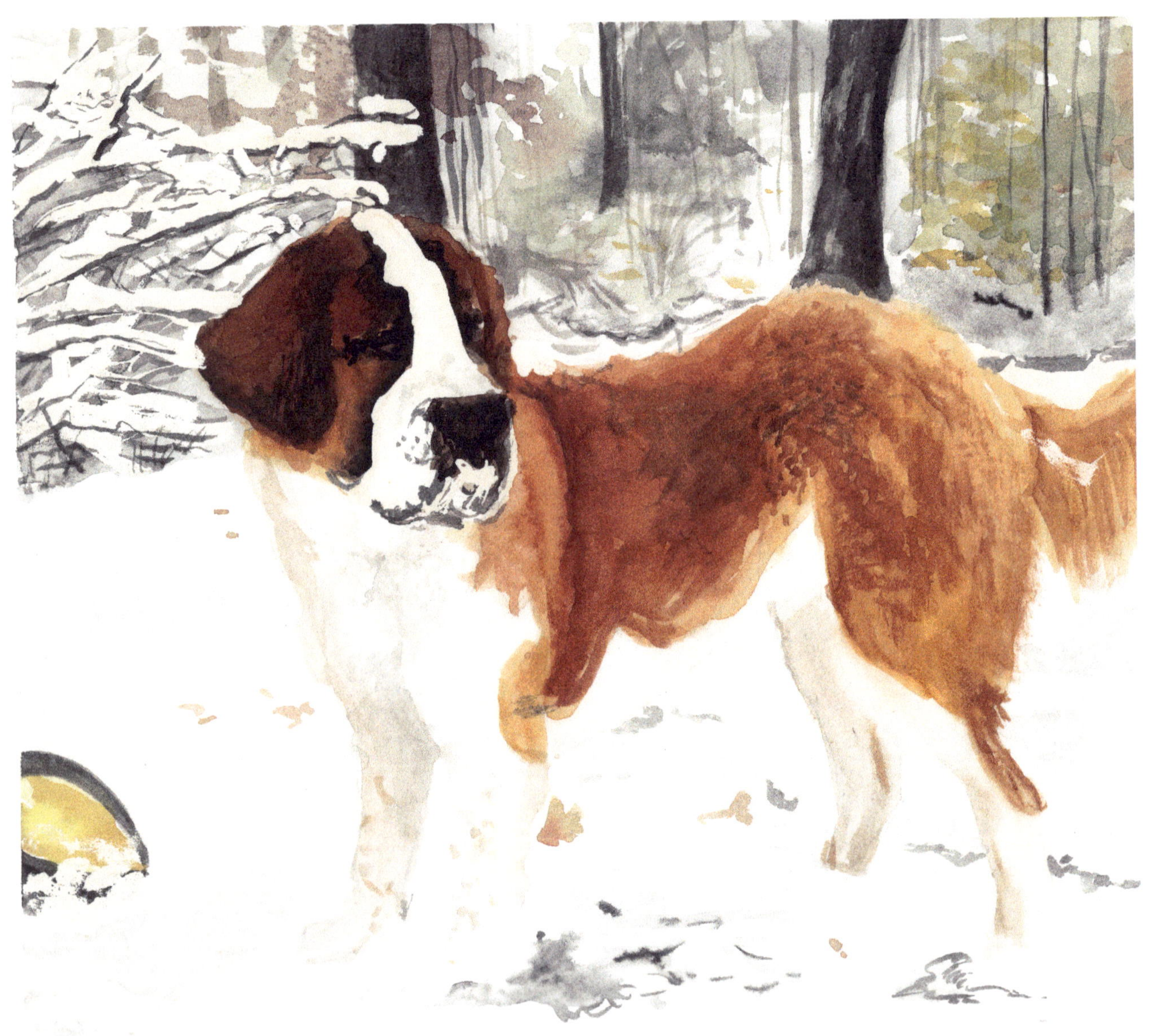

match/enemy

EASY BOY/GOOD KITTY

obedience training   panting   neediness   slobber
whether of dogs or saints she tends to think
why bother   though that muzzle in her lap & tugs
from a *medicinal* flask sound nice   particularly
given this arctic fallout so late in the season
what happened to Spring   she'd dreamed of the beach
thought she'd shave   now she wants nothing but blankets
& Doris Day   has no energy to argue the merits
of cats   or her distaste for getting "saved"
maybe she doesn't want anything to change
let's face it   a dog who's a saint is leagues better
than a saint who's a dog but far less common   so the fridge
is bare & the car snowbanked   no problem
she knows how to live on anchovies & ramen

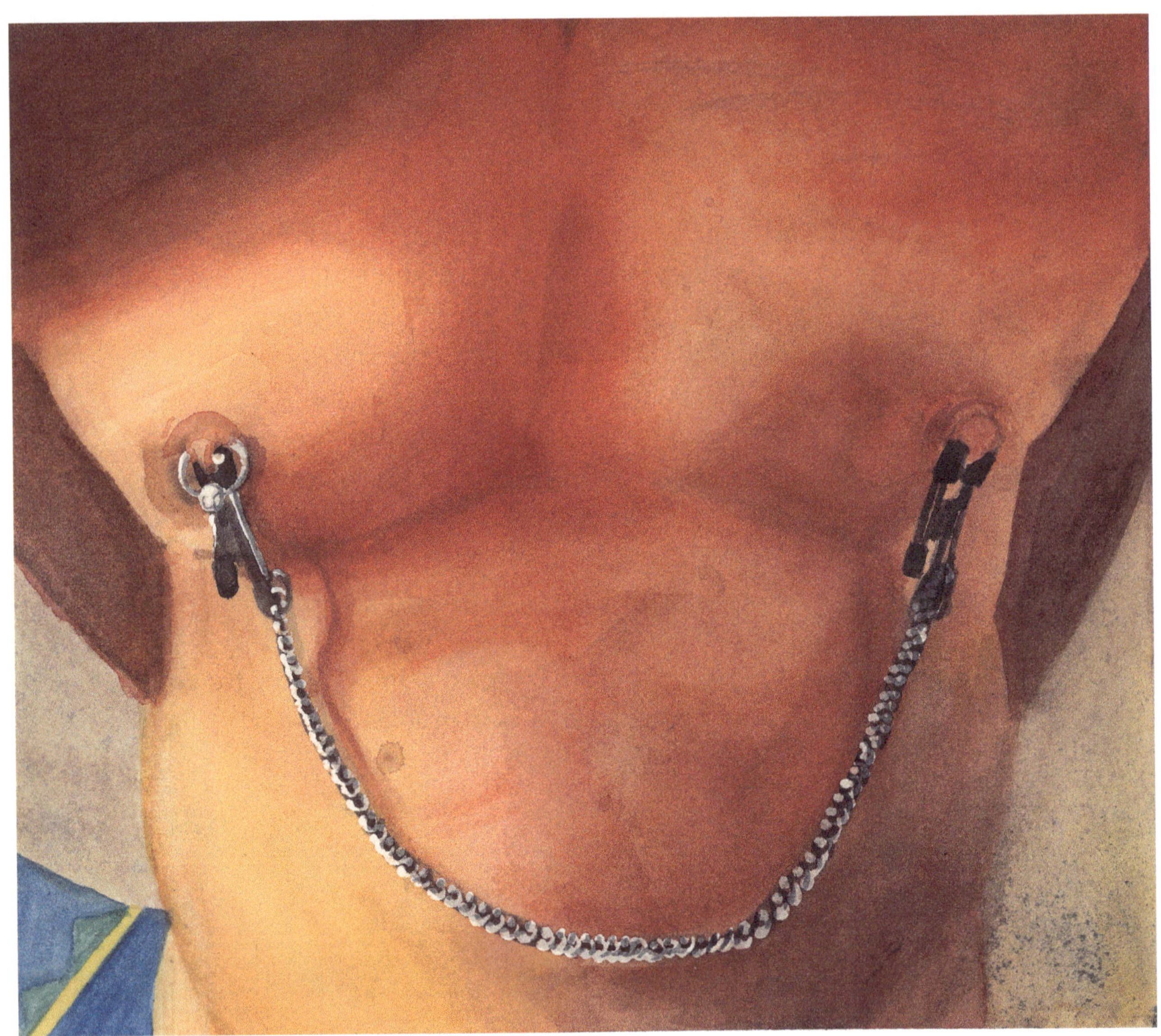

DOUBLE DOWN

one means to serve   the other   to service   one
w/ a cast iron handle   the other w/ hands
clasped politely behind his back   (bonus!
the stainless alloy swing slung in front!)
she'd like a grip of either off screen
was never precious about her metals   loves
iron's heft   the surgery of steel & oh

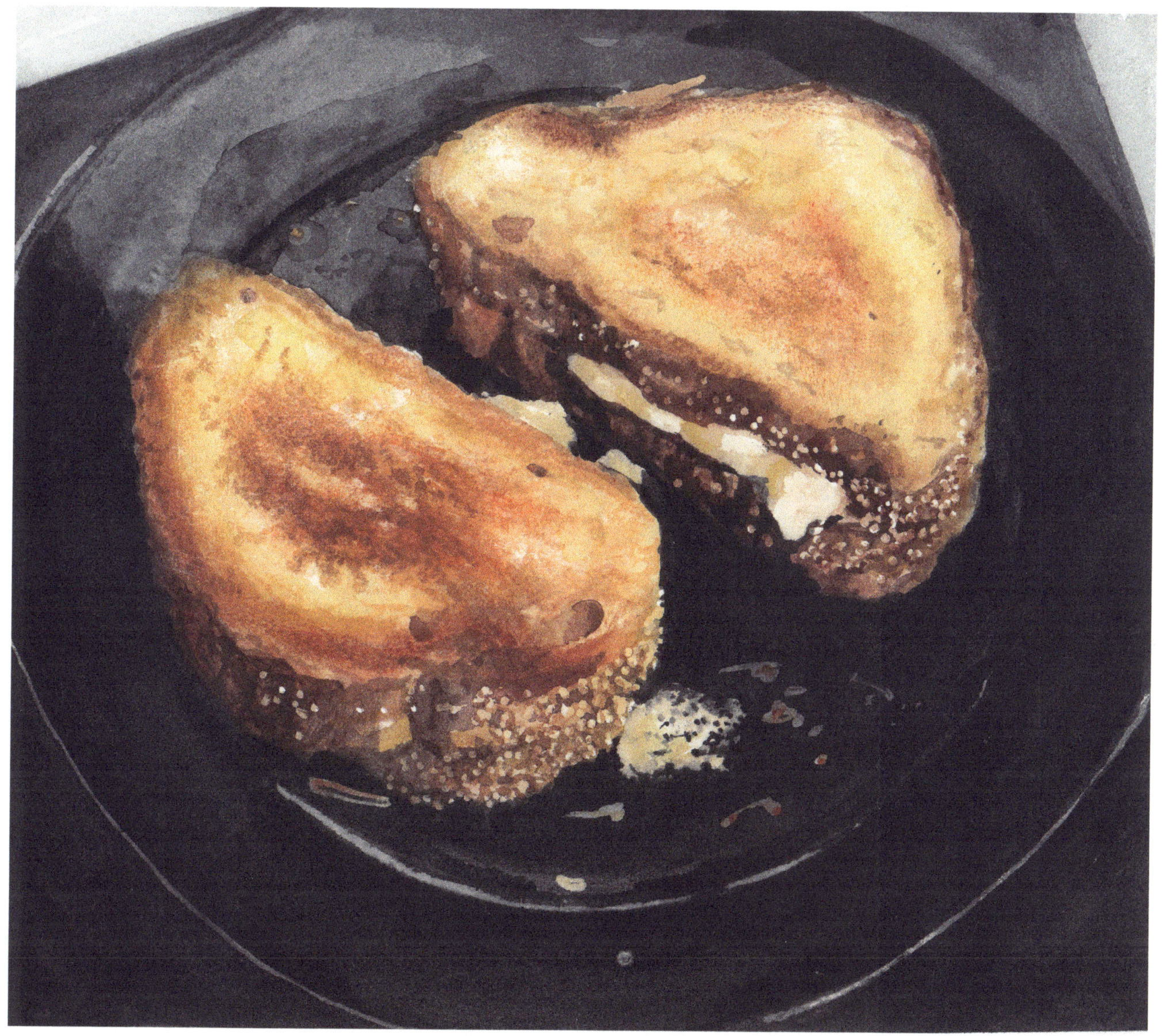

the implications of symmetry   *you could pierce
yours too   make* me *your supper* doubling both
form & content/ment   so much cheese! oh
she'd whip him up some eggs   saltlick his tum
that skillet—HOT! however will she choose?
nipple to nipple or melt to melt? would
consuming both at once be overkill?

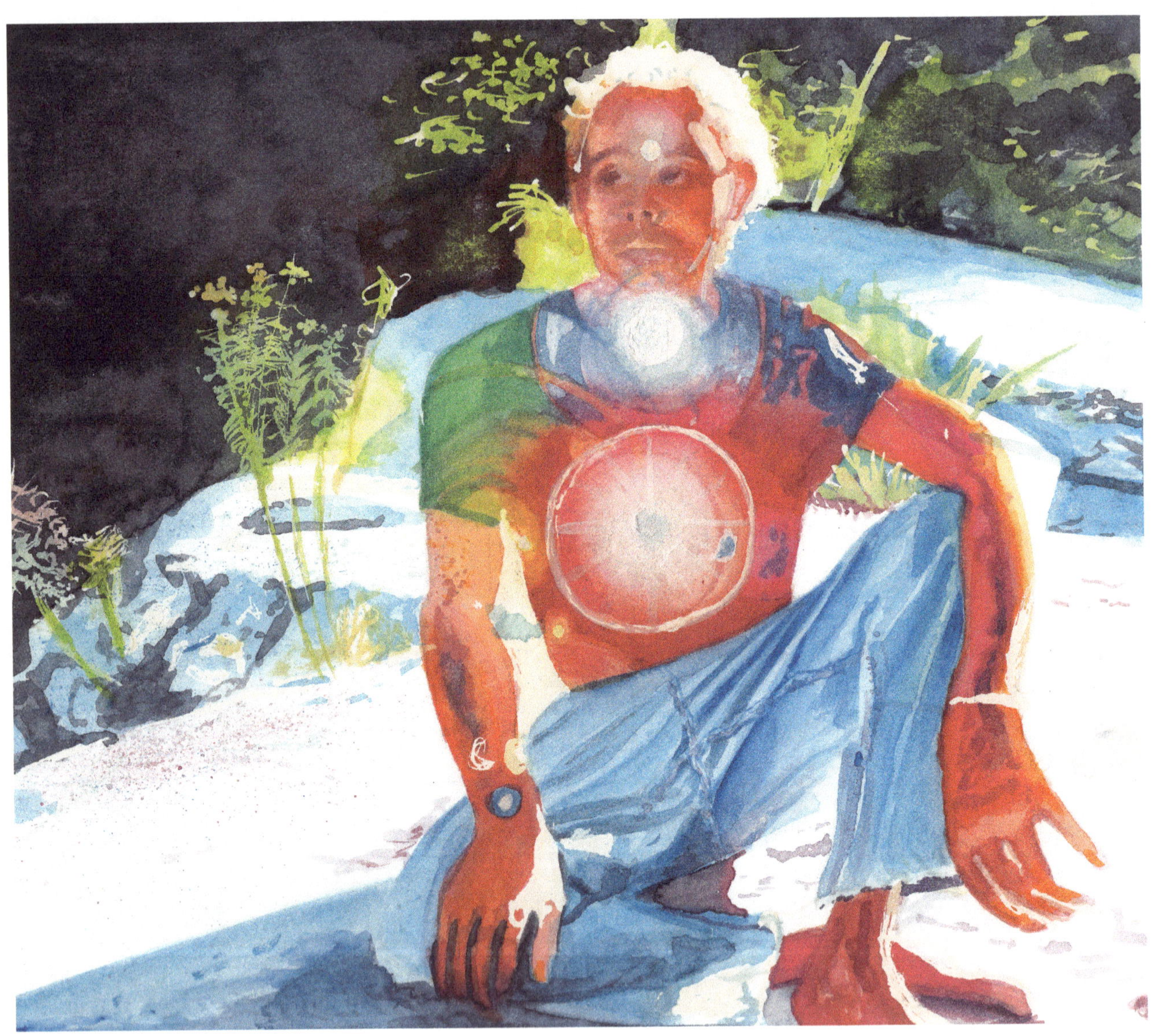

match/enemy

OK BUDDHA

this one wants to be the bodhisattva

has made of his body a light to ease suffering

does love require suffering?   is suffering love?

maybe he just wants someone to look at him

& see stars   better than being blinded by the dark?

at least she can see his eyes   all three

& she wouldn't mind his dietary restrictions

much   she just wouldn't mind   but he seems

less enlightened than bored   another mask?

there's got to be a zipper in the back   inside

a litter of puppies   squirrels   a pair of koi?

maybe love is best ruled by serenity's child

but she can't help wondering what's been lost

each time she comes across so blank a canvas

OK *ASTRONAUT?*

no *diver*   same suit   different rude abyss
but *she* longs to visit neither outer space
nor lower depths   her inner depths are rough
enough   some nights you don't come back from
even w/ air to spare   still   she appreciates
his willingness to *go there*   the viscera
of that first abyss   trouble is   the suits aren't made
for two   they couldn't screw   or even kiss   plus
she's claustrophobic   even sleeping bags
make her panic   in planes she needs the shades
drawn up to see beyond her little room
is she doomed?   if she can't manage being sealed
submerged & assailed by gloom   how can she be
the guardian of her dearly beloved's solitude?

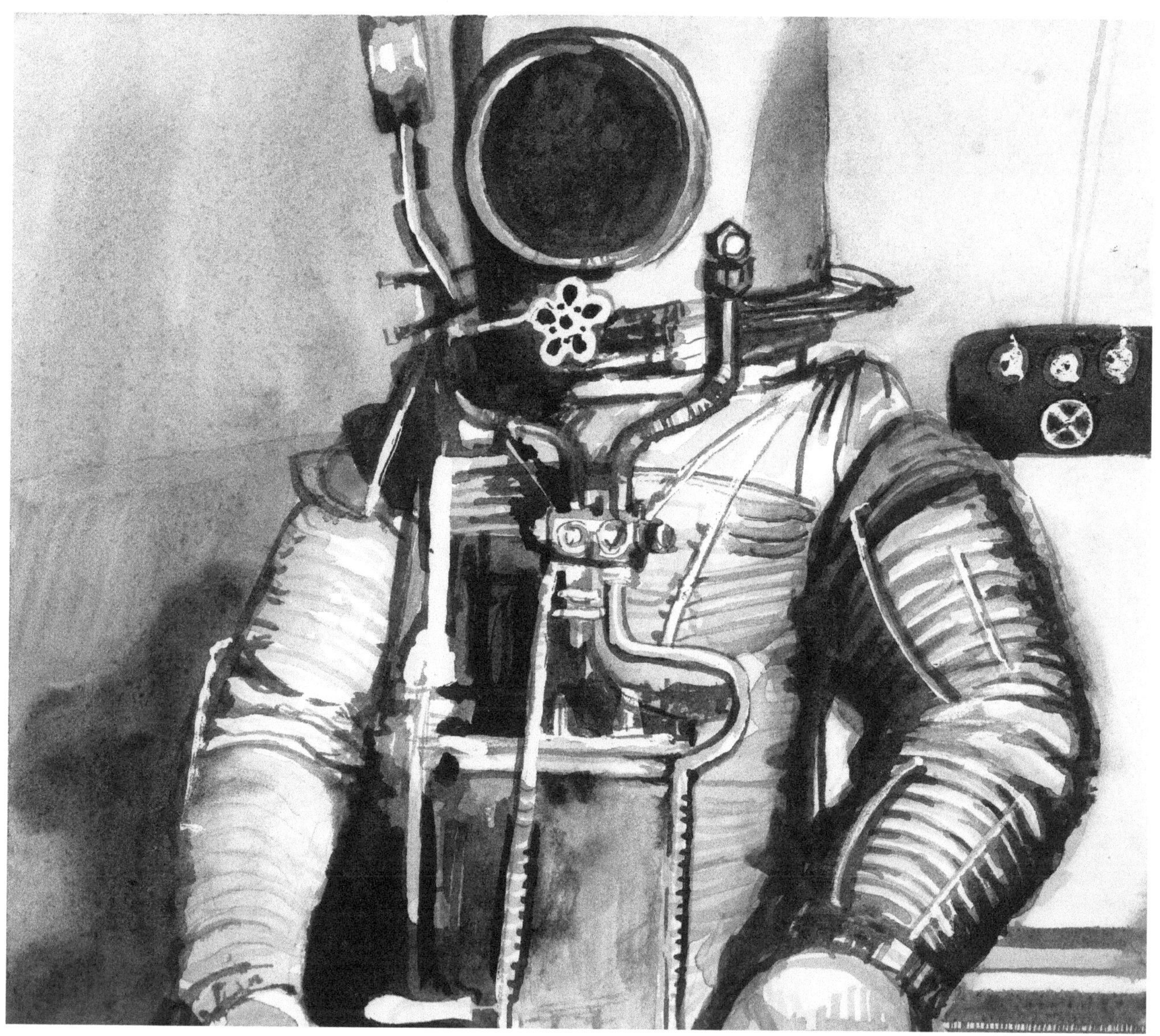

match/enemy

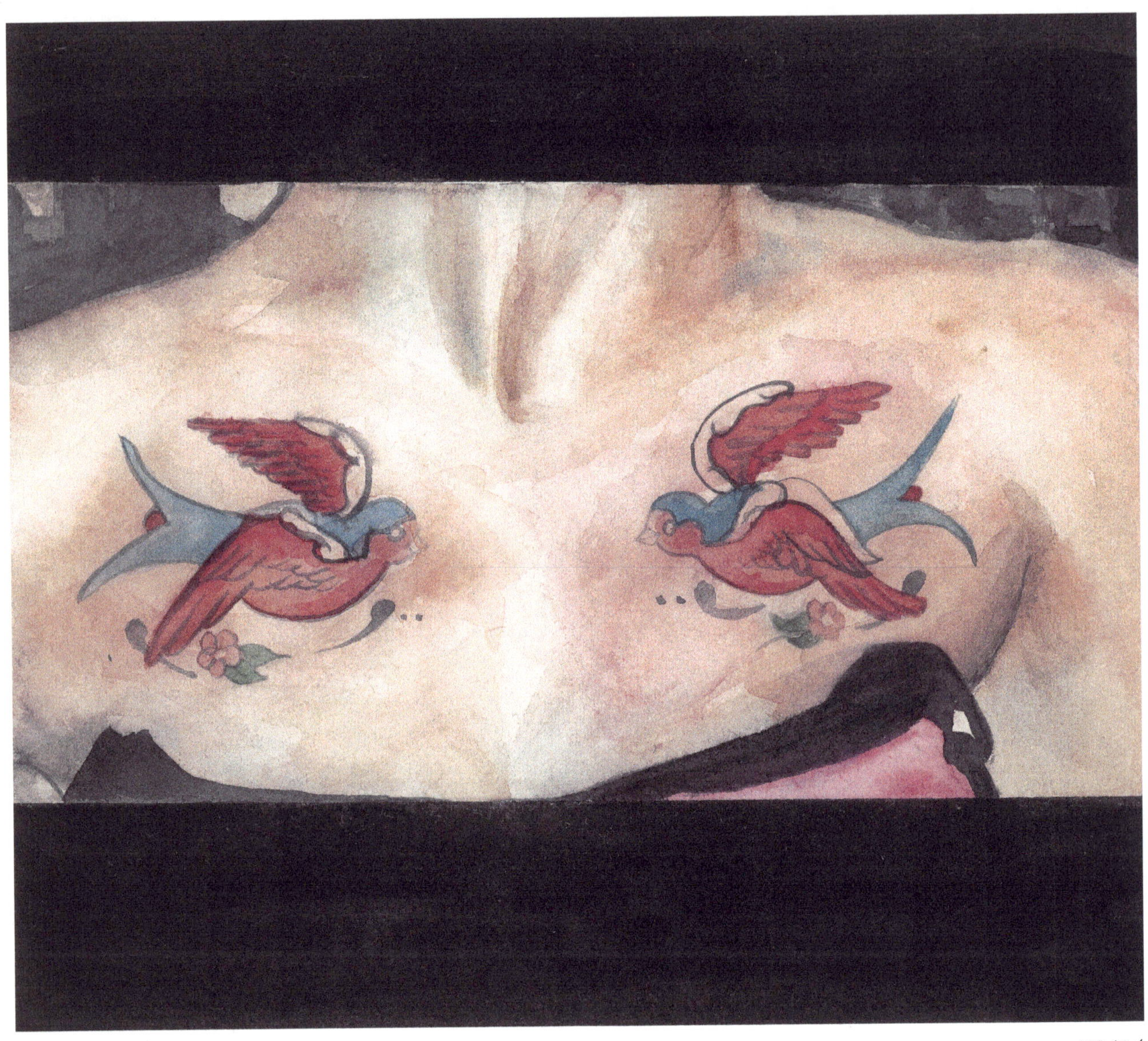

match/enemy

DECORATIVE ARTS

hard not to wonder what tension was levered
against the spring hinge of his spine when these cherubs

were penned to ornament his clavicles
how much has he hurt? we have so few ways to fly

& one is the sympathetic nervous system
i.e. desire i.e. danger i.e.

penetration   pain   memory   *say please*
wear pink   flower   this *is* her color

& she loves embellishment   especially
decoupage Victorian drag that could tweet

in the skinned sky quaking over her head
as he flies into her eye & liquefies

everyone has a wing that needs to mend
a needle isn't half as scary as thread

OK LOOK

it's not that keeping house is shameful   is it?

but seldom is scrubbing linoleum selfie terrain
one thing to brandish messes   confess the lessons
sublimity's slop & spill   another to vaunt
the body doubled over the bill   so he
obliterates the part a creep might say

only a mother could love?   & there's the rub

his reader wants not to witness his shame

wants not of this servile submission to be
afraid   prays his crudely excised visage
was carefully saved   to grace deflated breasts
in the long descent of an eighteen-karat chain
embraced by one who taught him not
to grovel but to consecrate

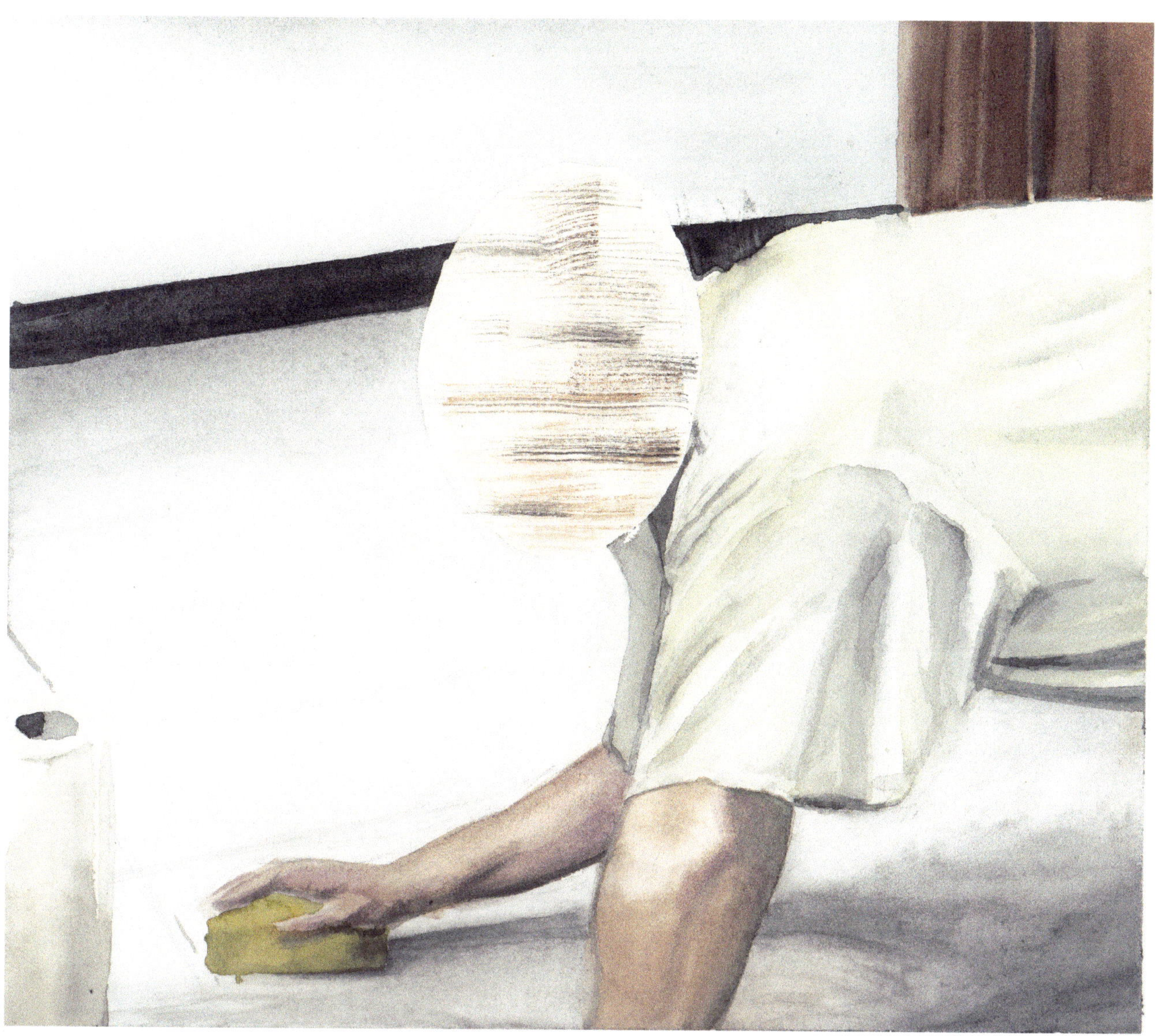

match/enemy

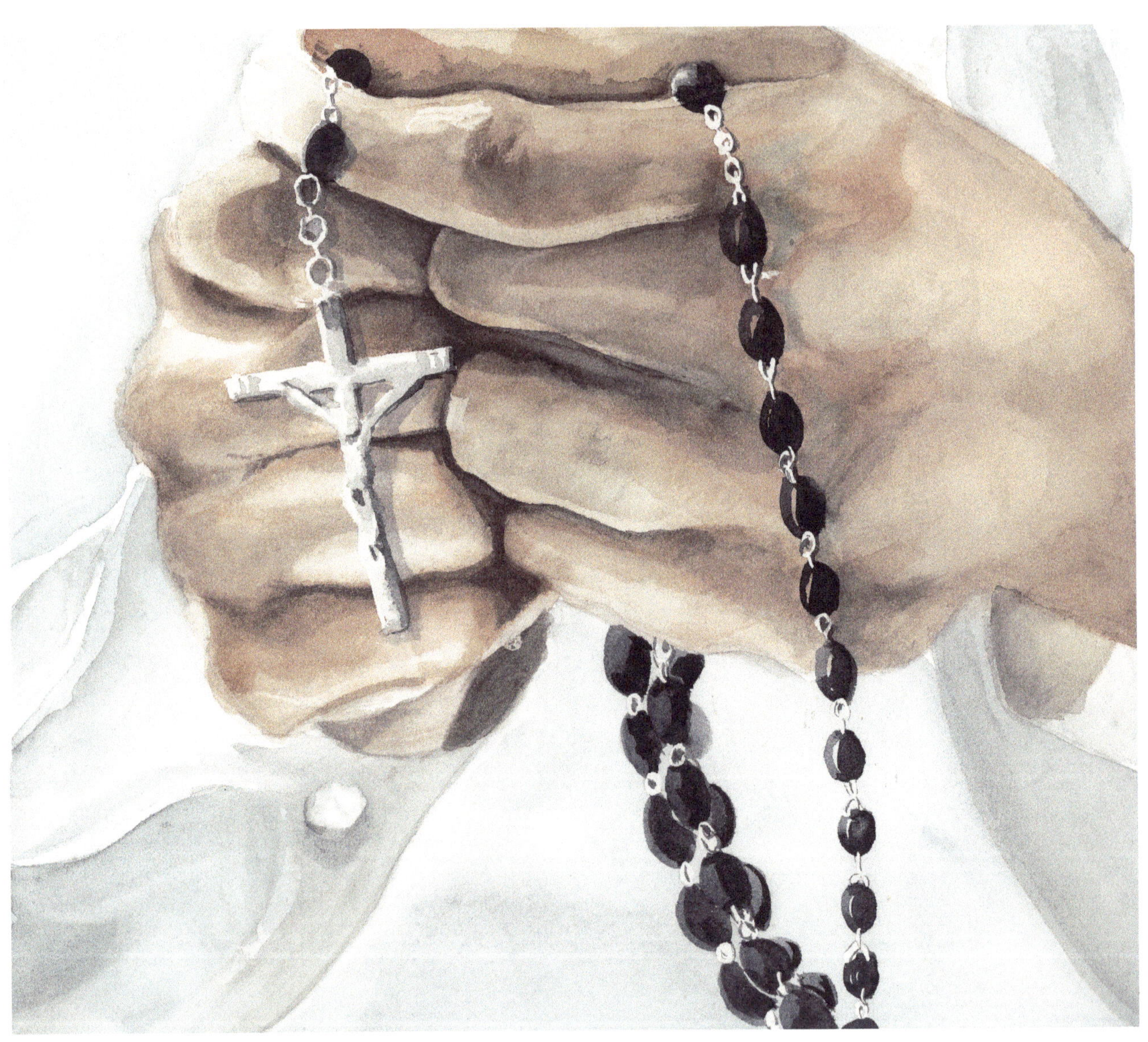

match/enemy 47/45

A LAP OR THREE AROUND THE ROSARY

don't pretend you won't get punished she recalls
w/ a grimace   it may be true Hail Marys
can reduce a sinner's sentence but they never
got *her* out of detention   if it weren't
for that blasted cross she'd tuck the beads
insider her   practice her Kegels   which
who's to say   isn't a better way to atone
for her sins   keeps the road to heaven narrow

his hands might be skilled   (on so many beads
rehearsed (& O the murmuring lips))))) but
in this congregation God only knows
they could be cracked   calloused   hang nailed
capable of miracles   or murder...
she falls asleep w/ her laptop open....

DREAM WEDDING

she falls asleep w/ her laptop open
dreams she's been cuffed to a fresh corpse

tossed in the Pacific   how does she know
it's the Pacific? there was a sign

my word is my bondage   said the corpse
or rather said the red felted letters

ironed onto his tee   it's odd how little
a pair of handcuffs sunk in wrinkled

satin sheets resemble wedding rings
but misery loves company   like a judge

loves to throw away the key   some marriages
are made in heaven some make hell

seem sheer delight   at least this pair
doesn't pretend she won't get punished

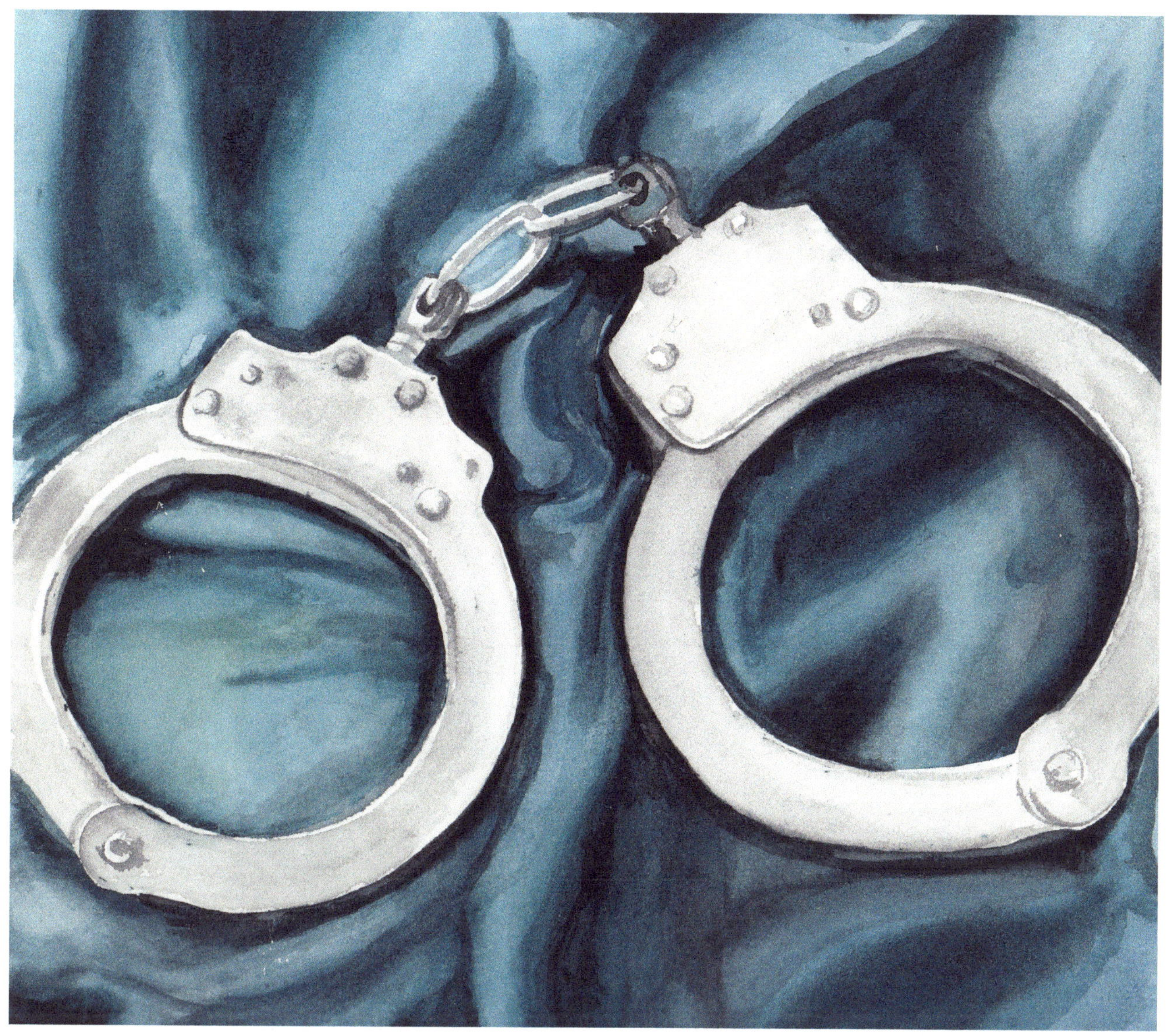

match/enemy

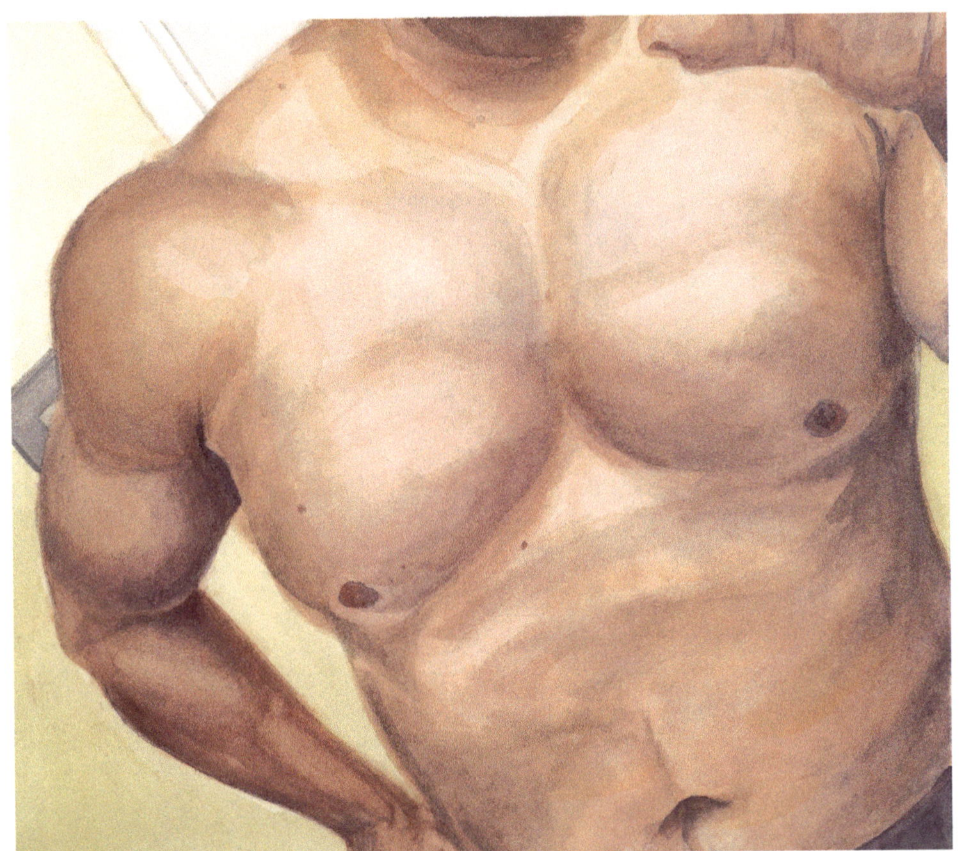

match/enemy   46/37

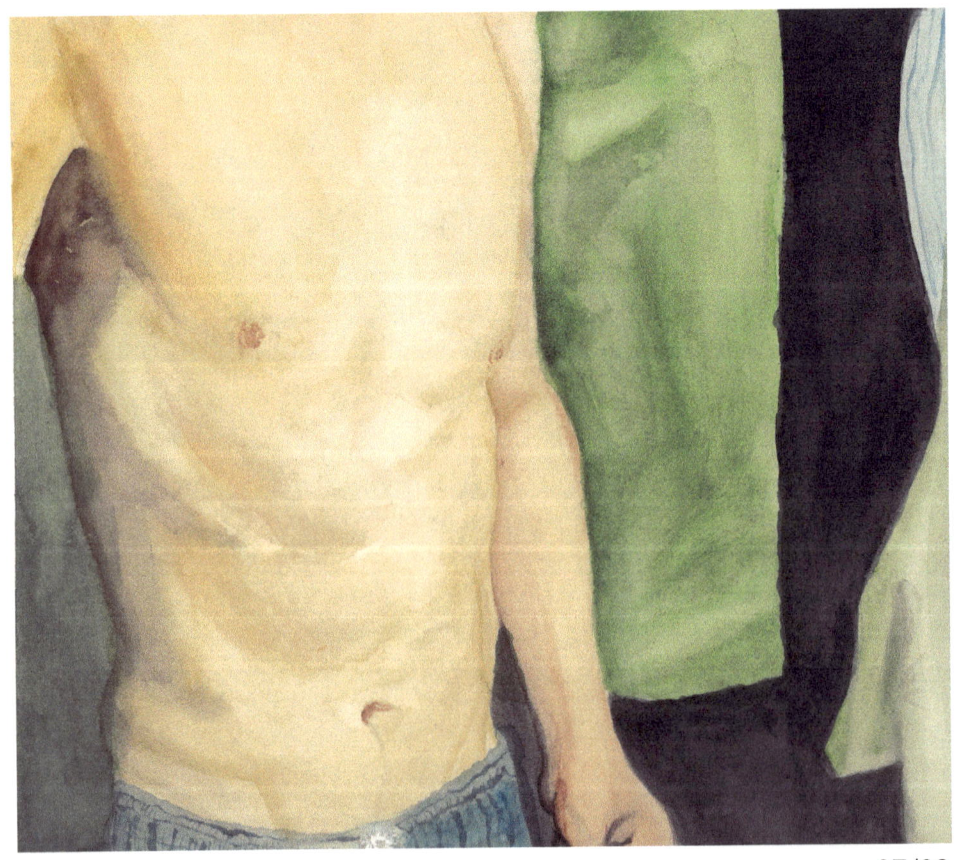

match/enemy   37/39

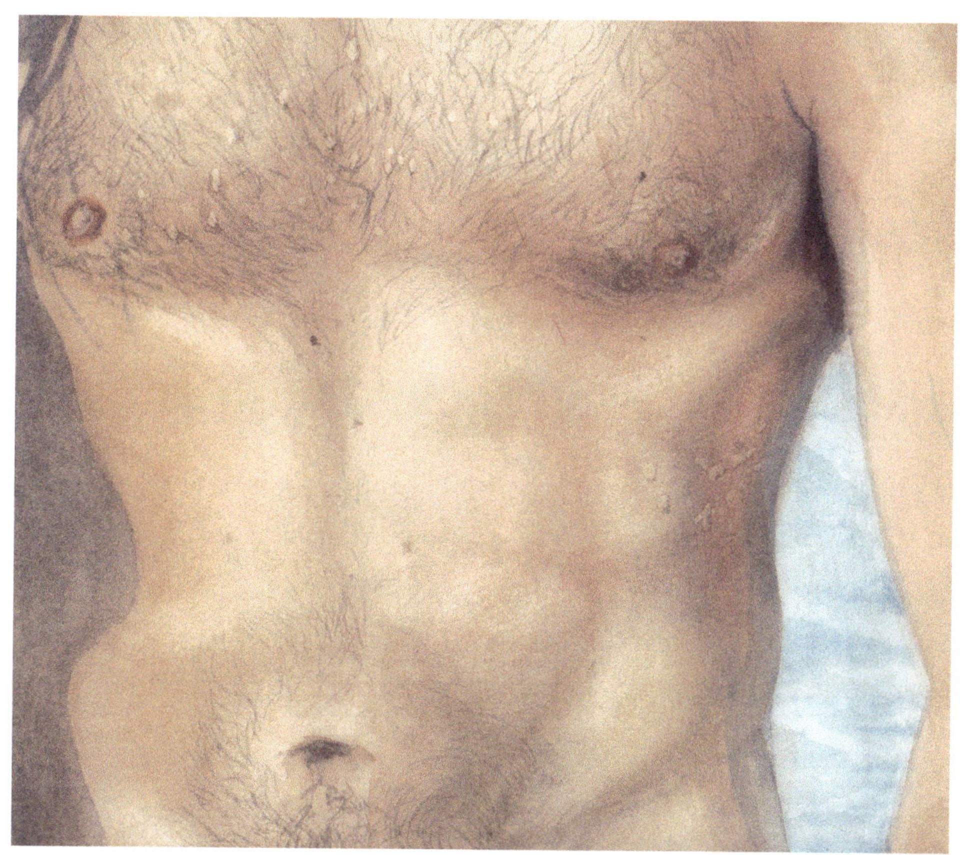

OK ARCHAIC TORSO OF APOLLO

after Rilke

so many skins beheaded   a contagion
of hides half-cocked   assuming she wants
what?   a barkless trunk? the arid dream
of a marble bust? some sun god blunder?
perhaps to inspect the caged suite where beats
the cardinal valentine   scrutinize
for hypotonia & moles   in truth a body
reduced to box checking comes so close
to nothing she wants sometimes to scream
in the speculum of a dormant screen   mascara
skids betray that ancient morbidity
loneliness is such an eclipsing disease
doctors & shadchans be damned   what she can't
see in him exposes far too much of her

OK LET'S PLAY

1.   hard pass

                    look at
                    my boner

                    look at my
                    boner look
                    at my look
                    at my look
                    at my boner
                    look at my

                    boner my
                    boner my
                    boner oh

                    like my oh
                    love my boner
                    o boner my boner

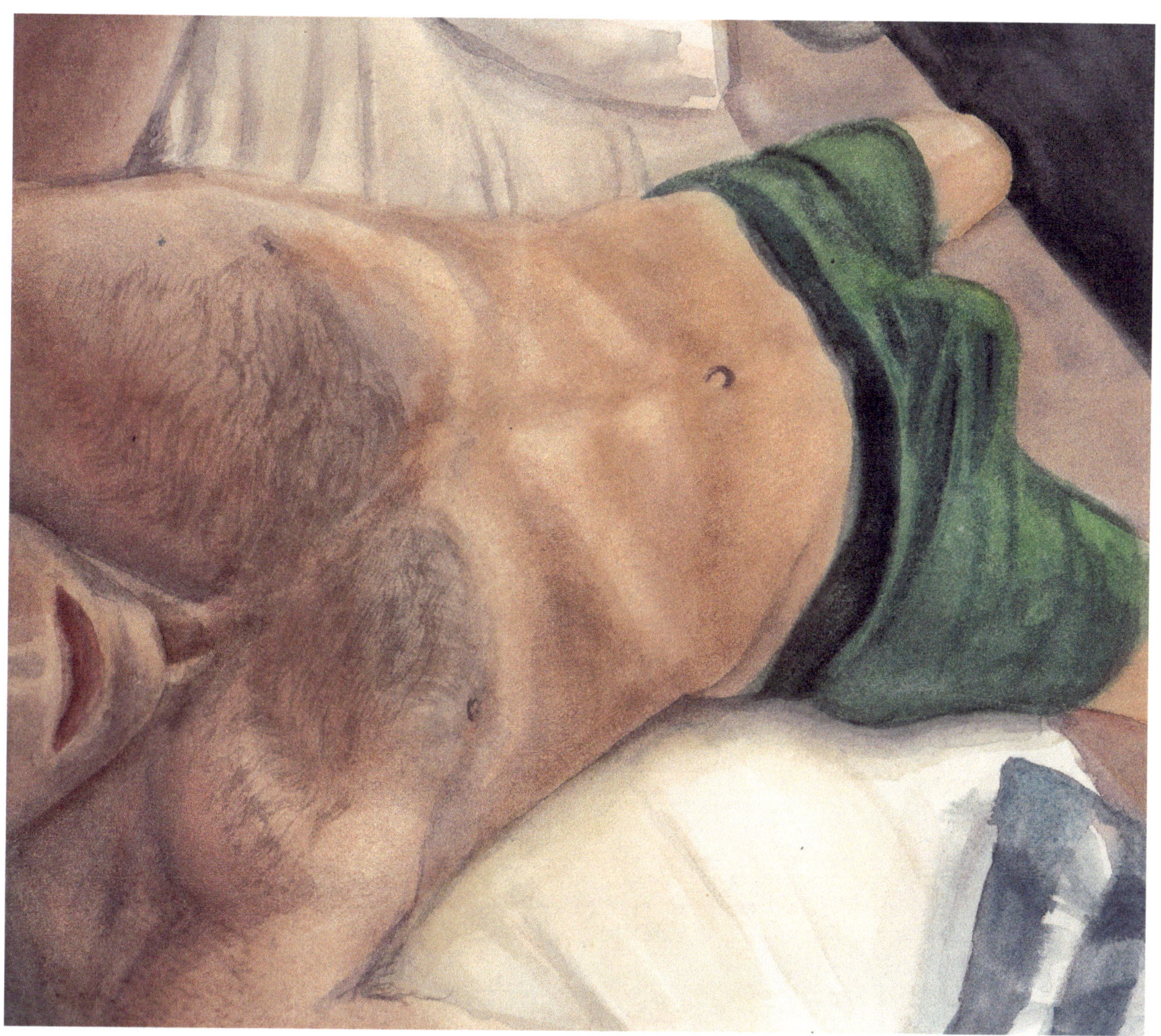

match/enemy

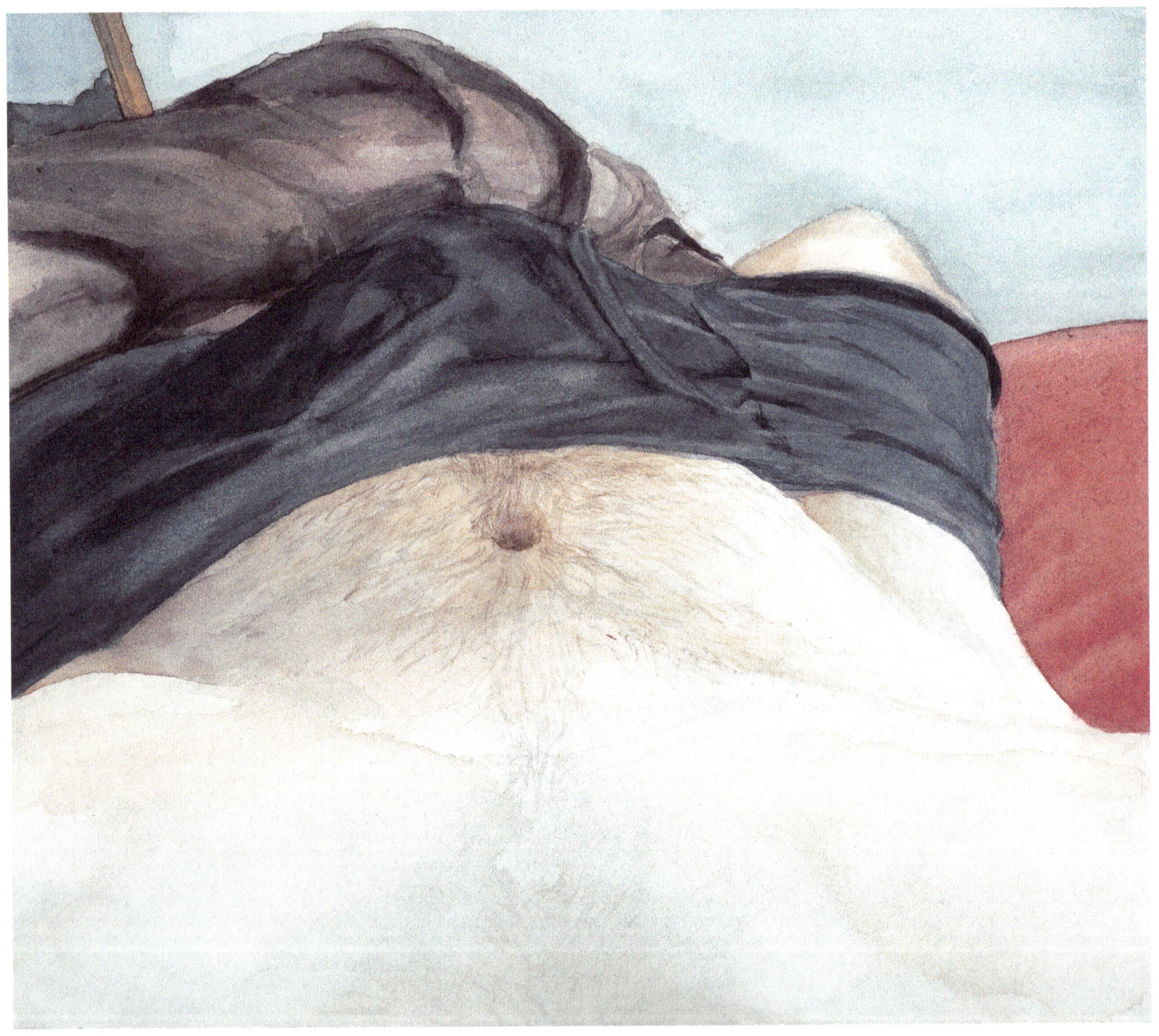

match/enemy   00/50

2.   O longest running show

look at my boner look at my boner
look at look at look at my boner
look at my boner my boner my boner
look at my look at my boner
my boner would you like my boner
would you lick my boner
i'll give you a boner if you like &
you lick my boner's your boner
you give me a boner let's play w/
my boner I play with my boner
(my boner's my boner) high boner
low boner your boner my boner
o boner o boner o boner O

3.	Her screen her bed a private theater

for his perennial one act play

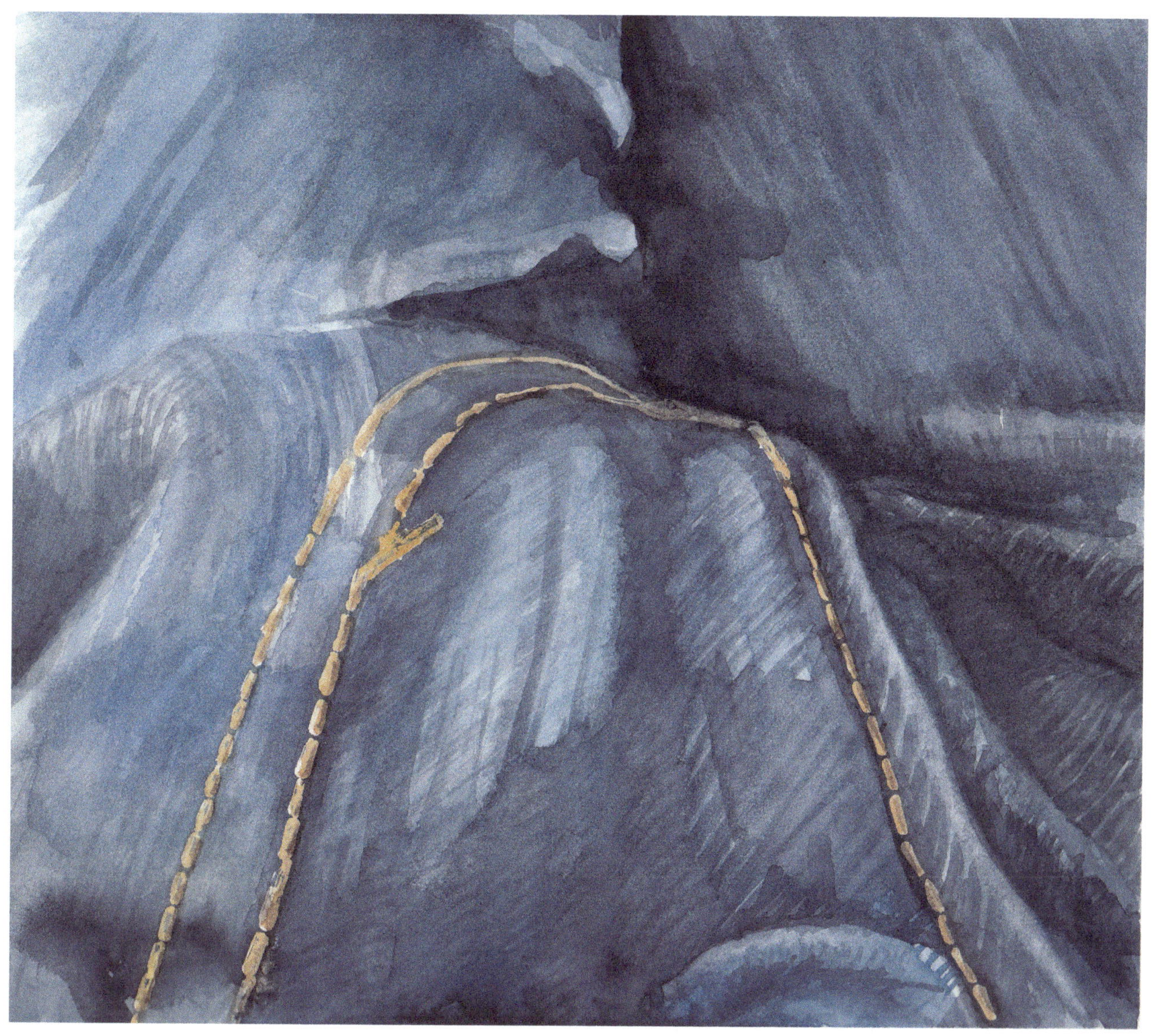

match/enemy 45/47

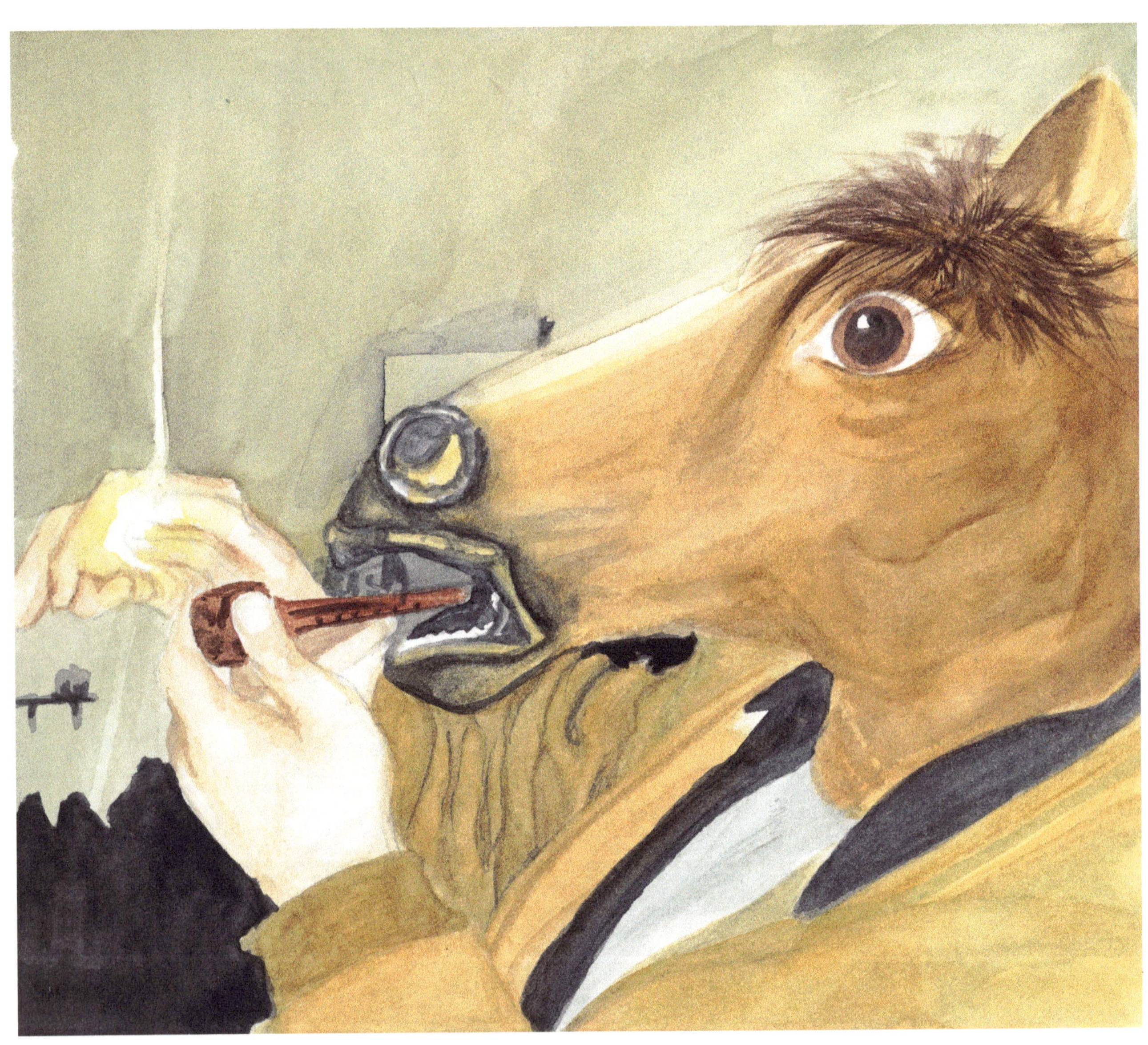

match/enemy   33/38

LET'S NOT PUCK

so Titania's roofied again & the ass
hat Bottom's up   till cordial & quarrel fade
the fae will play   our Lonesome played the Jack
in high school   less boys than parts   her lines weren't hard
to memorize   she made the mask
herself   on scene Titania nuzzled her make
shift muzzle   beards   suggests Bard

be wildlife refuge   forsooth teenqueen
preferred ladies (sweet lion among
the ladies) but Big O's hands were everywhere
as here where beauty reigns only almost supreme
just after muscle & muscular drugs
better to self-dissemble & disappear
our survey suggests male suitors agree

THE COMPARATIVE ARTS

some friends have been married since before dating
went viral   tomorrow: cocktails to celebrate

D's divorce *Inferno* she just read
is a midlife crisis poem   O woe   O saint

O dead   Beatrice   now here's a guy who wants
to show her   *what?* vacation pics with his ex

their perfect storm? portrait of the love
that spawned locusts? can't he see the ashes

disseminating from their laced silhouettes?
it's alluring *yes*   their slant symmetry

the slim hourglass before all hell breaks loose
beauty wrought from agony may be the first art

but who wants to leap from this virtual plague
of loneliness into memory's idyllic noose?

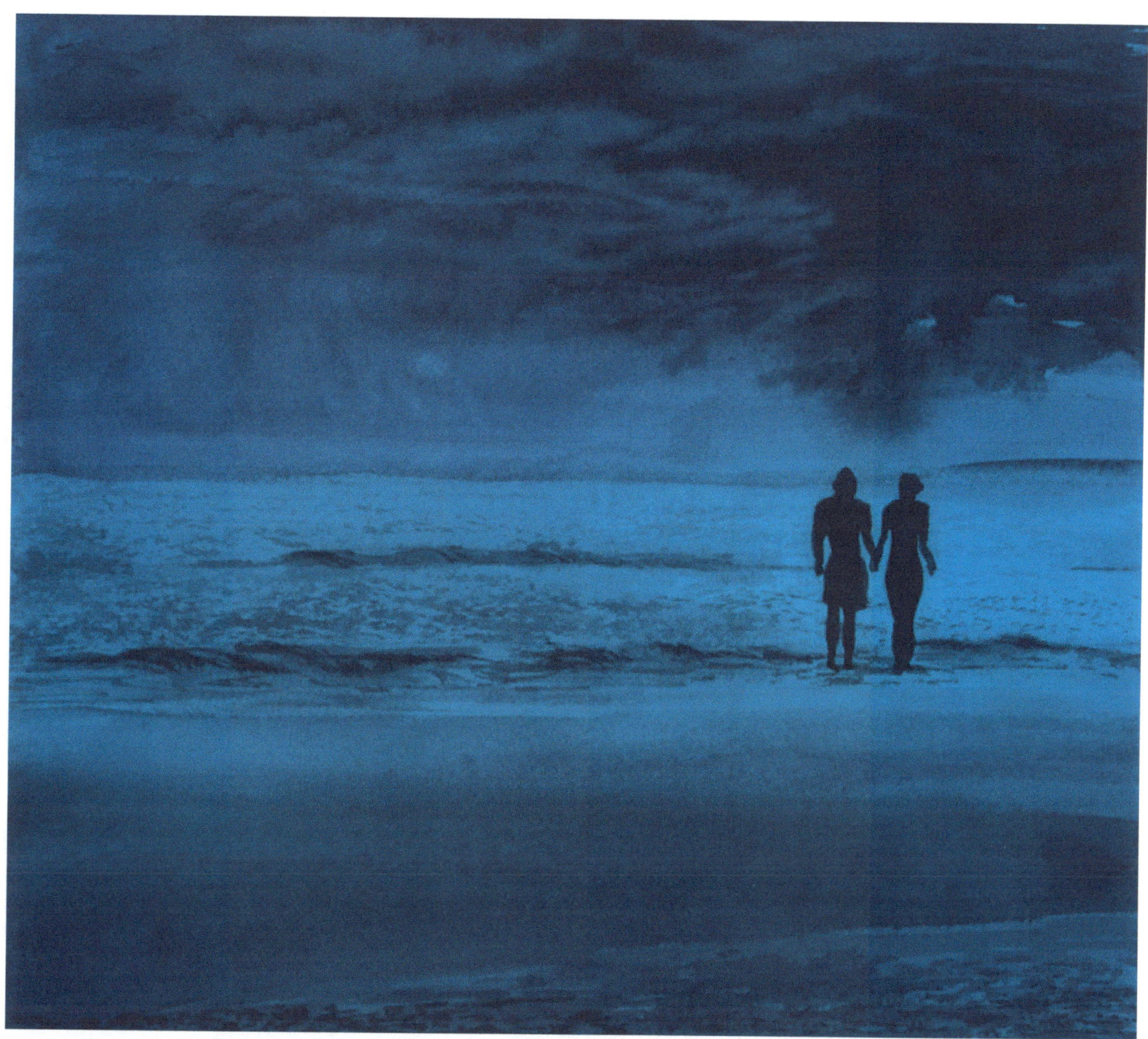

match/enemy 76/23

match/enemy 89/19

OK PACK A FLASHLIGHT

some say marriage is made in heaven some
in the rear end collisions on Gross Street

Dante says delusion is an egregious sin
but it's merciless chance   that blind pair of die

that fills us w/ terror   duh   this from a book
she bought to read w/ her bae before she saw him

reading it w/ his *wife*   what're the odds?
Huxley said six monkeys striking keyboards
at random for millennium would eventually key

a sonnet   had she known it all along?
what difference lies twixt love & chance if both

are blind? a sentence revised for clarity
may be a mercy: *this from the book
she bought....the night of the blackout.*

OK GROVEL

the problem w/ shame is it just can't stand
to let go   she can't expunge him from her mind
imagines him tall   wouldn't he be tall
before the fold to hands & knees   the peak
cut down to an oblong square   *don't*
be a square she self corrects having never held
a whip   oh she's been   whipped   been made to crawl
berated for things she could not control   why
would you want this she wants to ask of him who's made
his wants explicit (knowledge of which makes her
complicit?) whiskey & cat hair he'd scrub from her floor
denuding downy baseboards   filth he'd flush
from bloody porcelain bowls   here's
the dirt   the heart wants   the pain it knows

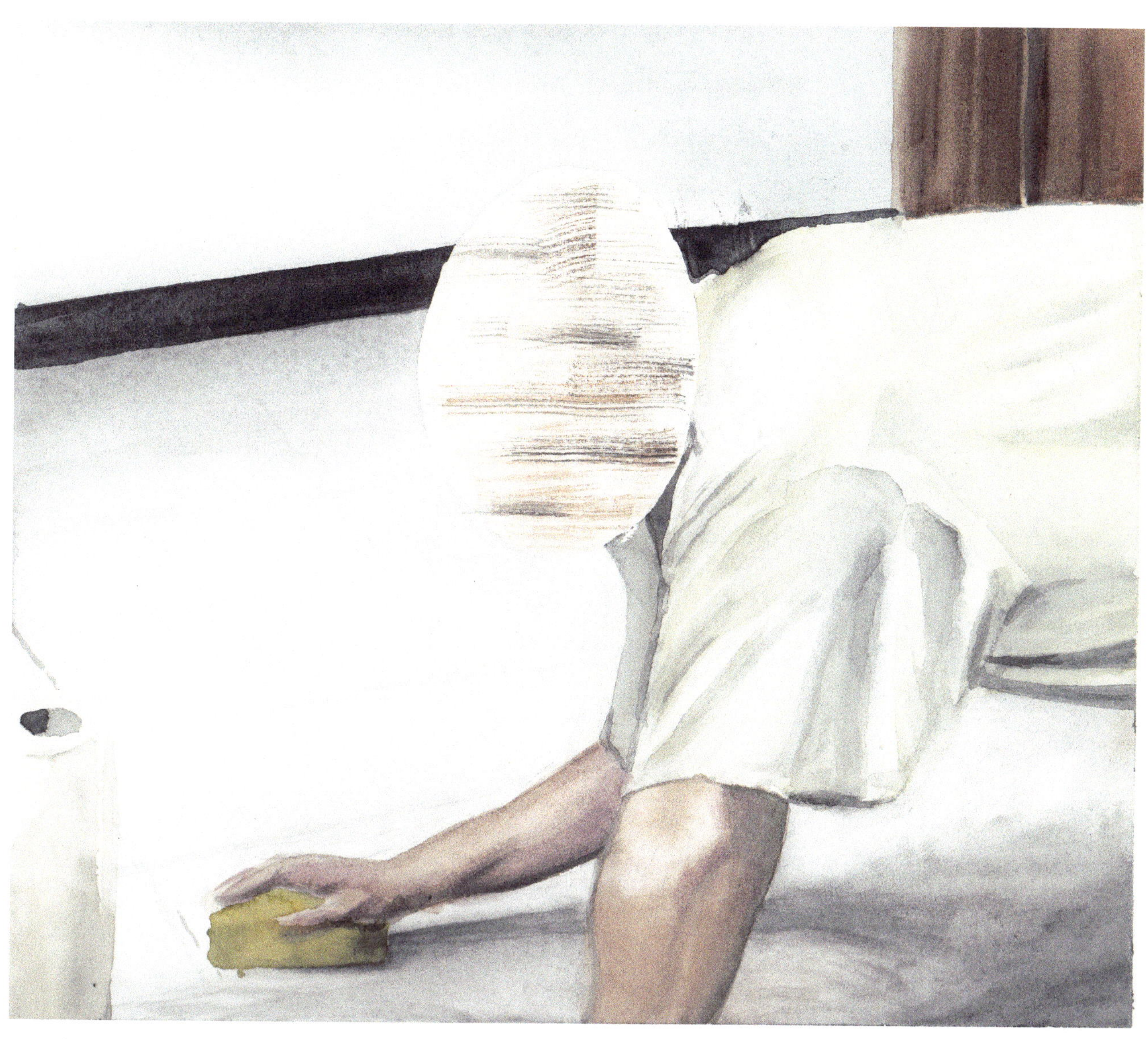

match/enemy   45/38

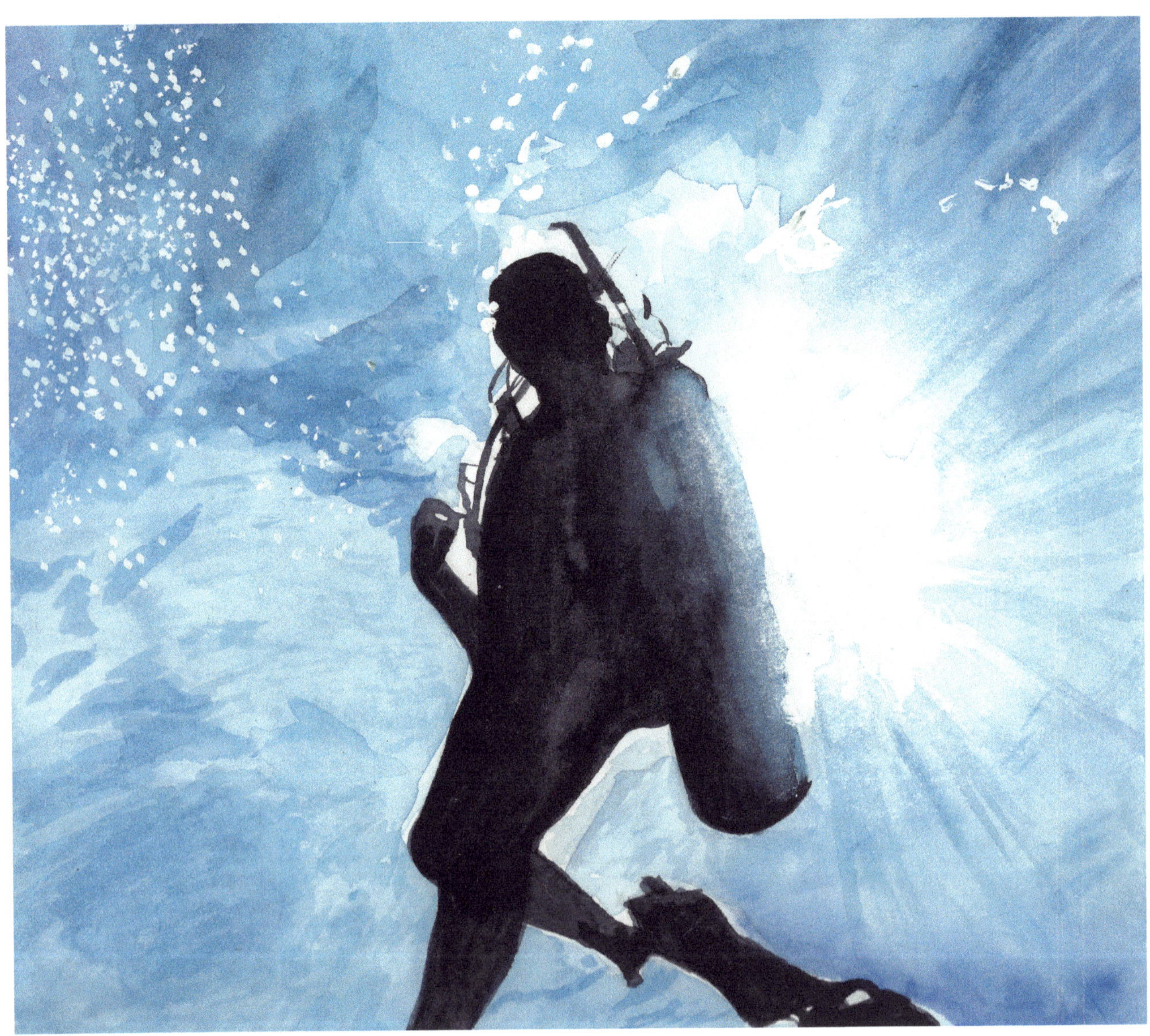

match/enemy

94/06

OK ~~ANGEL~~ GO FISH

suspended in light   not weightless   not
bodiless but   as if newly begot
an angel alight   adrift   in slow descent
twixt heaven &
                              surely the father of lies
isn't angel but *us*—diviners of portrait
of image   futile attempts to fix to stay
to say   *yes! this is me!*   falling through water
& glass   through salt & time   to record the mass
replay the play   once we were masked
& flippered things   the light behind   the dark
before our knees buckled under the weight
of a recirculating tank   o angelfish!
what hell or heaven-sent lover
can assuage the gravity of our fluidity?

OK SWITCH

some hands whip some hands smart some play w/ feathers
some w/ tar what's the difference between life & art

between role-play & reality? not even dogs
love unconditionally   even they know the difference

between humility & humiliation   so does she
though some postures she cannot bend her mind

to imagine she doesn't have to   a body recalls
being struck by someone it loves   the open hand

slotted spoon   spatula   belt   it never felt
like love   like this   how to distinguish human

from instrument? even that upturned gaze intimates
no scrim of defiance   no twitch to retaliate   even

to stand
                but maybe she's about to face her fears
maybe she's got an open corkscrew in her hands

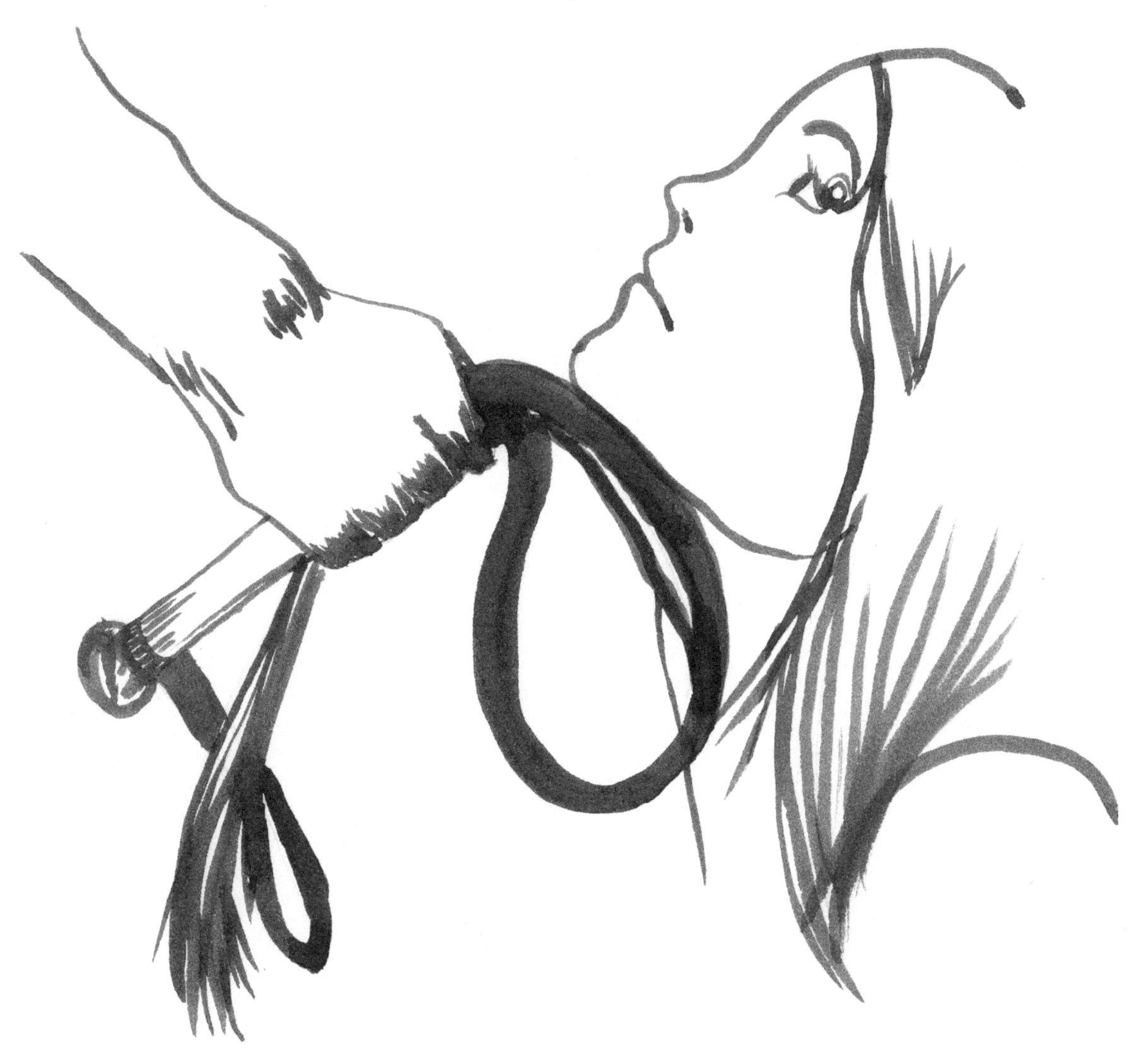

match/enemy

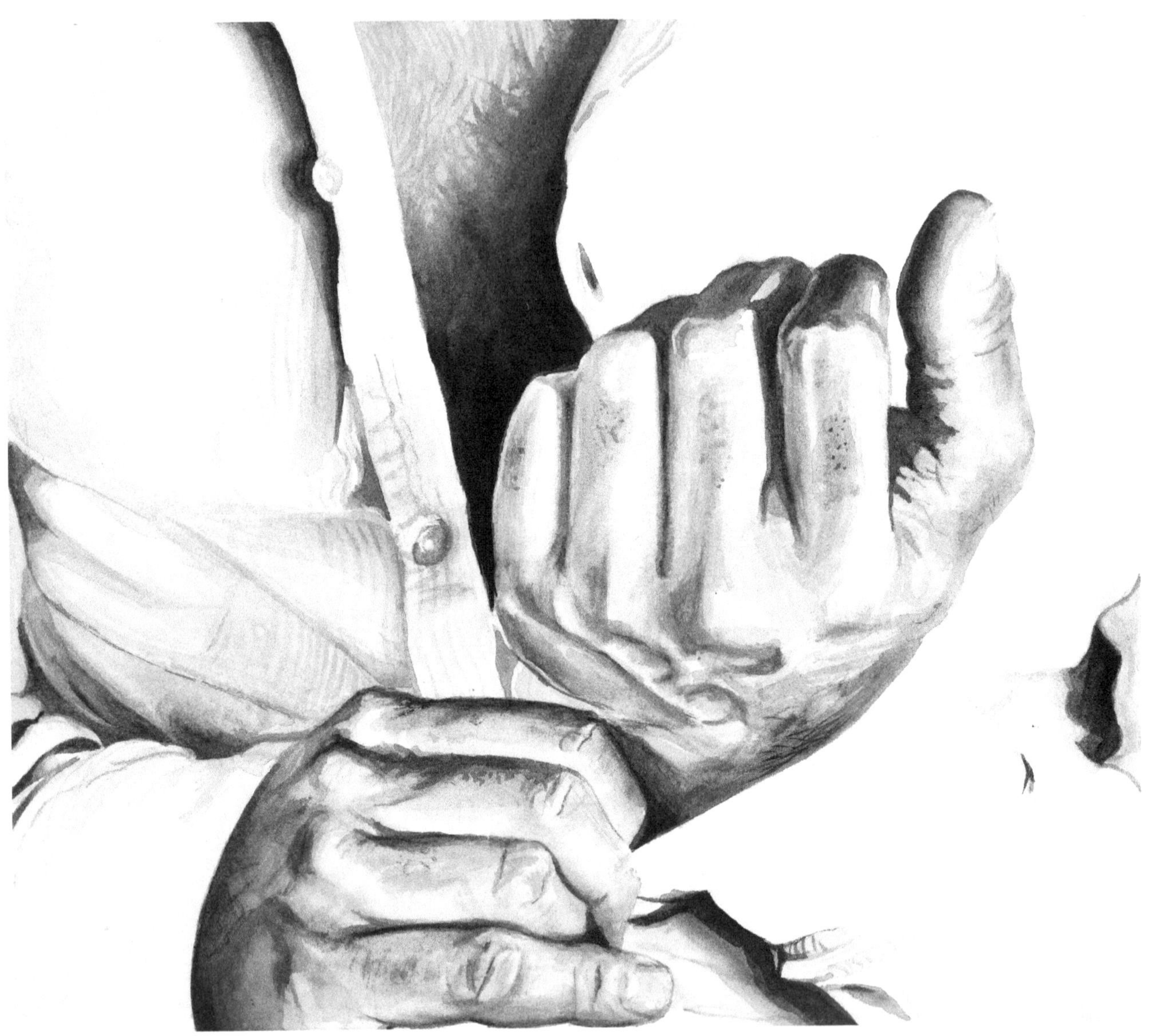

match/enemy

PAN TO THE HEROINE

a lover once referred to her as *investment*
she thought   *mutual bonds?* but he was all liquid

assets   soon divested   no chance of return
so cut to the crop of hands caught in scrim light

between billable hours   an overexposed black
& white   glimpse of the animal mid-skin

the deed done   blood rinsed   opposable thumbs
buttoning up his linkless cuffs before back

to work   the boss   the wife & kids   pressed & starched
where life is good & good *Love* is dull

is Hollywood to blame for this tragedy? maybe
it's not power but plot that defines what's sexy

we flirt w/ what we fear   no accident then
we call it *heroin*   that most addictive drug

GHOSTS IN THE MACHINE

she misreads *marriage* as *miscarriage*

trick of the screen   fatigue   the fallible eye
which brings her to his   suspended in light

pupil like the giant barrel turned tunnel
at the park   where kids pretend they're hamsters   or hide

or wish they were never born   *I hate you!*
she heard one shout at an apologetic mother

juggling another kid   two bags of groceries
& a coffee   some faults are hereditary

he's turned the gaze back on her so might as well know
she wears glasses   Coke bottles almost since birth

avoids contacts   it's not that she's lazy
only she likes sometimes to turn the world off

it's so easy to drown in this limbo

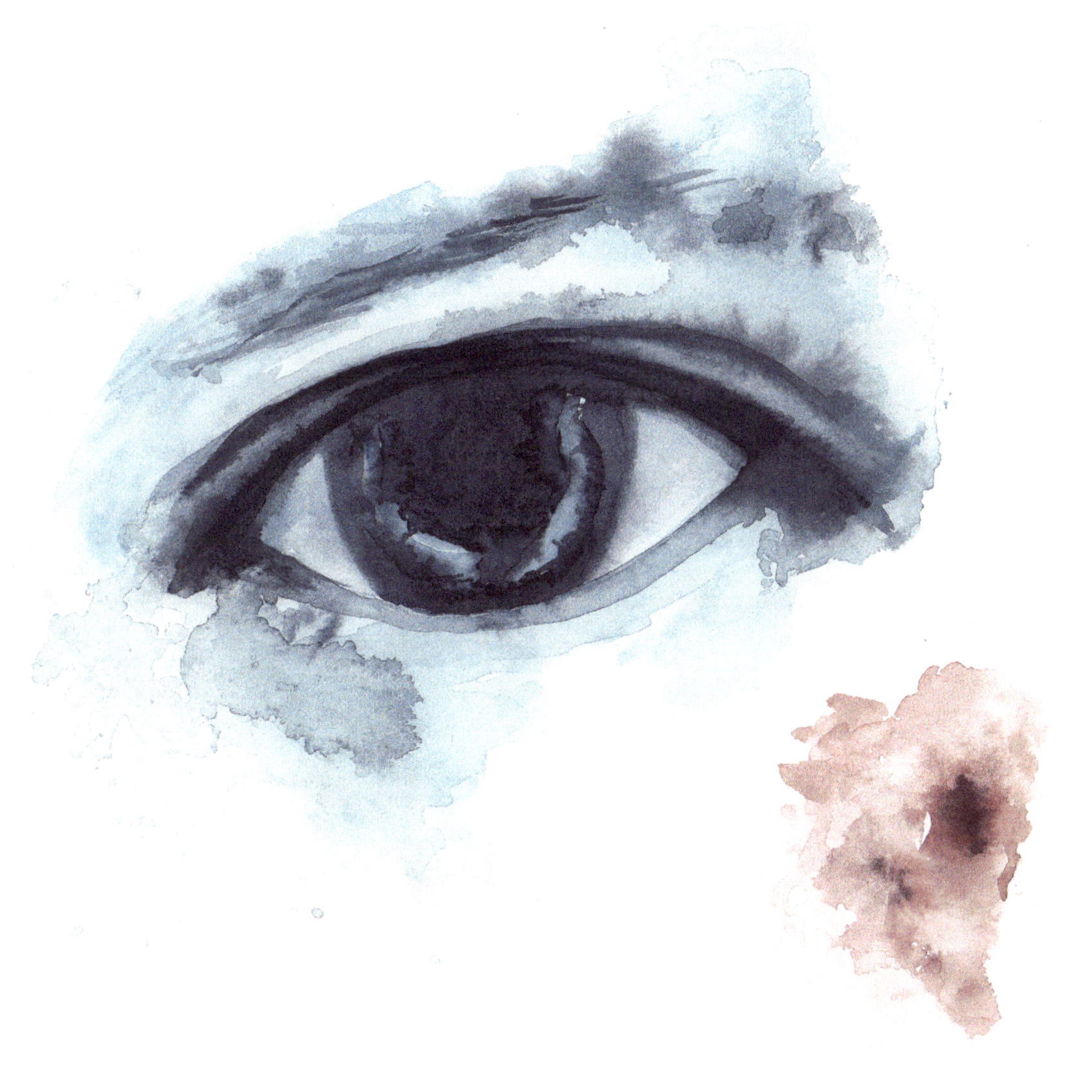

match/enemy

76/22

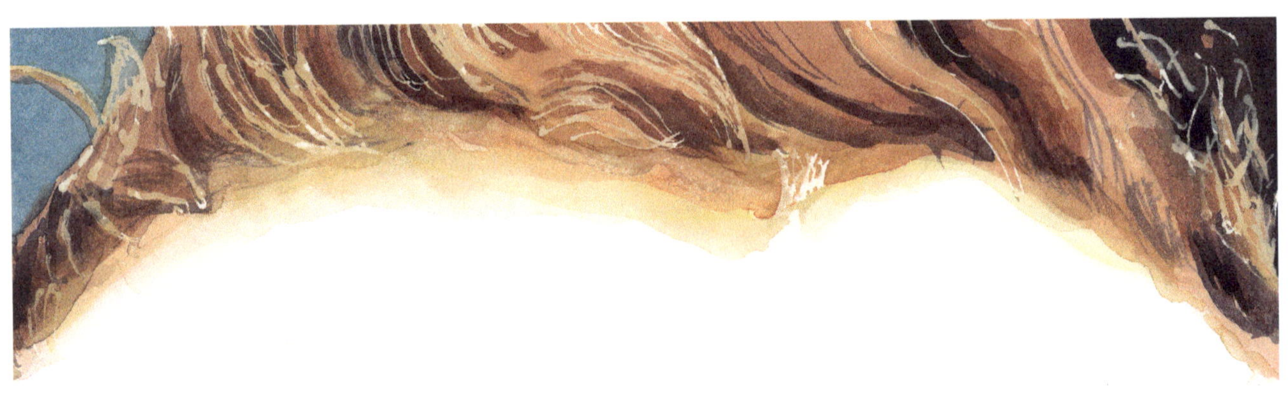

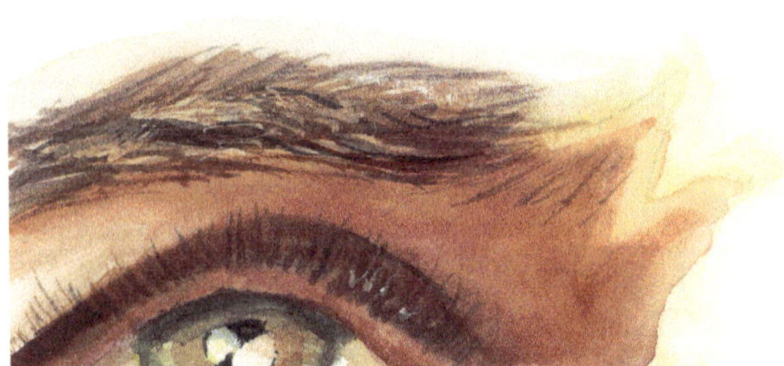
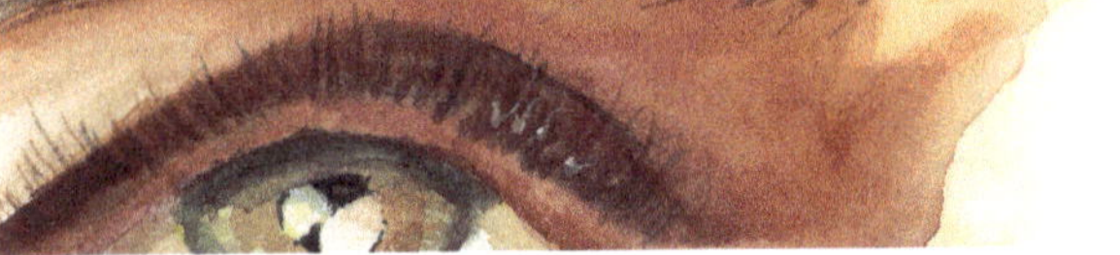
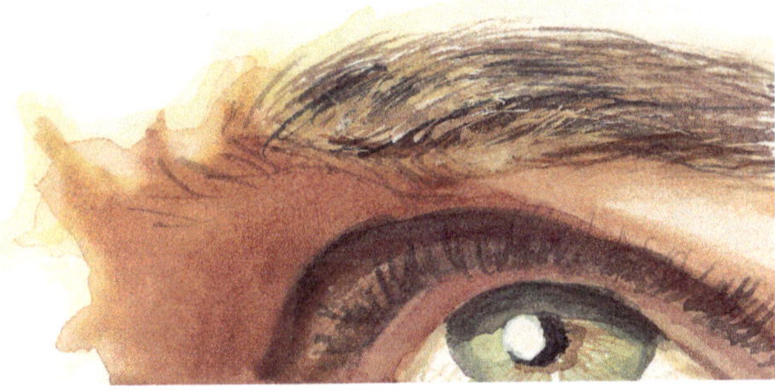

match/enemy

it's so easy to drown in this limbo

the Sears catalog of singles   swipe left
swipe right   bring the vegetable dish assigned

brace oneself for disappointment   be part
cavalier part cadaver always prepared
to MacGyver   it's exhausting   a friend says

nevermind   says every marriage falls
into misery   misery like a path

less wood   misery like a soccer field
refereed by leopards & she-wolves
no shin guards   impossible stains   impossible

to wash dishes w/out wreckage   where
we bury the fetus   flies   for this
for this   why send out a search party

for this   why send out a search party?

& we w/ satellite TV   why watch?
but behold seven new Goldilocks planets

are we there yet? to Earth abort? meanwhile
in another part of the world   one half
dressed teen pushes another from a chained door
to peer through the keyhole   how much will each
be sold for & how is the sum ascertained?
they squat suspended in the rank bowel
of an invisible cargo vessel
preborn   the thin one in the corner almost still

where's big brother now?   got any siblings?
want kids?   she considers the sentence again

misreads *miscarriage* as *marriage.*

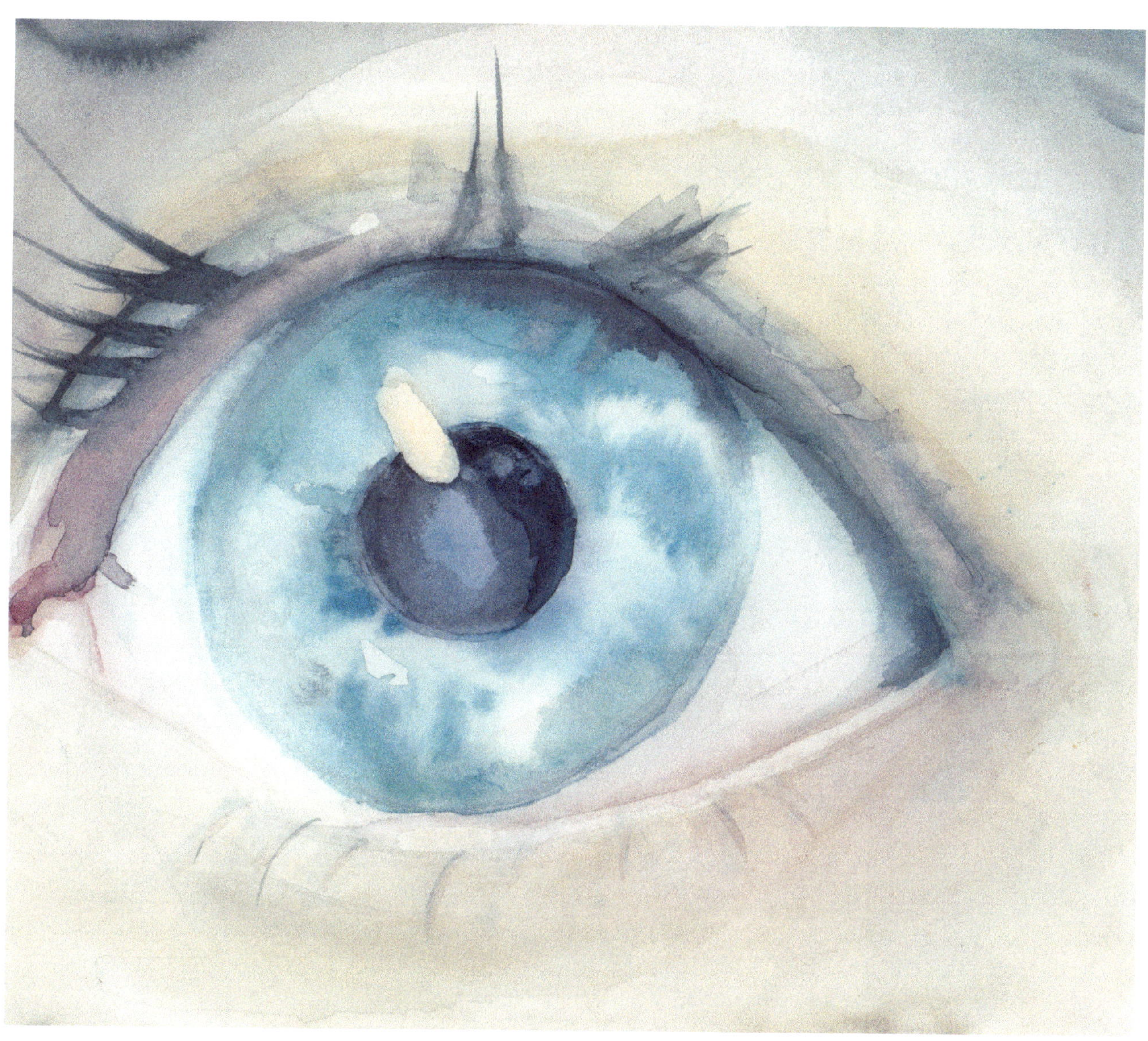

match/enemy

02/43

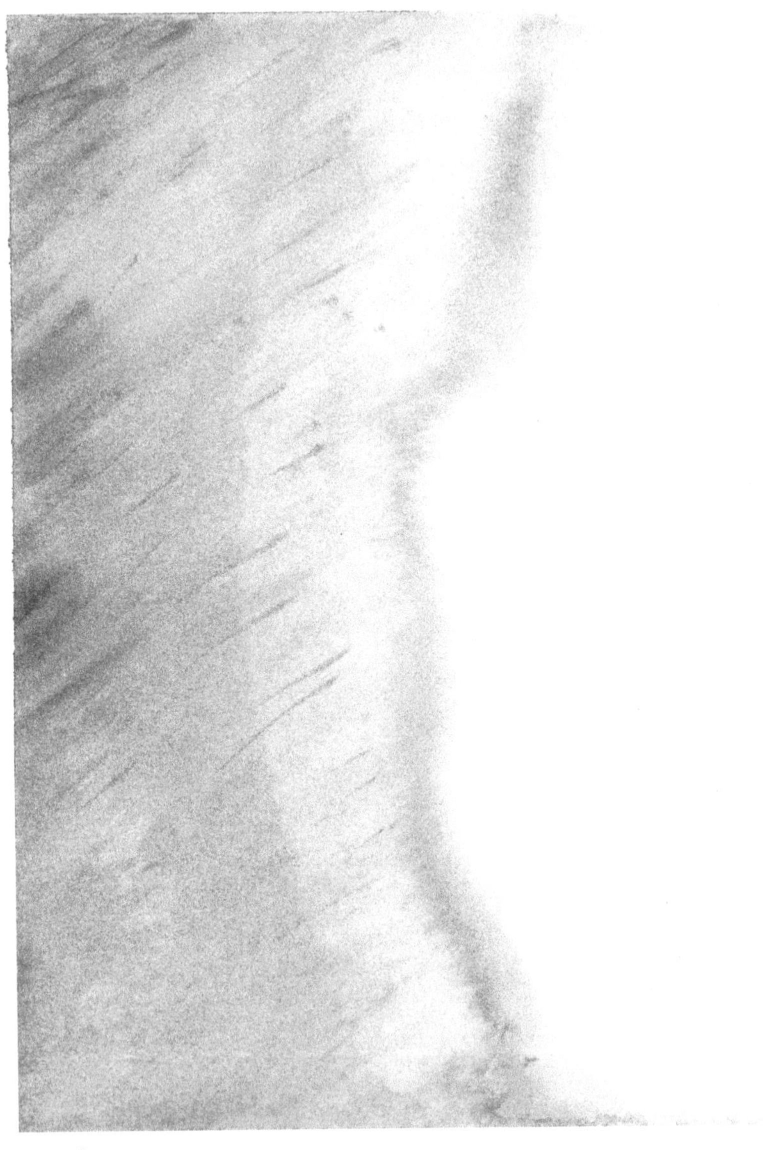

match/enemy

53/25

SELF-PORTRAIT AS SLAG HEAP FOR DATA/GRATIFICATION

her head's in the cloud   haze   a likeness in bytes
strip mined   war gamed   at sufficient scale

every brain's a universe   looks/the same
siphoned through servers   siloed on farms

think hillside pastures w/firewalls   a grazing green
tumbling gently into the sea   & counting to sleep

some sheep get lost   the wolves   tagged & tracked
only after they're caught   & anyway

aren't wolves just   another kind   of farmer
who nursles before he smites   (these faceless suitors

are mostly White)

                              this one wants to watch   wants
to see her tassels sway   a blow   by blow

of her last   date/lay/surgery/fantasy/shipwreck
they say it's a seller's market   buyers believe it

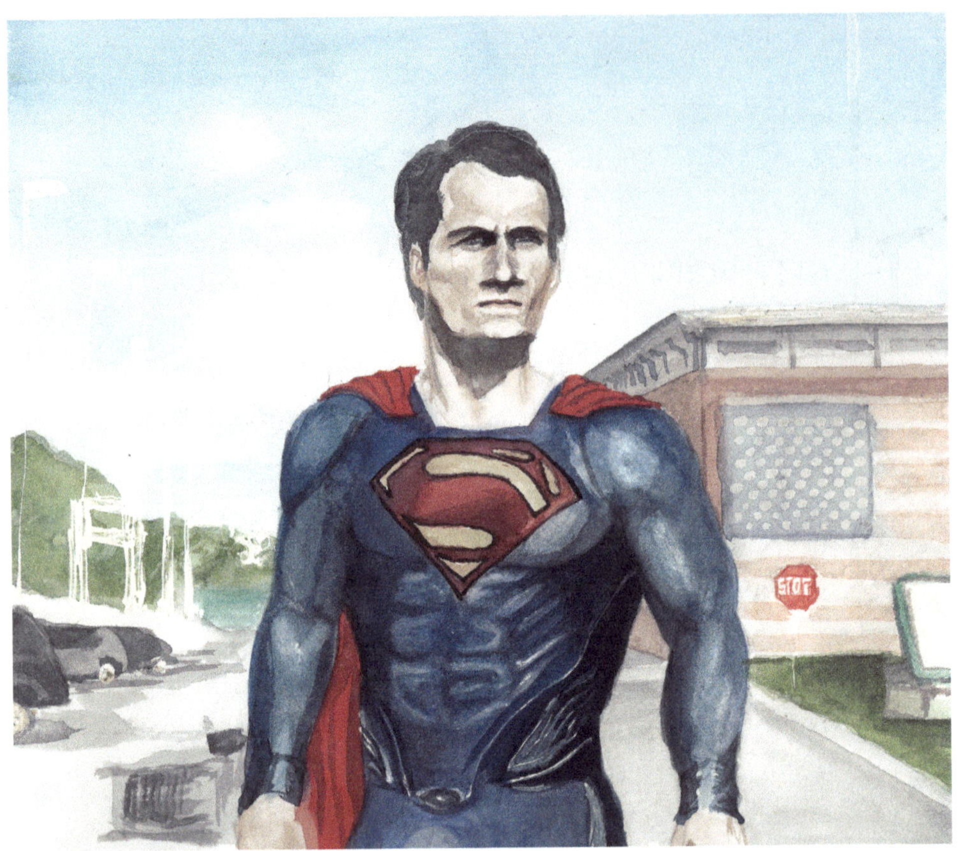

match/enemy   58/48

OK SUPER

S for salivate S for sandwich S
for sanitary S for snake S for swindle
S for sensitive S for sherbet S
for shake S for yessss S for damsel
S for distress S for stag for stagnate
rhinoceros extinction S for sad
S for lads in swimsuits & swole suits
sanguine capes & shrapnel vests S
for saviors & scurvy knaves sperm banks
& single dads S for supersonic
secrets & subatomic stimulations S
for strongmen to strongarm sacrifice & stipulation
for standoffish for soaring for swollen for shaft
for siren for solo for spent shell for sag

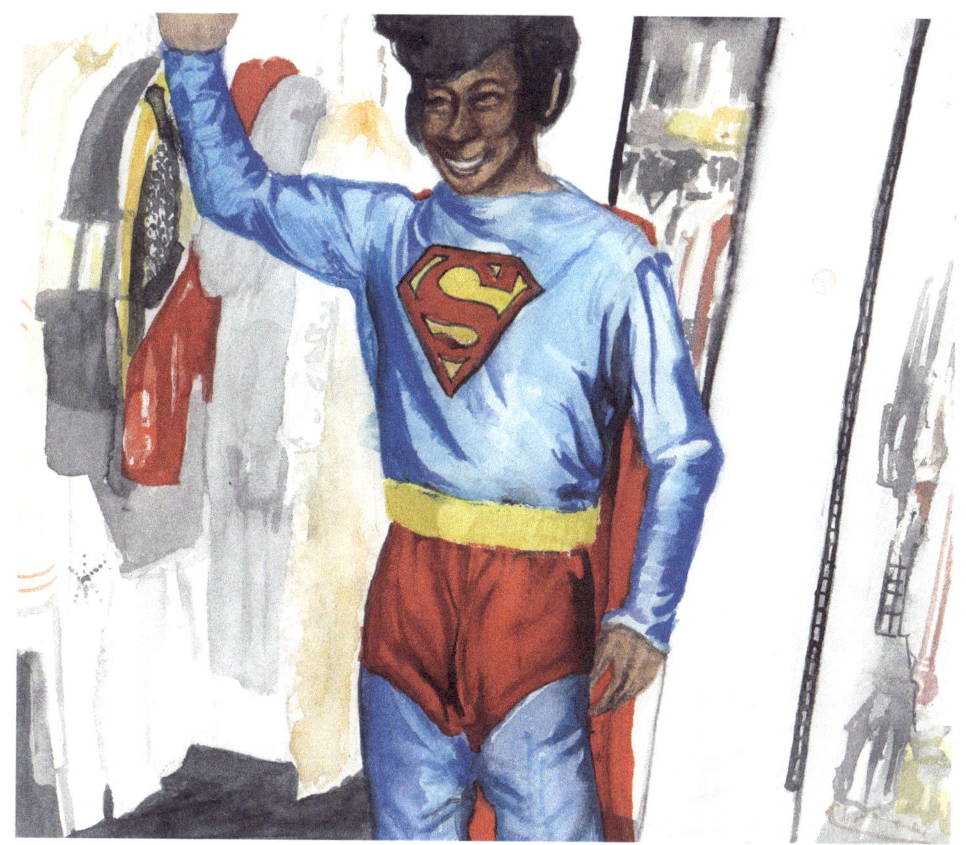

match/enemy   08/50

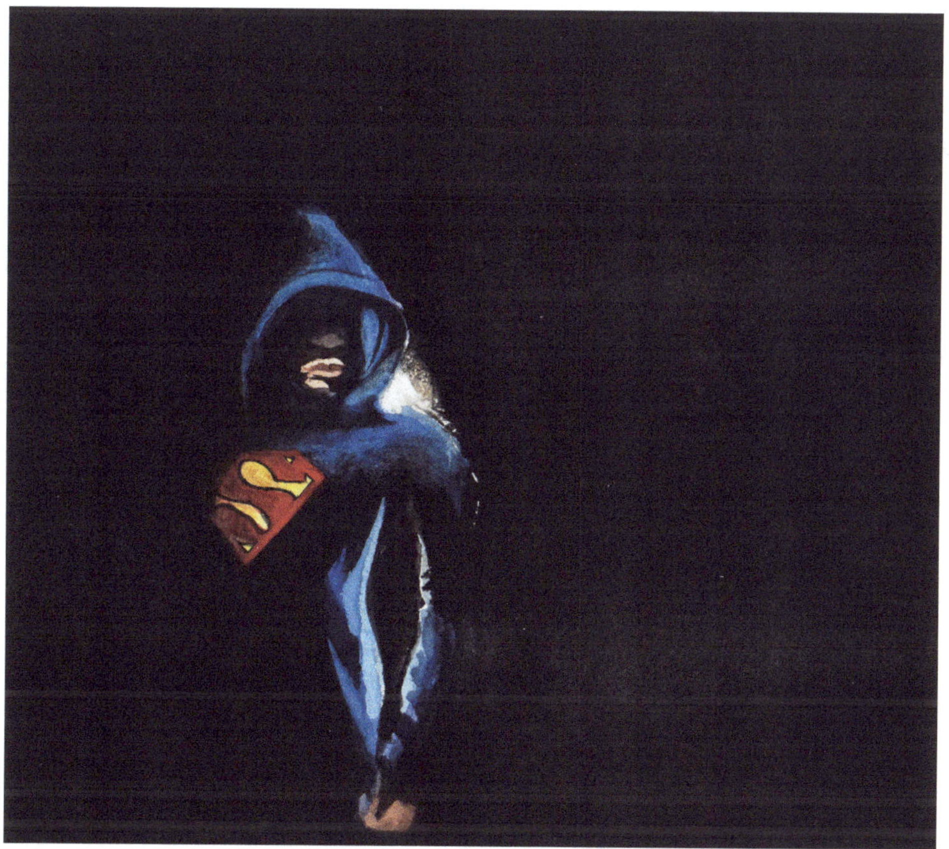

match/enemy   0/0

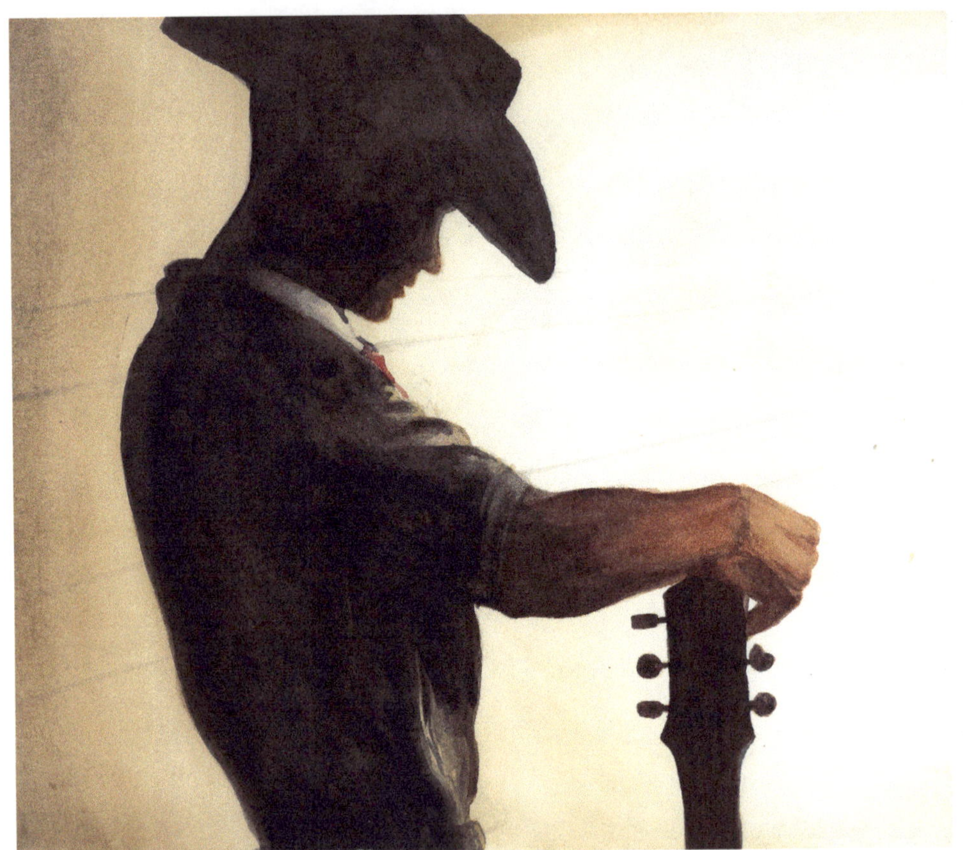

match/enemy   91/10

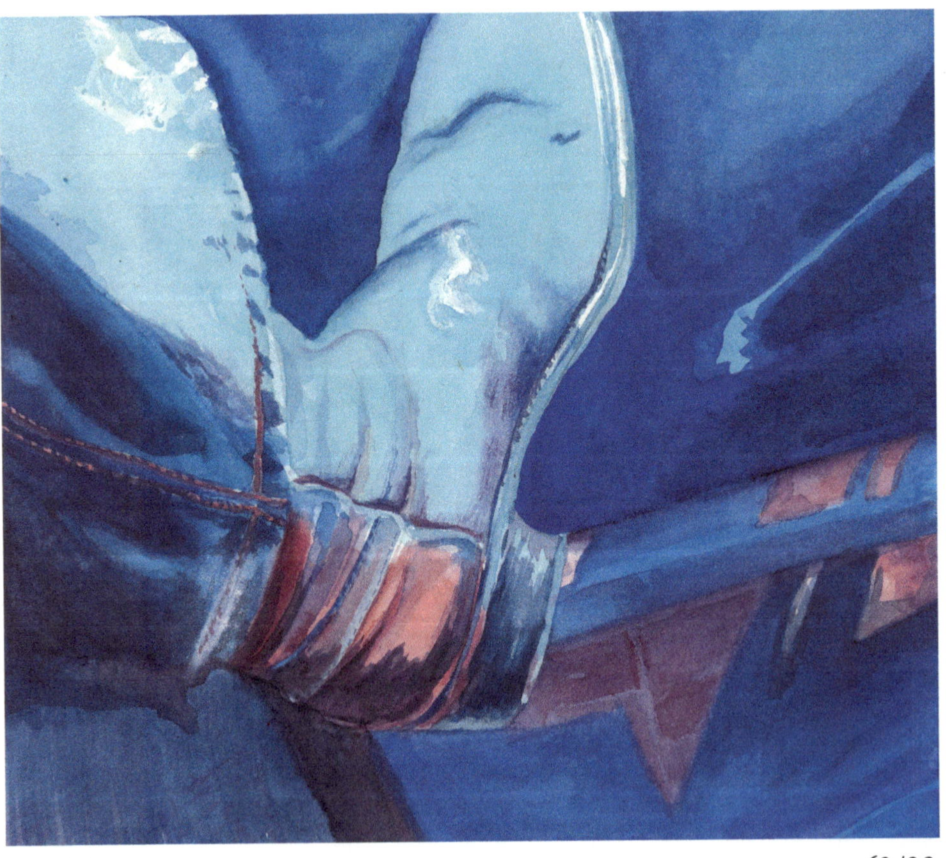

match/enemy   63/29

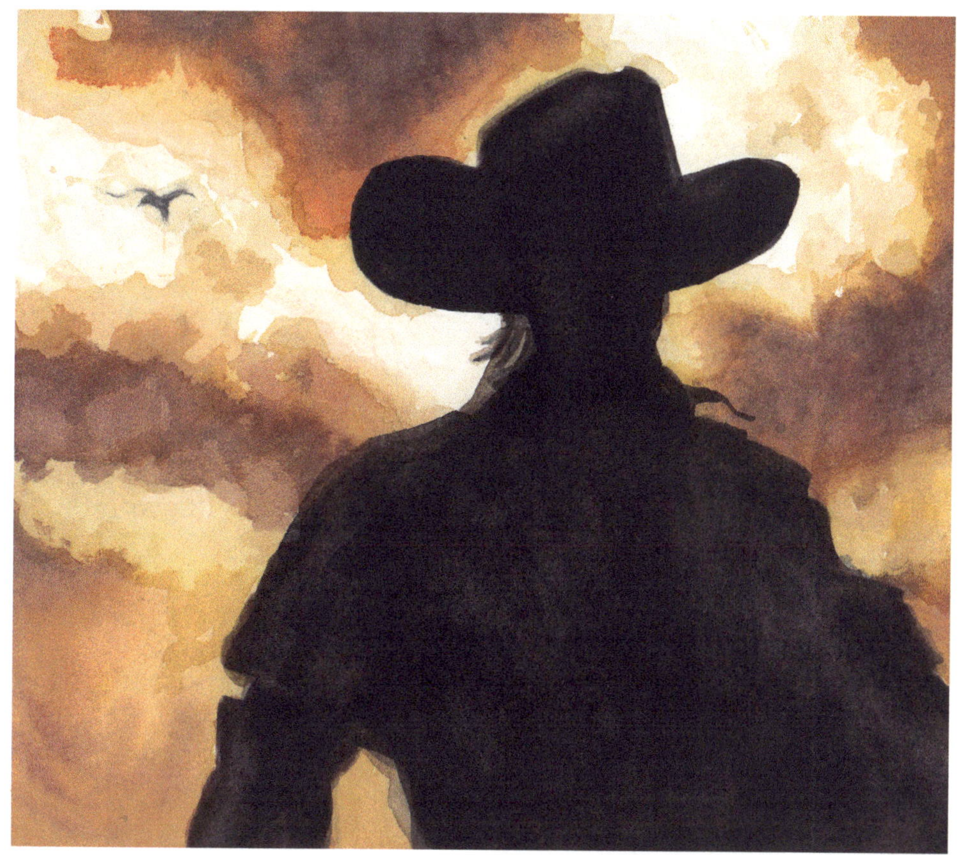

match/enemy   79/20

ON THE RANGE

home home outside
a box? any range w/
ends is also a cage
like a belt   might be
one way   to claim
what a feller likes &
to keep the strays in

a box? can a belt be
a fence &well notched
to buckle what's not
sized to fit cinched
to keep drawers up &
like branded   skin
in range   of a rifle

sight check your six
your self your calm
collect only burrs
check the category
what got caught
what's that in your
holster what's not

check the box check
cool &   collected
or maybe a loner
best describes you
in the cross hairs
pocket your empty
remains in the frame

OK BLOOM

she loves the mess a flower makes
dogwood's
snowy dandruff salting manicured
lawns   roses rouging driveways
& trees!
mulberry's sticky ebony stains
or sugar maple's four-season debris
how even deepwinter boughs
sap-sucked   take power lines down

& loved she no peacock much as when
she learned the lesser-known plight   of peahens
though Darwin viewed the cock's train-rattling
his opulent iridescent shimmy
w/ vexed
avowed disgust *such*
brazen vulnerability
to what end!?
the end is known to hens   whose unfair sex
selects what beauty will
or not   bare consequence

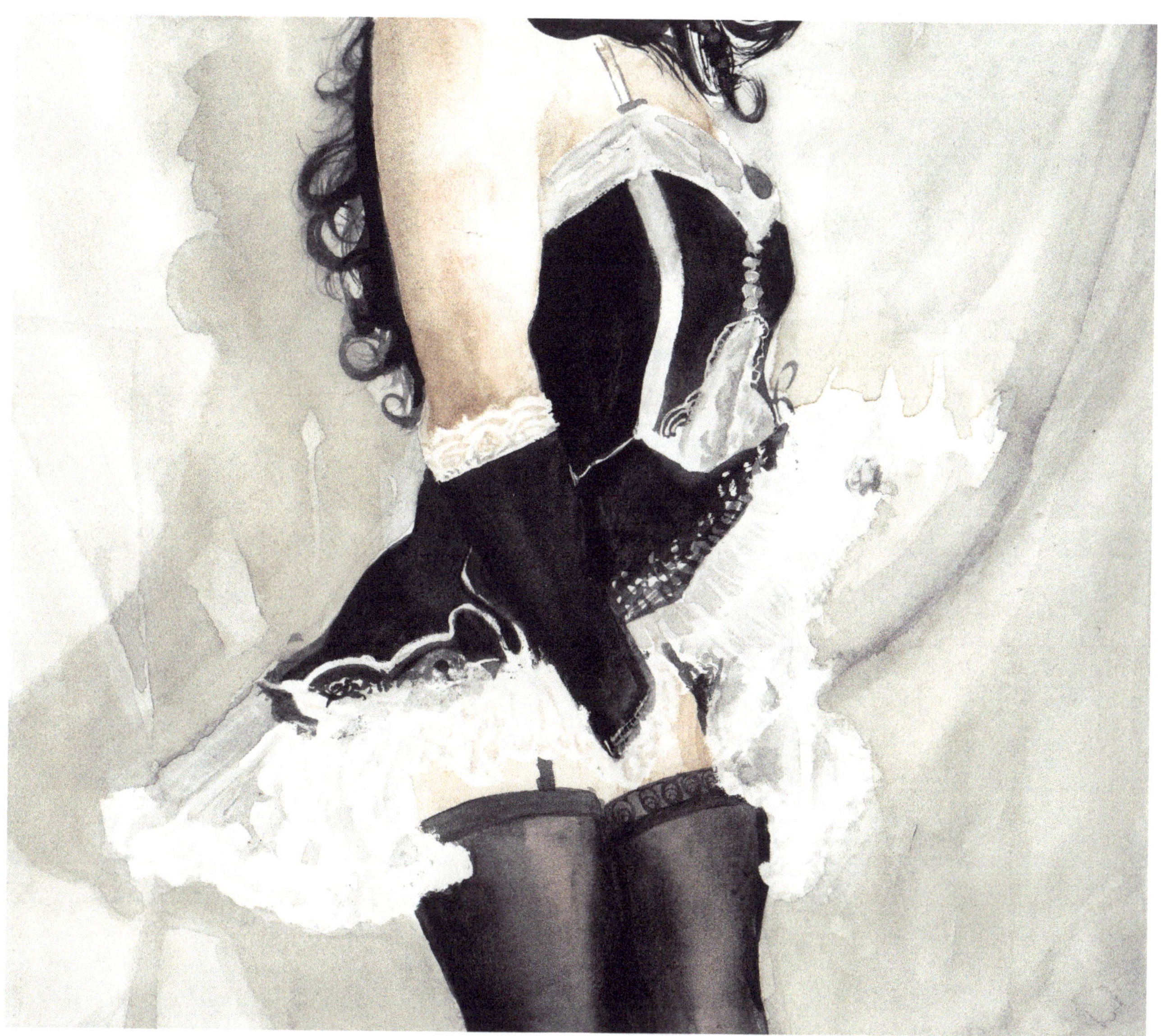

match/enemy

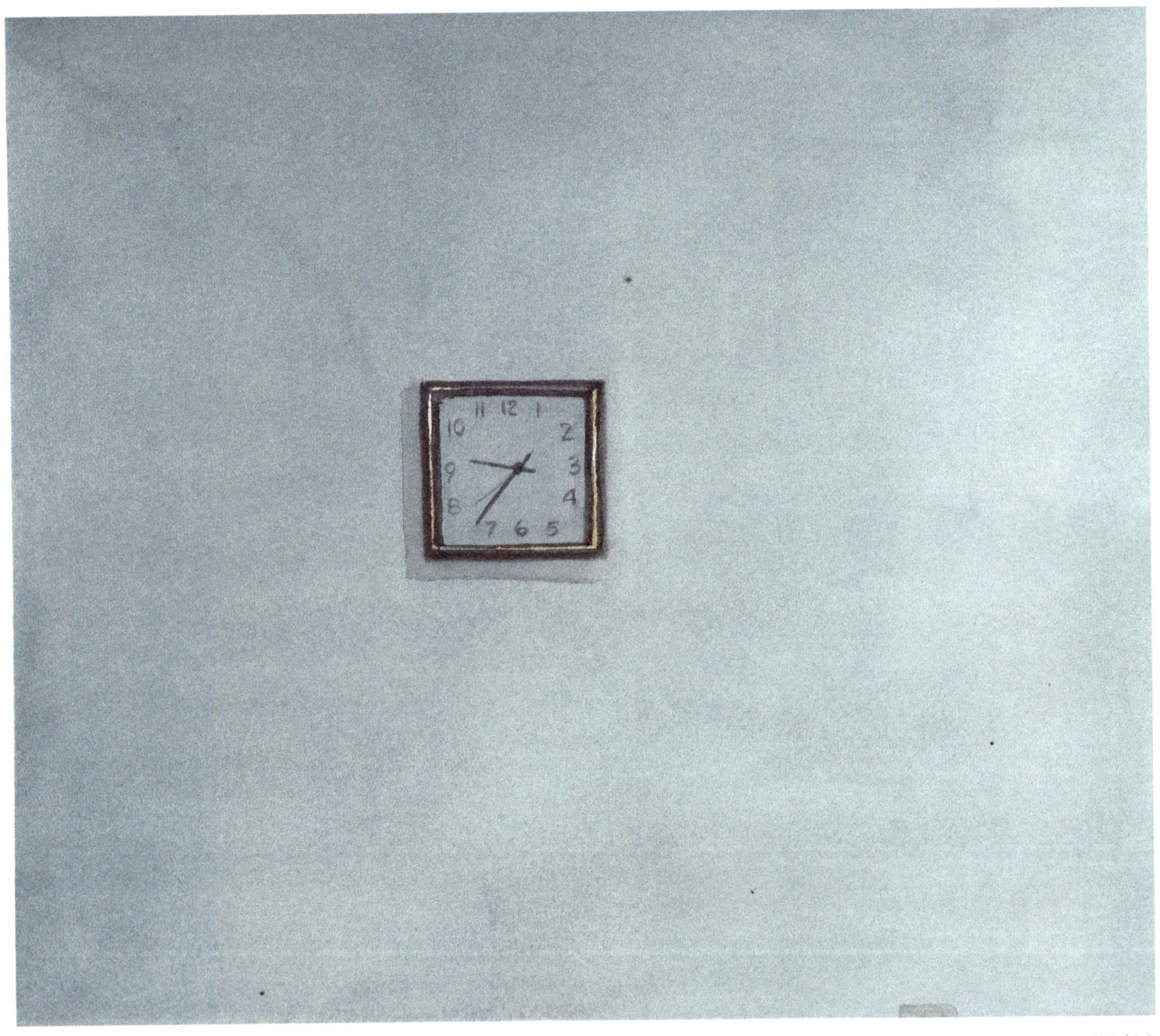

match/enemy   00/90

NO SUCH THING AS FAIRIES NO SUCH THING
AS CAPTAIN HOOK

O blue mirage of wall   keep still
keep still! o steadily troubling hands
the hour chimes   the hands align is she
too late?   is he a prayer?   beyond the wall
a train wails too far gone to catch   beyond
the train a river cuts the mountain's girth
in half   the river laps the cliff face   moon face
watch   the river rots the timber   rusts
the iron of abandoned docks   so much for portrait
potions to snag a leg/a love/a life
tick tock!   so much for flights of fancy   behold
the circling hawk   the cloak falls back no face
blinks back   no Never Never time   nevermind
nevermind the eclipse of moths in the closet

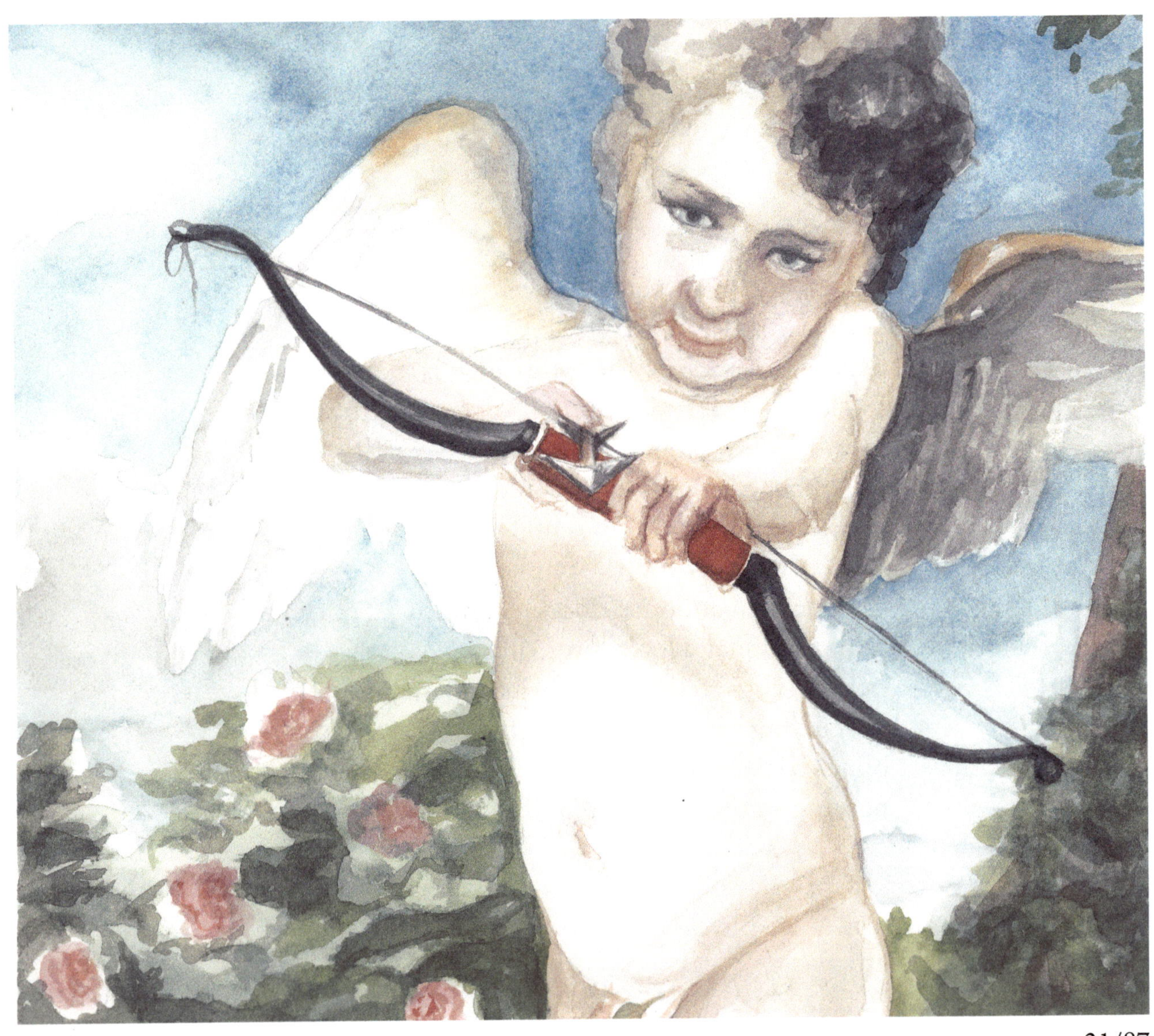

21/87

IT'S NOT OKAY, CUPID

& yet he's here at the door again naked
but for the unsleeved arrow   no defense

now algorithms figure prison sentences
insurance rates   whether he'll beat his child   again

& homophily suggests she's just / like him

it's not an exact science   but a quiz
reveals her self/sabotaging behavior   her

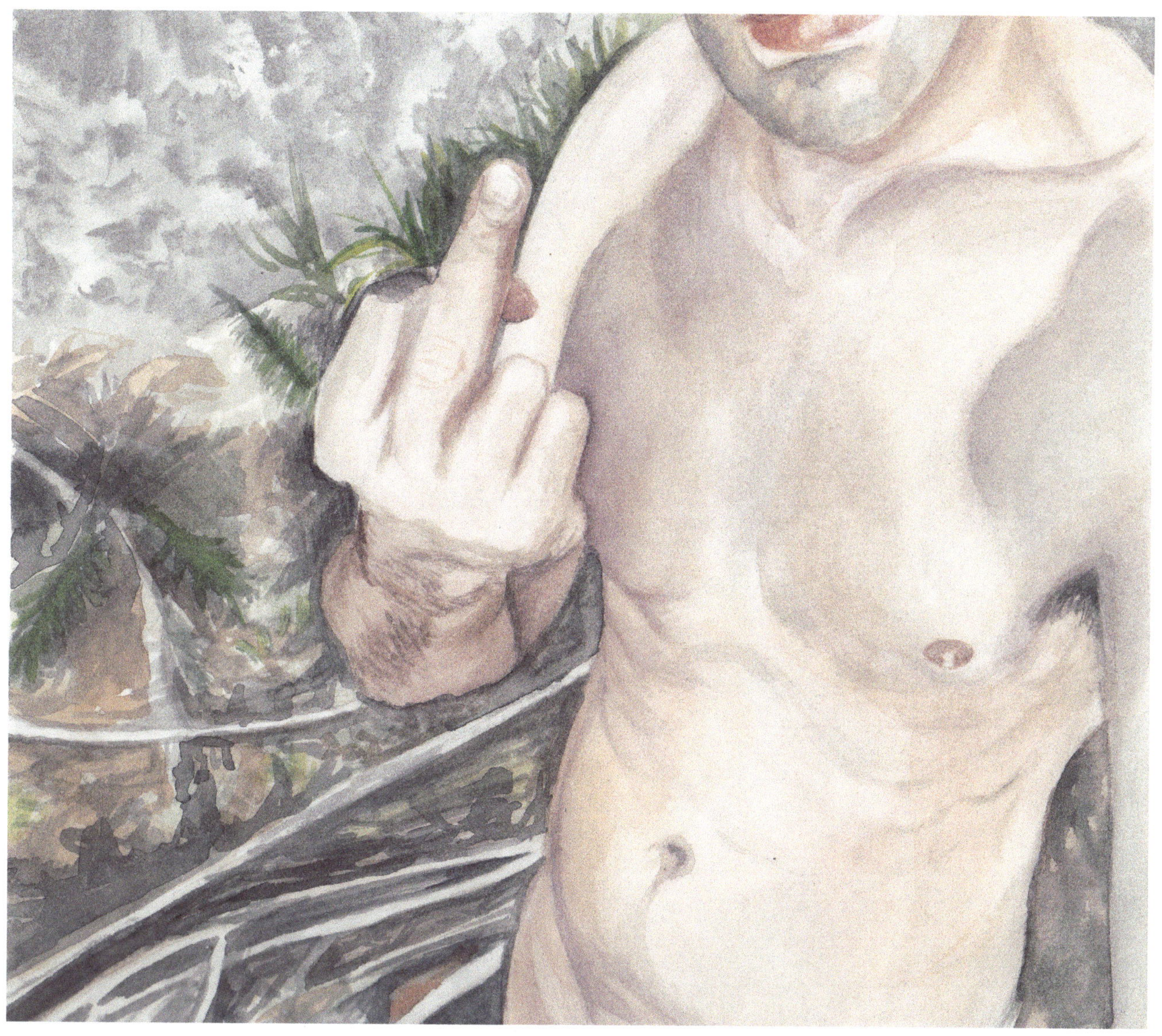

match/enemy

harpoons   white whale dreams   the winedark sea
flesh that never saw sun   flensed & boiled

to moodlight ballrooms   it's true she signed up
for this Mystery Date serenade

for this faceless sniper poised
o'er coconut canopy   apex predators

know too well   entanglement is dangerous.

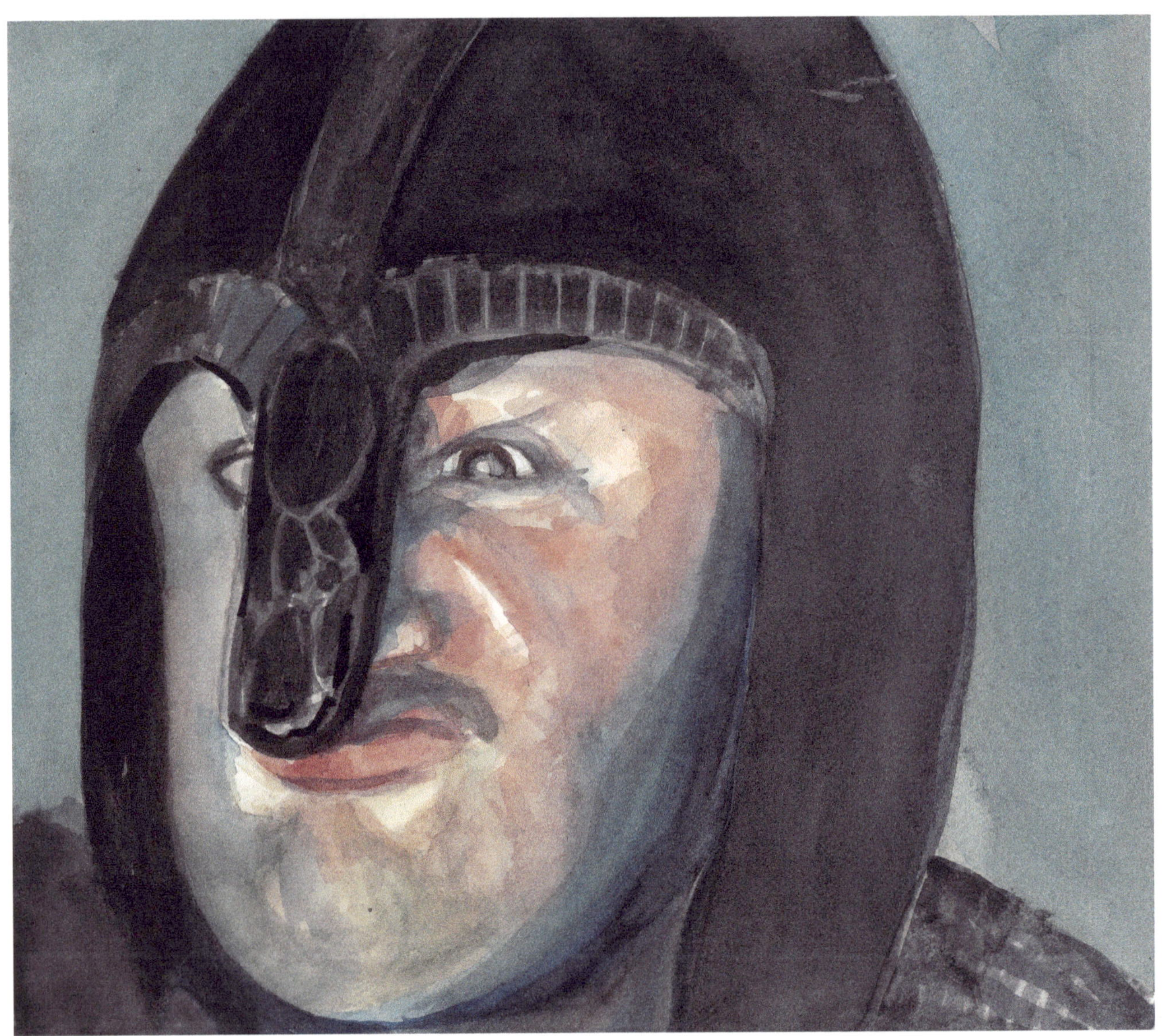

match/enemy 73/13

OK HELMET

has he pledged sword to queen

                                    or bros
fruitless unless attack mode?
attack mode   she knows   can be a relief
the spring's release   hasn't she cocked head
bent knee   laid trembling ear to earth
for song of infantry   held breath
all shell-shocked night lest infant wake
come helmet   tin foil hat   faraday cage
come chainmail to cloak her email
broad sword to smite the ultrasound
O for sub-submarine w/built-in
erection ejection seat   a ground
to air defense against foreskinned
attempts to repatriate the grail

OK KING ME

   or Elvis through The Looking Glass
an erasure...

  the mirror logic tools our think
our sense of   shrank
   we ghostmask real & present ends
  our selves a blip on newnew hop
scotch whirl windsyncs as Alice
          found
   when Al/ice went to crowdsource
      friends
   [replacing self   w/plate
       to feed
    the mirror alpha
       bet] *should* we
  Kaczynski target
       tech? embracing cop
 y copy copyweapons?   ~~art~~
  obscura ~~king~~ re placement feat
  of optics aero   space genetics
mirror portraits con   & vex
  the wo/man loo/king @~~herself~~

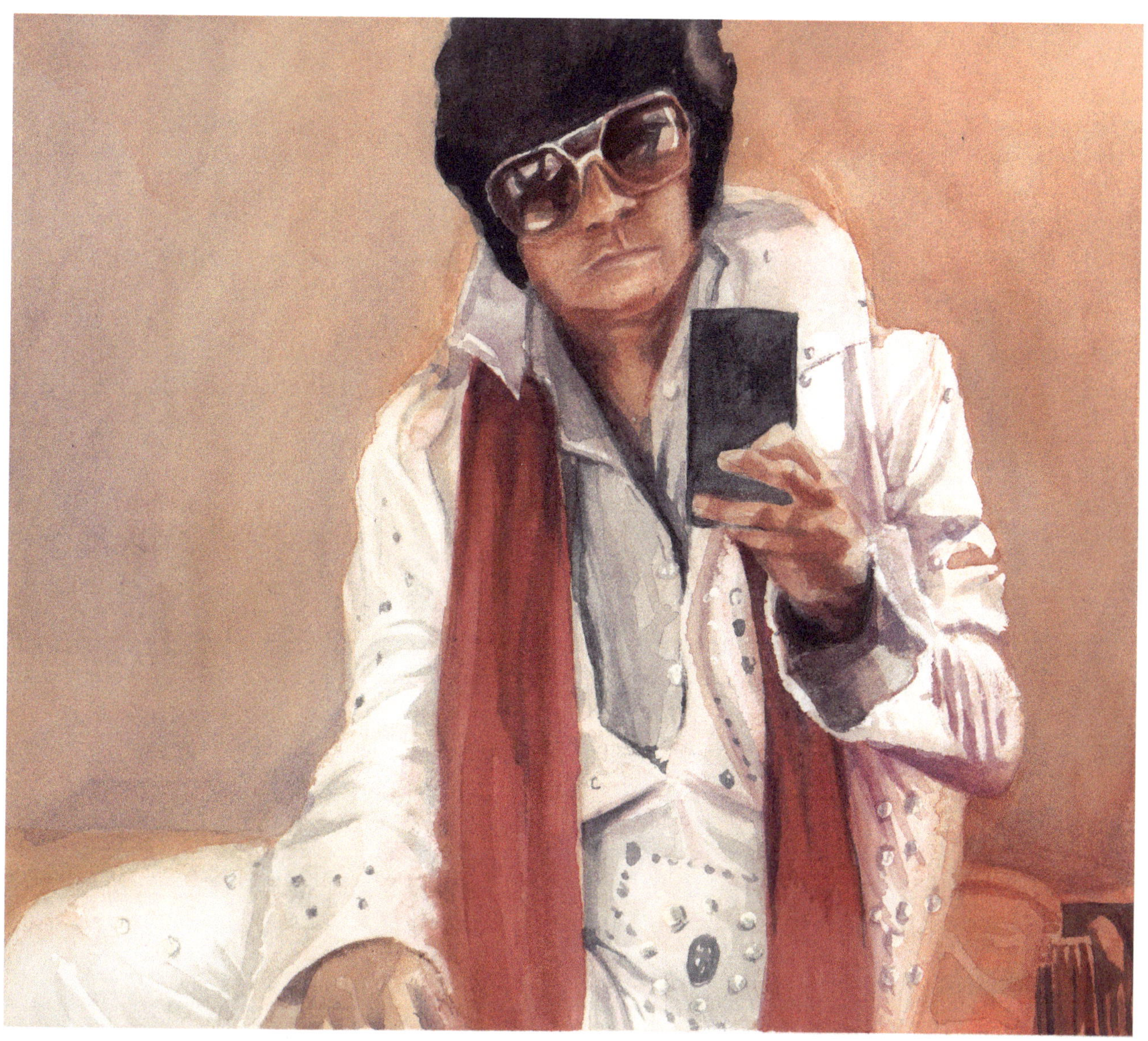

match/enemy

0/99

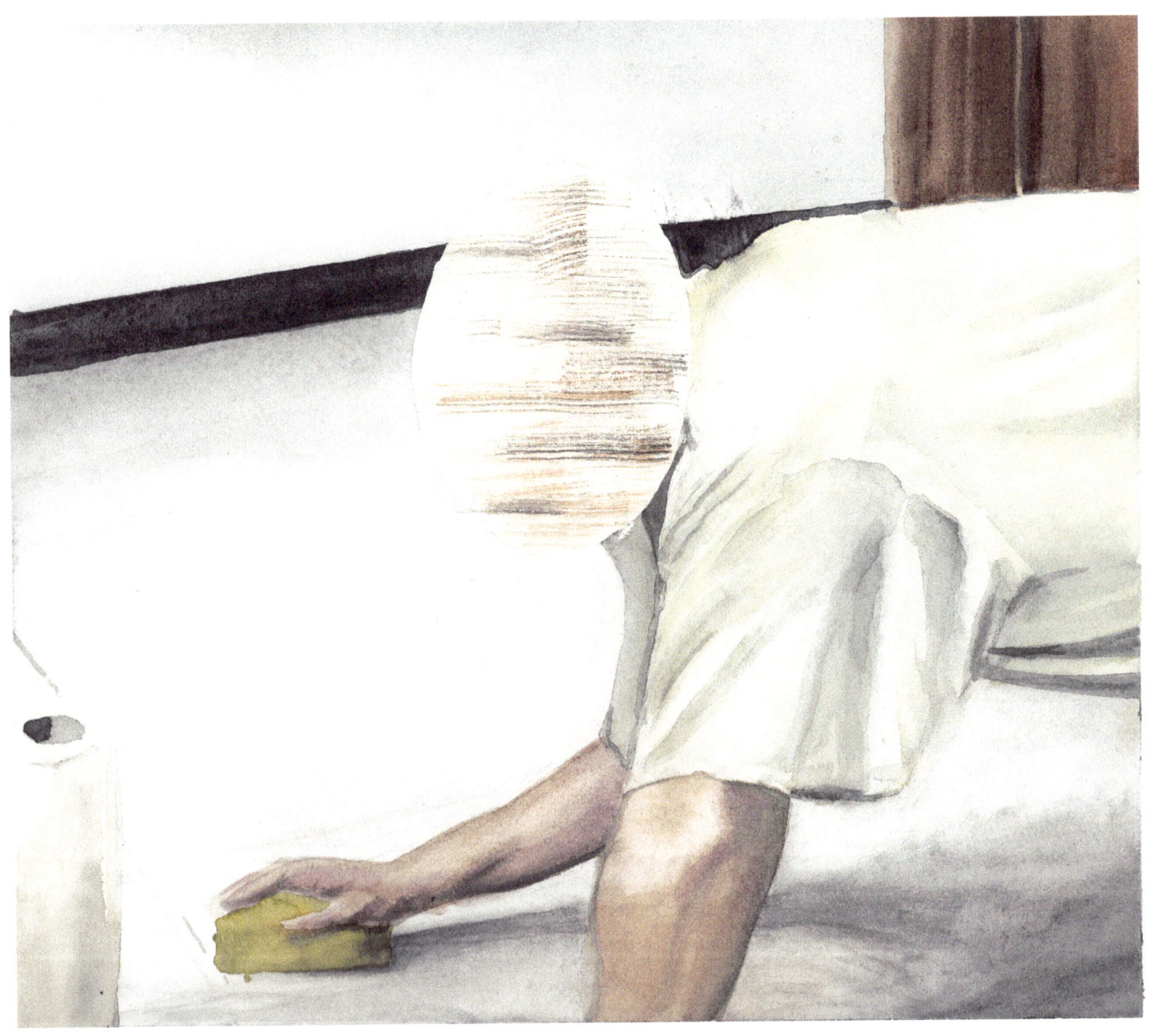

match/enemy

45/38

OK KNOW ME

the problem w/love is it doesn't fit
in boxes   or planes   like the preacher spilling out
his private jet to deliver the sermon
on washing feet like the preacher spilling wine
into the mouths to deliver us from ourselves
once a woman knelt before a dusty
sandalled traveler poured the last of her
precious oils her jet hair her only sponge

& here again this man w/the sponge asking
to be whipped only w/words to embrace only
his own shadow to meet the fecund earth
teaming beneath him missionary style
& who can blame him? the problem w/love is it's just

never known better

she's not sure what she's looking at but can't seem
(is so tired of seeming) to stop looking   has she
ever felt such fondness for toilet paper rolls?
maybe as a kid   some Bible school arts-n-crafts
one end capped w/ wax paper & a rubber band
the room a sudden choir of makeshift kazoos

so easy then to *make* the world   to *make*
the world sing!   & if now she bent to peer
through those cardboard binoculars   that improvised
View-Master™ what beyond the blue dress
of a bare wall would she see? or if she donned
those rubbish spectacles & spun round & round & round
                                                    who
in the slantwise unfiltered unphotoshopped light
would think her happiness a ruse?

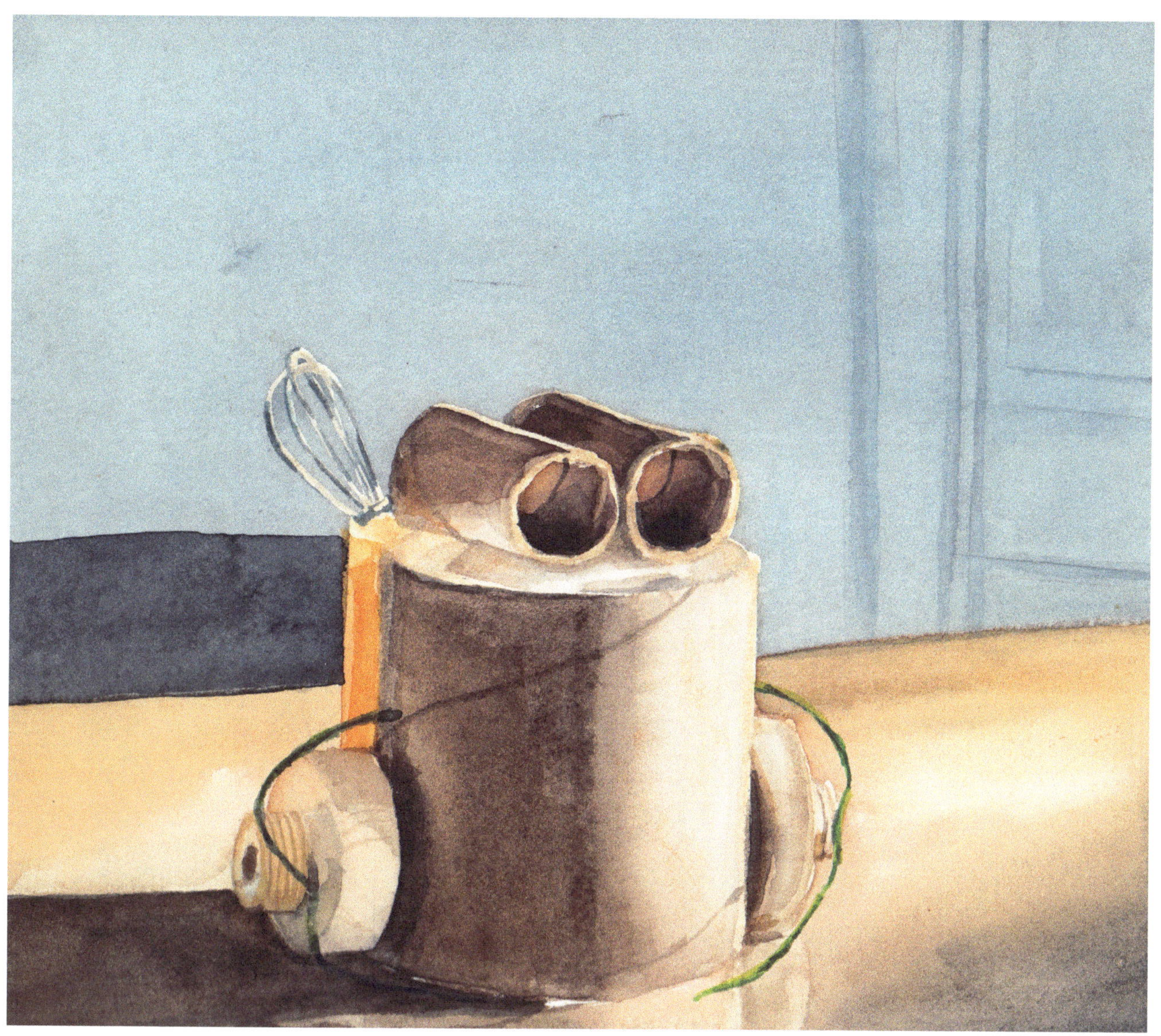

match/enemy   68/16

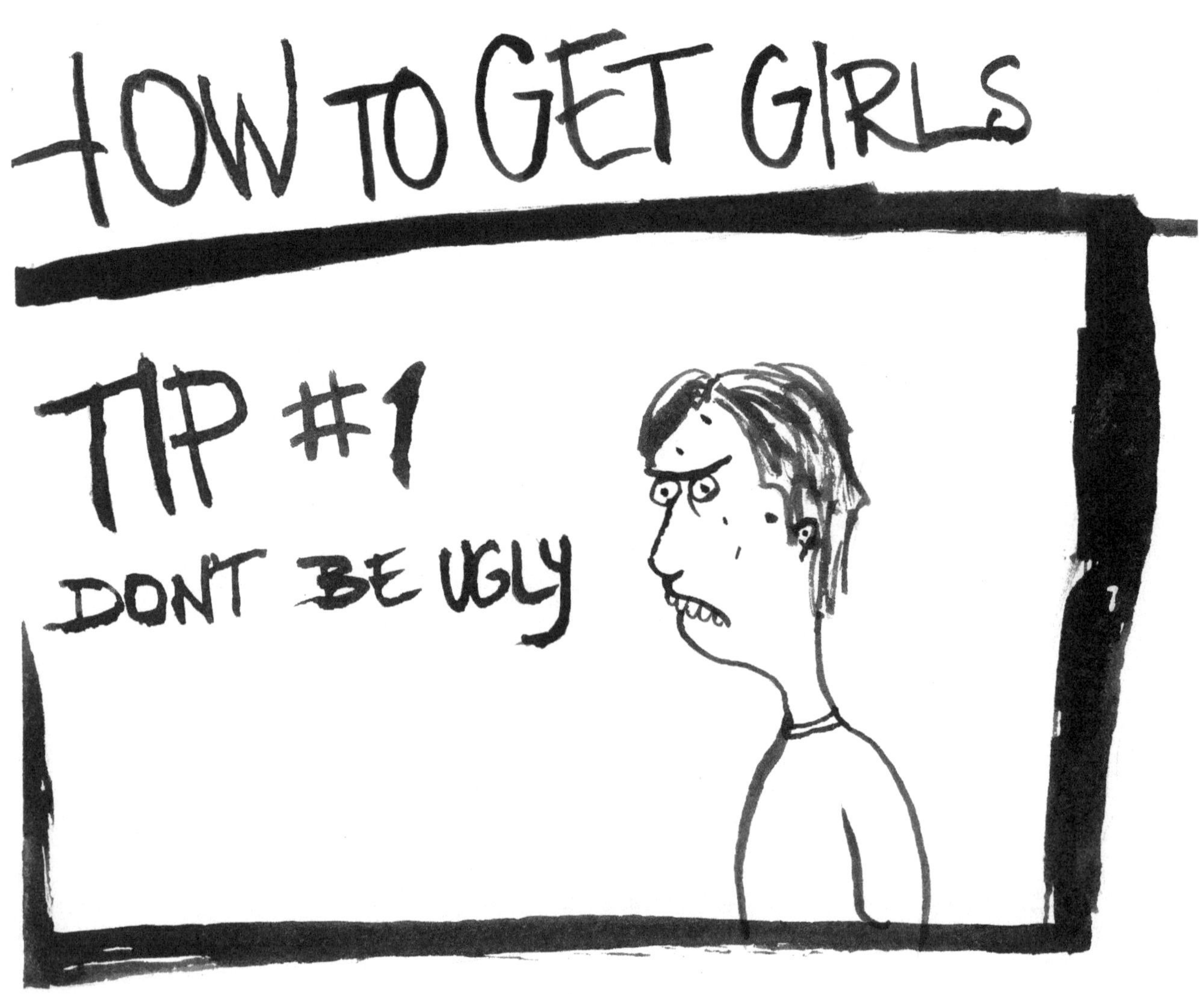

match/enemy

SANS ALLURE?

O creep toothed dorkling   O placid buttress
of fat & fart jokes   O snarling   O pockmarked
you're in luck   as it happens there *aren't* plenty
of fish in the sea   just ask the tuna industry

our fathomless depths run dry   which brings us
to poor man's lobster aka ugly fish
aka frog fish goosefish monkfish now
a bonafide cash cow! in other news

we love the Geek Squad™   whiskers   four eyes
androgyny   the pickled brain salad is delish!
wonder might be our only limitless bounty

what can't be fixed via laser or knife
if only we could appreciate the delicacy
of delicacy we'd be licked & licked...
                                        & licked...

PROTAGONIST REX

like he's posing for end time footnotes
by half-light side stroked   the looney befuddlement
a shortfall amusement   it's not despicable
to be caught mid-scowl in a grinning henchman sandwich
not now—in late descent—it's medicinal!
yellow pills so sweet they rot the teeth
so they attempted to steal the moon—big deal!
they failed! & wasn't the point how villains & minions
are just
                like us
                          failed heroes trying to survive
the swan dive   nursing wounds by firelight
screenlight laughing at evil brethren not just
demoralized but tenderized humanized
redeemed   ready to don again the humble
huntsman's orange fleece   return to active
duty   if only
                if only

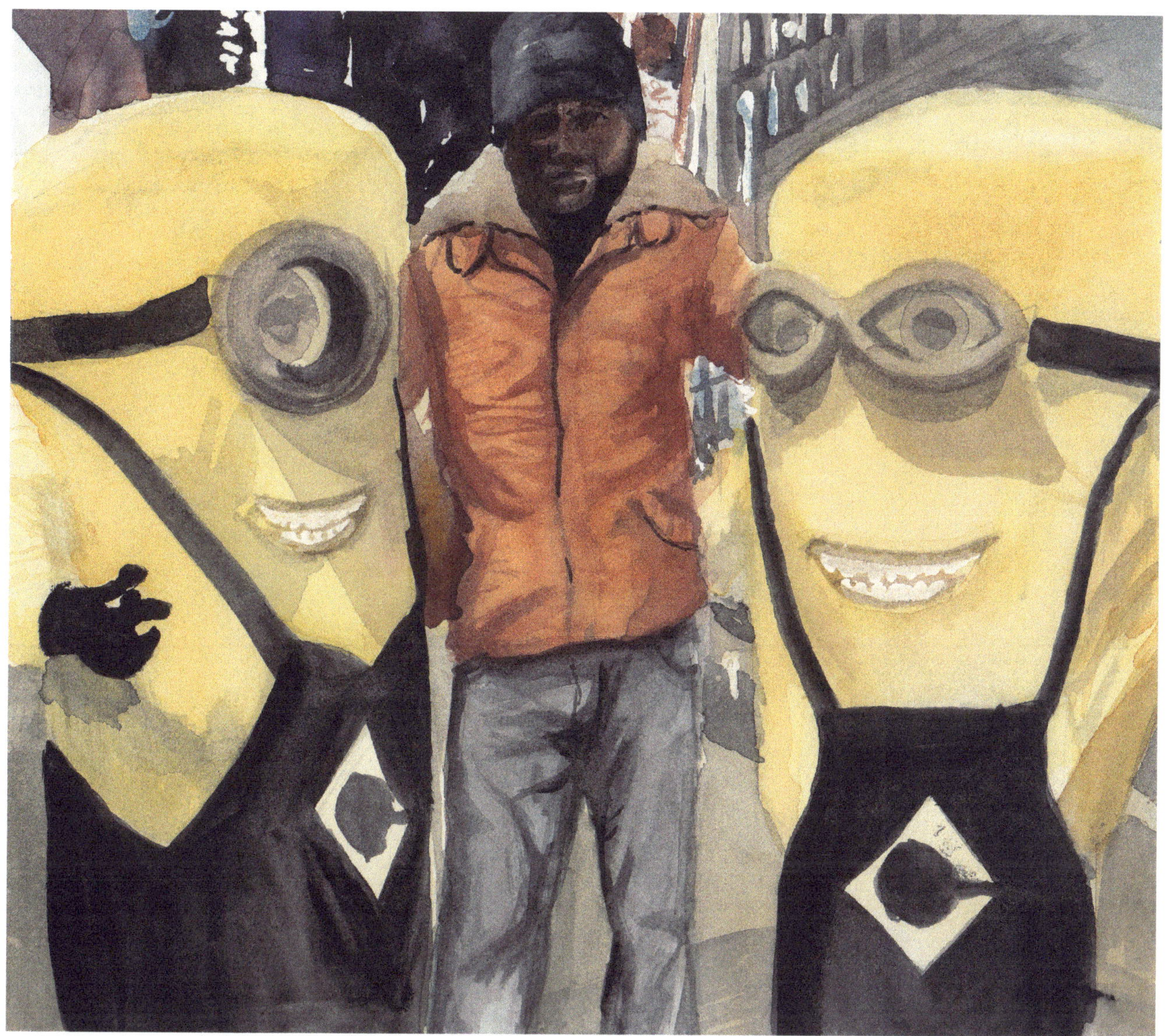

match/enemy　　　　　　　　75/13

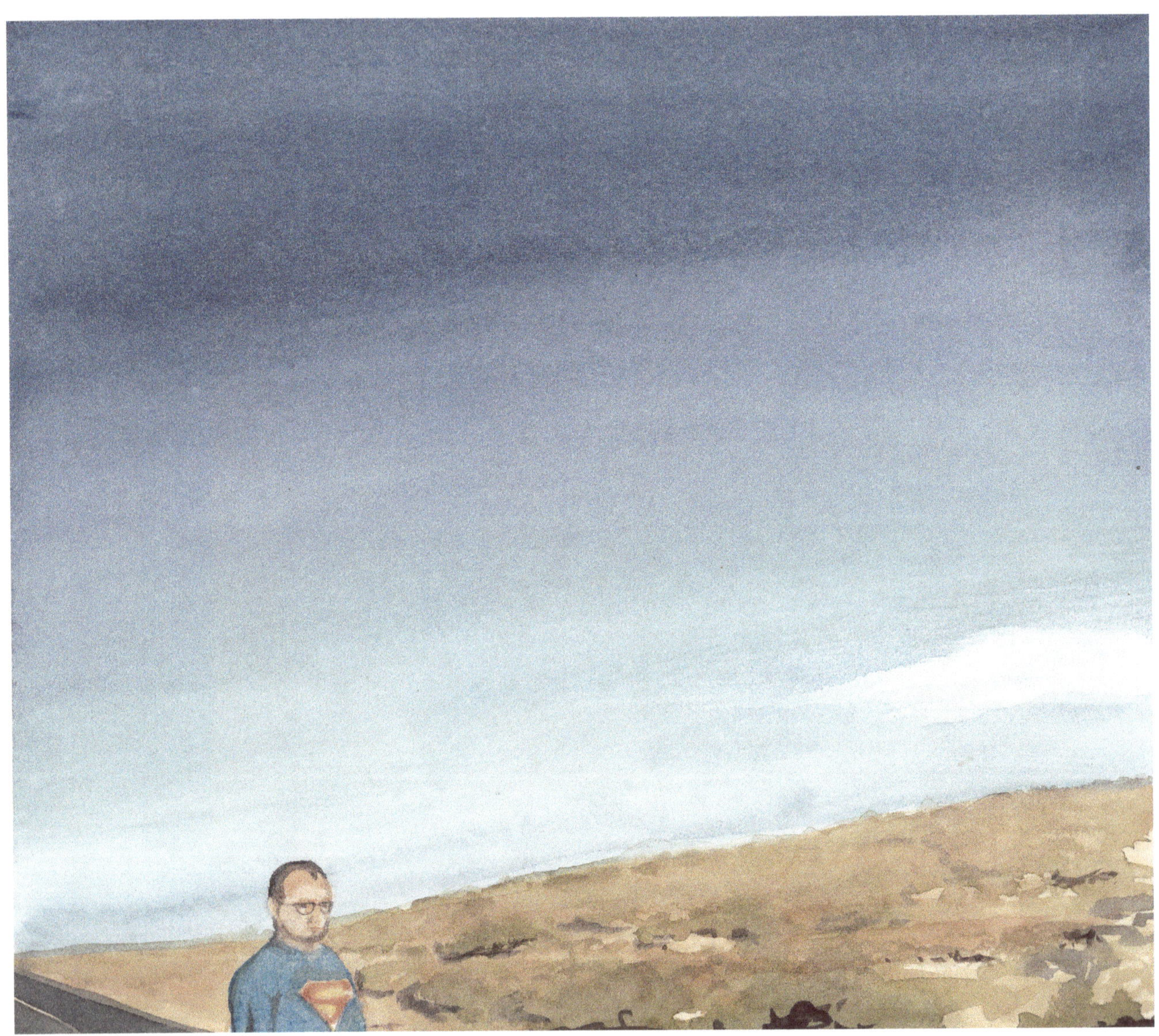

match/enemy

WOMAN WONDERS INTO A BAKERY

who might he be   this rangy super this
high/way dreamer who'd cut his own legs out
from under to deliver the unskyscraped
unsiloed unbillboarded horizon where even
the mountain's low outcropping drinks its fill
of ether where when he flies his shadow's just
another sage brush   a dust up   he's got
no hard-on for vacuous space   no plans to vacate
he's already New Worlding Krypton's asylum
besides there's plenty hostile planet here
to terraform   logistics fixes yet to farm
what makes none sick   plus bodies suited more
or less to gravity w/o which hearts atrophy
terrestrial beets to stain red velvet cake

at last a fool who almost lets her   see him   as through bars   the strings drawn
taut   noosed trick of latex   O simple art   displacing air   (keep breathing) (breathe!)
w/ unburst!childhood!dreams!   of He   O helium! whose thoughtless levity is naught
but off gas trash of radical radioaction   \   faint memory of most brutal instabilities O

memory! let too   thine noble gasses
grow inert \ let it   not hurt! were he in
strument oh how   she'd pluck \ & join
the loosed kaleid   oscope aloft   or let
they together (O   fumblingfingers) un
do flexile knots   releasing what will
slip through all   the O/zones of us
oh oh to deep in   hale that god all
seeing by whose   light we play at
oath k e e p i n g   star on whom
no human jelly   must ever gaze
she'd huff fumes   of that bright eye
for daze they'd   translate every
song they knew   to chipmunk tunes

they never sung as kids like kids they could begin   again   w/tinny practice promises
writ in helium   O atomic abstract of violence   O impervious isolationist O nuclear bond
the envy of wannabe   Beaver Cleaver families   (forever?)   cleaving two   lonesome
(gee Wally) protons into one \\ they might have fun //flirting w/spontaneous combustion

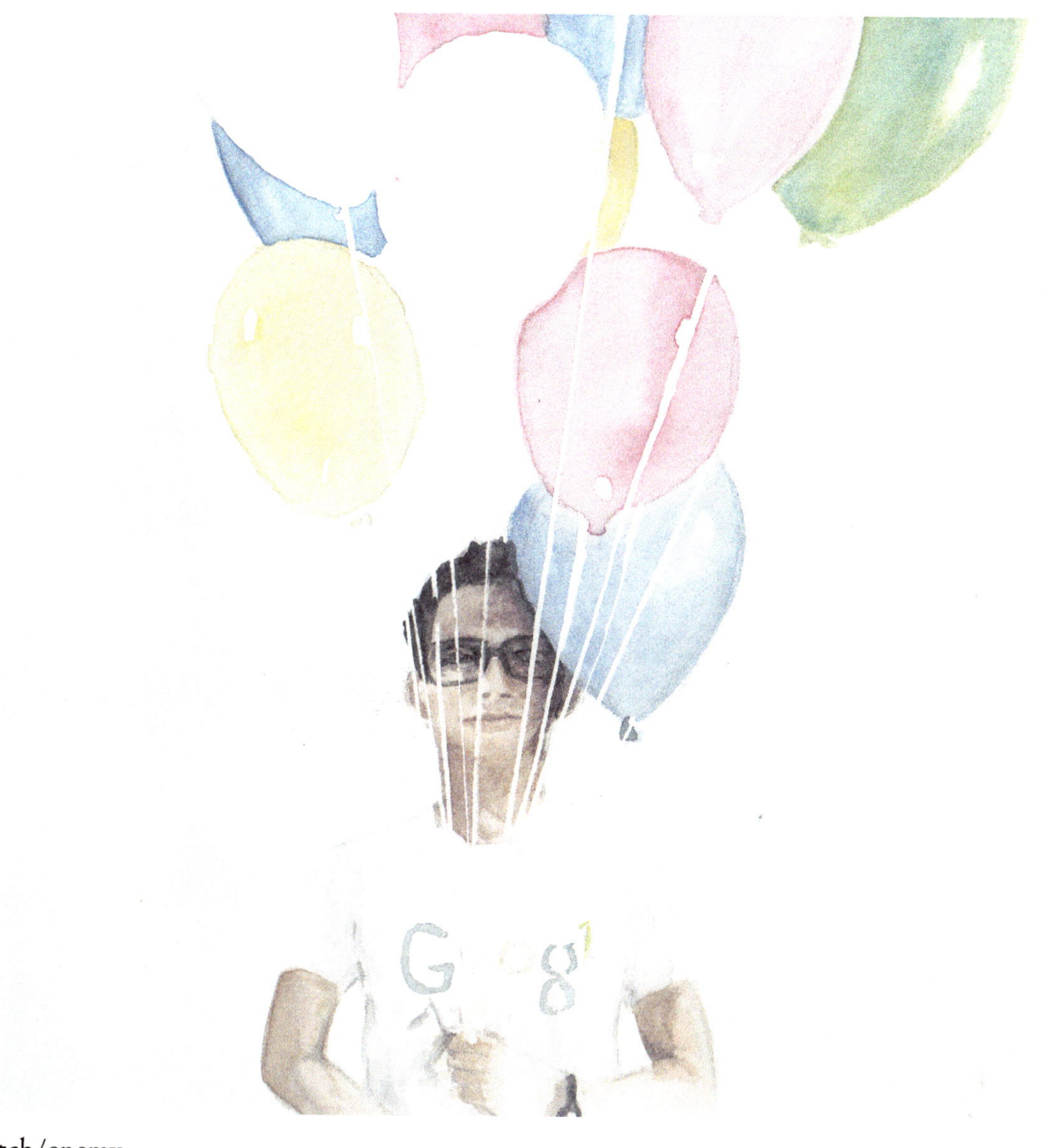

match/enemy   56/42

at last   a fool   who almost   lets her   see him   as through bars   the strings drawn
taut   noosed trick of latex   O simple art   displacing air   (keep breathing) (breathe!)
w/ unburst!childhood!dreams!   of He   O helium! whose thoughtless levity is naught
but off gas   trash   of radical radioaction \ faint memory of most brutal instabilities O

memory! let too   thine noble gasses
grow inert \ let it   not hurt! were he in
strument oh how   she'd pluck \ & join
the loosed kaleid   oscope aloft   or let
they together (O   fumblingfingers) un
do flexile knots   releasing what will
slip through all   the O/zones of us
oh oh to deep in   hale that god all
seeing by whose   light we play at
oath k e e p i n g   star on whom
no human jelly   must ever gaze
she'd huff fumes   of that bright eye
for daze they'd   translate every
song they knew   to chipmunk tunes

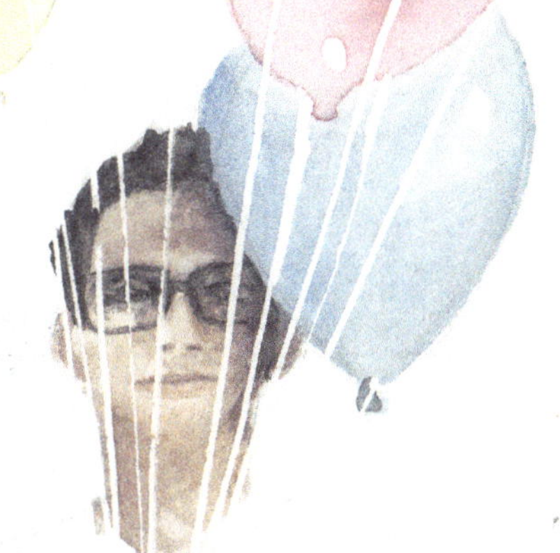

they never sung   as kids   like kids   they could begin   again   w/tinny practice promises
writ in helium   O atomic abstract of violence   O impervious isolationist O nuclear bond
the envy of wannabe   Beaver Cleaver families   (forever?)   cleaving   two   lonesome
(gee Wally) protons into one \\ they might have fun //flirting w/spontaneous combustion

match/enemy   56/42

II.

SPECULUM₆

(((of a midlife⁷
Gen X poet
of 50 years
25 **married**)))

from topside
a tumbling

down

down

down

the **rabbit hole**⁸

---

6 A) in medicine, an instrument that expands the portal, the better to see; B) in ornithology, re: plumage, the extra dazzle; C) a **mirror**, esp. as part of a tool advancing sight; D) in the 1960s & 70s a tool whereby women taught women how to view & so reclaim their nether regions.

7 Is it bad luck to call 50 the midpoint? Like **Dante**,* she can hope.

8 A) portal to a **rabbit**'s burrow, to the subterranean complex of a warren; B) route by which Alice **blunders into Wonder;**** C) a metaphor for bizarre, **labyrinthian** experiences; D) in the 1999 dystopian **epic**, *The Matrix*,*** a metaphor for the way of enlightenment via **red pill;****** E) the practice of falling through cascading internet hyperlinks...as the poet has polishing the **glass** of this Speculum.

---

* Alas, though **Dante** set his midlife comedy (his speculative autobiography?) in his 35th year & proclaimed it "halfway through life's journey", he died 14 years shy of 70.

** *See also* **"White Rabbit"** by **Grace Slick**: *one pill makes you larger...*

*** In the film, "the matrix" is a manufactured **dream**, a **mirror world** uncannily like our own used to eclipse the post-apocalyptic reality in which humans are unconscious slaves powering sentient machines.

**** Had *Matrix* diehards read the film as "transgender allegory" as writer/director **Lilly Wachowski** intended, **red pill***** might be an emblem of progressive consciousness. Instead the film became a key text for disaffected men populating chatrooms in the early aughts,*⁶ who now march openly. Their **red pill** revelation? This is a woman's world. *See misandry.*⁷ *See* **manosphere.***⁸ Behold **incels**,*⁹ PUAs (Pick Up Artists) & MRAs (Men's Rights Activists), the medicine cabinet of pills in every hue. *See* **anonymity** swap hoods for handles.*¹⁰

***** *See also Total Recall* (1990).

*6 Why? Is it the groundbreaking fight scenes? The **neo-noir**, **cyber**punk aesthetic? The plot?—see a **dungeon** dwelling **hacker** turn invincible martial artist (via Neuralink-esque uploads), get the girl & save humanity from **AI** tyranny.

*7 Prejudice against men, claimed as equivalent counterpart to misogyny.

*8 Umbrella term for online sites & forums advocating for men in opposition to feminism. Rooted in the men's liberation movements of the 1970s & 80s that began as a critique of gender normativity & devolved to anti-feminism. Around 2010, the **manosphere** "tipped" from fringe (cringe) to mainstream industry.

*9 Portmanteau for **in**voluntarily **cel**ibate, ironically coined by a queer woman blogging her dating frustrations in 1997. Studies indicate that the online posts of men who self-describe as **incel**, often broadcast misogyny, racism, depictions of physical violence & **rape**, as well as self-loathing, depression & extreme loneliness. In one **survey** of 300 **incel** men, only 30% reported having one or more friends.

*10 In 2017, the subreddit **r/incels** was banned for violent content, followed by r/braincels in 2018 & r/MGTOW (Men Going Their Own Way) in 2021; several mass shootings have been linked to those belonging to these & other groups that reorganized on more "tolerant" sites . In 2018, the Southern Poverty Law Center added *male supremacy* to their hate group watch list.

Algorhythmix...no relation to the British pop sensation which brought us **"Sweet Dreams,"**[9] nor the Dalcrozian system devised to incarnate music & train would-be players...no relation we know of...though the latter lent some DNA to **Nijinsky**'s ***Rite of Spring***[10] which (like Annie's[11] **dreams**) got lots of folks hot & bothered.

par/allel beauty... in a 2015 talk at **String Theory**[12] in Philly,[13] **OKCupid** founder, **Christian Rudder**, infamously declared that people complaining their matches are ugly must be ugly, since, in addition to pairing clients according to preference & personality, **algorithms** "objectively" assess **portraits** to enforce a water-finds-its-level parity (parody?) of beauty.

As if the laws of attraction were universal. Quantifiable. Neutral. Swiss. As if the eye of any beholder was not a singular juice box of nervy siphon squirts but a **code** (genetic? kinetic? magnetic? bilateral? hieroglyphic?) to hack. As if **sex** could be certified as **Fair Trade**™.

infinity-mirror...to replicate via opposition what catches twixt the **glass** ad infinitum, ad nauseum, until the re**doubling** distance dissipates with the exponent's exponent's exponent, obscurum per obscurius, ad delirium, ad deliquium, ad glorium.

homogenize...application of heat & high-pressured squeeze to prevent cream's rising.

level up!.. See hypergamy.[14] *See cheat* ***code.***[15]

---

9 **Sweet Dreams (Are Made of This)**, title track of a new wave album released by the **Eurythmics** in 1983. A sonic mickey slipped to an 8-year-old w/a **Walkman**™*, pumping her backyard swing.

10 Inciting a riot at its 1913 premier, the modern masterpiece conceived & composed by **Igor Stravinsky**, aka ***Sacre du Printemps***, also incited the rapid decline of choreographer, ballet super**star** & **sex** symbol **Vaslav Nijinsky**.

Inspired by Russian folktales & pagan ritual, the ballet depicts the **sacrificial "marriage"** of a maid to the sun **god**, a consummation whereby the **virgin** dances herself to death. Agitated by the dissonate composition & anti-balletic choreography, the Parisian audiences grew so loud that dancers could not hear their cues & **Nijinsky** took to shouting the count from atop a chair he dragged to the edge of the stage.

The score quickly established **Stravinsky** as a musical genius, but for **Nijinsky**, *the very perfume of the rose*, the great danseur of his age, (as **Baryshnikov** of ours), the **sacrificial** rite in *Spring* proved prophetic. Deemed by many to be a failure, the groundbreaking choreography, recorded only to the dancers' passing memories, was soon lost & despite a history of **romances** w/human sun **gods**—a prince, a count, the famed director of Ballet Russe—following *Spring's* failure, **Nijinsky**, *God of Dance*, entered a hasty hetero**sexual marriage** & spun into madness.

11 **Annie Lennox**, Scottish singer-songwriter, political activist & half the **Eurythmics**, whose queer aesthetic "defied the male gaze". The girl w/a **Walkman**™, may or may not have likened the dusky **croon** & defiant posture to another unflinching **femme** & early idol, **Lauren Bacall**.

12 A charter school. Also a theoretical explanation of everything in which everything is already partnered.

13 Philadelphia, city of brotherly love. Where the girl w/the **Walkman**™ lives briefly (late adolescence, early 90s— forget Chicago/New York/London—here is Gotham) to apprentice w/brotherly love ballet. Trades tutus & pointe shoes for raves in the broken mouths of factories, in the vault of an empty bank. Stalks taxi-less corridors for a quarter & a working payphone. Abandons the **dream**. Likewise **virginity**. Lets strangers take her home.

14 To enter **romantic** partnership, esp **marriage**, w/a person of superior social or financial status.

15 In video **games**, a secret command **code** by which players gain unadvertised advantages.

---

* The headset culture launched in 1979 by Japanese tech giant Sony foreshadowed today's app culture & like today owes its pre-"viral" viral appeal to influencers & product placement (see *Risky Business*, see *Pretty in Pink*) & to the **sex** appeal of youth culture & "indie" aesthetics.

the **Queen of Hearts** *says off with their heads...* **Carroll's**[16] consummate **bully** is so distracted, or her subjects so heedless, though the monarch dispatches four death sentences, we witness zero guillotined stumps.

Alas *you*, gentle reader, must begrudge or forgive us these many headless **chicken** runs.[17]

*she sees herself from outside herself...***John Berger** not unproblematically depicts the internalized male gaze in his seminal BBC series & subsequent book, ***Ways of Seeing.***[18]

> *Men look at women. Women watch themselves being looked at. This determines not only most relations between men and women but also the relation of women to themselves. The* **surveyor** *of woman in herself is male: the* **surveyed** *is female.*[19]

the foe in the **looking glass**[20]...**Mirror** as revelation. As nightmare. *See also* **Dorian Gray**, Jekyll & Hyde, Slim Shady.

The Victorian era saw a proliferation of **portraits** of women holding **mirrors** as a testament to their vanity (again, thanks, Berger), though who painted, purchased & owned the figures poised to revel in their own beauty is worth reflection.[21]

---

16 **Lewis Carroll**, Victorian author most famous for ***Alice in Wonderland*** & *Through the* **Looking Glass** & for perhaps pedophiliac proclivities especially as regards one Alice Liddell (whose name so slantly **echoes** Lewis Carroll).

17 The case of **Mike the Headless Chicken** (born April 20, 1945, decapitated September 10, 1945, died March 17, 1947 (a longer run headless than not)), put a name & uh...face/lessness to the gallinaceous propensity to gallivant haphazardly post axe. Nevertheless, the analogous phrase goes back six centuries, suggesting the headless **chicken** dance—a waddle made possible by **bird** brains that extend well down the neck & a mysterious organ w/mechanosensing capabilities, call it a second brain which, like a human's, is located in the pelvis—is surprisingly, alarmingly common.

Less common, of course, is sustained, free-roaming beheadedness. Beyond his not quite dumb luck (the **bird** could almost cluck) Mike's deadhead days came at the pains of his assailant & would be gobbler, Floyd Olson. W/watery milk & an eyedropper, the Colorado farmer kept the Wyandotte **cock** alive, transforming Mike into a touring sideshow **star** that fetched a quarter a gander. At his best, the **cock** grossed $4,500 a month (70K a month today)—no chicken scratch.

One wonders if the miraculous **bird** was the namesake of Magic Mike*, *those* **cocks** strutting their stuff, or if his acclaim (a feature in both ***LIFE*** & ***Time***) led to *Michael*'s nearly 50-year reign as most popular boy's name (a **game** Mike loses when we consider not longevity but frequency to (ahem) Jen/Jennifer/Jenny).

18 In the later 90s, expelled from Philly, the **dream** turned darkly, **Walkman**™ **Girl** now college girl, reads **Berger** & thinks—*duh! did women not already know this?*—wonders (before the term but not the ubiquity of *mansplaining*) what girl wouldn't scream off w/his head? what blade bearing woman wouldn't answer, *which one?*

19 A) If you think the internalized **gaze** is kind, think again. B) If you think the rise of social media marks the advent of body dysmorphic disorder, put down the **mirror**. C) What is the **surveyed** inside men?

20 The **looking glass** in which one meets one's foe might apply to those lining the walls of a ballet studio, pet shop window, a junior high bathroom, a hotel bathroom, a filling-station bathroom, the surface of skyscrapers, **glass** of the bodega, the framed photo of your mother, father, sister, brother...the **spectacles** of anyone you want *to know.*

21 Now—at 50—does **Walkman**™ **G** know whether she wrote this because she knows this or because, way back in the day, **John Berger** told her so?

5   **The Wounded.**

Two Face/d....Obsessed w/duality, fate & chance, **Two Face**, aka **Harvey Dent**, a once upstanding, prosecuting attorney, is among **Batman**'s most popular enemies.[22] Origin stories vary. In DC comics, Dent's justice-begetting charm earns him the media moniker, **Apollo**,[23] until villainous trauma causing hemispheric disfigurement & psychological fracture render him arbitrator of good or woe pursuant to the land of a coin.[24]

In ***The Dark Knight***, Dent's split begins w/the loss of his beloved, a gruesome dispatch of the beguiling Rachel Dawes, w/whom our **hero**[25] too, is in love.

Tomorrow & tomorrow & tomorrow...it seems, like Harvey, MacBeth (one more **hero** turned **villain**?) can't screw his courage to the sticking place w/o his Lady.

6   **Don't Look Down.**[26]

35mm: once the affixing eye's arresting notion of choice, gone w/the dark rooms, halide crystals, **double** exposures[27] & canned cheese.

---

22 How we love to hate our enemies.

23 Greek **god** of light, logic, music, healing, law, poetry, beauty...**twin** to **Artemis**...who **Walkman**™ **Girl** learns in college poetry w/**Diane Wakoski** (fan of **Nietzsche**), apposes **Dionysus**—god of wine, fertility, **sexuality**, theatre, a tricksy interlocuter between the dead & the living, of **dark matter** (otherness, chaos, epiphany, insanity, ecstasy, **sacrifice**)—a male deity associated w/the wild "nature of women".

Nietzsche/DW says intercourse between the two is necessary for vitality in art & in life, but something of the gender representations make **Walkman**™ **G** angry, a ferment which monthly bubbles over in hysteria.

24 So **Apollo** becomes **Dionysus**.

25 And don't we love this, how he loves her & how she, thwarted by the **masks** of his maskless identities, can't, then can, then can't see him.

One wonders why, in *this* **survey** of suitors, the **Bat** is unrepresented, while **Superman** (spoiler alert) swoops in repeatedly. If **Hollywood** investment & gross yields are any indication, the travails of Bruce Wayne are far more popular—despite or *because* of his shadowy psychology. Certainly the Man of Steel seems a less troubled & troubling model—is he who men think their mates want them to be? And *do* we?

Walkman™ **G** prefers a **cat** who knows their way around a cave, wells, the **sex** appeal of cloaks, grappling hooks, a slick hood, spandex, growls. Though for long range missions she knows it's foolish to choose urban playboy over cornfed reporter & who wouldn't trade caves & gadgets for the **dream** of sky & might—for **flight**. Not to mention, as **Walkman**™ **G**'s very human **husband** points out, **Batman**'s got no actual powers. He's just a man w/a lot of cash.

26 Says **Superman** to **Lois Lane**.

27 If you've never known the pleasure of a dark room, if you've never calculated shutter relative to aperture, if you've never spliced a negative, timed the light, clicked the switch, tonged a high gloss sheet in the shallow basin of a plastic pan

Or:

If you've never dropped a roll of amateur **porno** pics at the quickie print...never returned for the pick-up, never met the **gaze** of the Sikh man behind the counter, taking your cash, making change, making familiar the strange, forget what you think you know about **double** exposure.

*Anyone can fall in love with a **double**...*Studies suggest people favor people who share their features, calling to question whether the allure of the familiar proliferated prior to the **mirror**[28] & if eternal bathroom dwellers are more beguiled by **doppelgangers** & if maybe for the good of the species, genetic diversity, etc. we ought shatter all the **glass**, phones, tempered sky scrapers, not to mention **Gelernter's**[29] **mirrorworlds**, the ones in toddling nascency & an onslaught in utero. But what would we do w/the rivers (that got **Narcissus**)?

***double**/black diamond*...a classification of slope for expert skiers/boarders/thrill seekers. Often, young, adrenaline junkies. As w/the gems, conquest requires luck/money.

9   There There.

There There...As in a nanny's placating coo or what **Stein**[30] says is missing.

prix fixe...in restaurant nomenclature, the prearranged **marriage** of the diner & their dinner.

O face... ... yes, *that.* Also a guitar pedal produced in Eugene, OR.[31] *See also* **rockstar**.

money back guarantee....speaking of truth-in-advertising, one site traces the strategy to J.L. Watkins, a traveling salesman hocking remedies in the 1860s; another credits Josiah Wedgewood[32] of fine, highly collectible pottery. A search reveals the tactic has many pros[33] & cons (there are many pros at cons) e.g. attracting bad customers.

***White Fang**...*by Jack London,[34] a novel from the perspective of an undomesticated **wolfdog**.

---

28   In the beginning, only a windless lake, lily-less pond, the bend of a slow river to make of oneself a picture. From the Latin, *mirari*, to admire. Ancient Egyptians polished bronze into flat disks to honor the sun **god** & their own face shone. The Greeks, of course, played w/scale—full-length reflections & compact companions—rimming each w/the likeness of deities, especially **Aphrodite** & **Cupid**'s foreshadow, **Eros. Glass mirrors** remained darkly inconsistent &/or deadly until Enlightenment, though the mercury-lined in China date to 500CE. A lady's most prized possession by 1600s & of the manufacturing technology Venice guildsmen, upon pain of death, were sworn to secrecy; as late as the 18th century, who so inherited the family **looking glass** was the most beloved beneficiary.

29   As described in his 1991 treatise, ***Mirror** Worlds: Or: The Day Software Puts the Universe in a Shoebox—How It Will Happen and What It Will Mean*, which predicted w/alarming accuracy our current digital state & the yet-to-be-consummated **marriage** of reality & its virtual **twin**.

For this, the young computer scientist & Yale professor drew the ire of Unabomber, **Ted Kaczynski**,* who nixed **Gelernter**'s **symmetry** via one of his last explosive missives in 1993, shredding an ear, a hand, an eye.

30   As in **Gertrude**, through whom might we consider *rose* as **infinity mirror** & expatriation as the ultimate **romance**. *See also* **Baryshnikov**. *See* **Eliot**. *See* **stars**.

31   Features include:
- *A soft-clipping diode configuration for high output, soft knee & a tube-like sound.*
- *Independent modulation for each overdrive knob.*
- *Rings in the pushbuttons to illuminate modulation waves.*
- *A tap-tempo switch for speed.*
- *A tap-hold for speed & depth.* [Don't come yet!]

32   & grandfather to **Charles Darwin**, obviously a purveyor of good genes.

33   & endless prose.

34   Witness the 19th century man witnessing 19th century man through the eyes of a 19th century **wolf**. *See also* **doppelgangers**, **infinity mirrors**.

---

* *See also* **rockstar**?

Aces to ashes. Luck to dust. Of course a riff on **David Bowie**[35] (& who doesn't want to be David Bowie?)[36][37] riffing on a burial from the *Book of Common Prayer*,[38] riffing off **Genesis** 3:19[39] which makes the end-all rhyme, the mortal rhyme, the cursed rhyme, rhyme.

got money to burn?... "Some men just want to see the world burn," says Alfred Pennyworth to **Bruce Wayne**, speaking, of course, of **the Joker**, another card[40] who's always in **masquerade**.

stop drop & roll...imperative of fire survival & back-alley dice...*luck be a lady tonight!*[41]

in the world of Hoyle...**Edmund Hoyle** of Cavendish Square, 1672-1769, gaming authority & high society tutor who wrote the book on whist[42], chess, backgammon & others.[43]

---

35   In the 1980 smash, *Ashes to ashes, funk to funky/We know Major Tom's a junkie*, **Bowie** resurrects his abandoned space argonaut* & shoots to **star**dom w/an iconoclastic (now classic) music video** featuring Bowie as 1) **a clown** among hierophants on an otherworldly planet; 2) a man in a padded cell; 3) **an astronaut** in a manufactured womb fed by tubes. *See also* Bowie influences on DC **Comics** & *The Matrix.*

36   But which **David Bowie**? Major Tom? Ziggy **Star**dust? Thin White Duke? Some say in "Ashes to Ashes" the iconoclast integrated all his **masks** into the singular, gender bending **rockstar** (*see also* 20th century **god**), known thenceforth as David Bowie.***

37   A lot of folks don't want to be David Bowie. *See* glossophobia. *See* scopophobia. *See* transphobia. *See* misogyny.

38   *We therefore commit this body to the ground, earth to earth, ashes to ashes, dust to dust.*

39   In the wake of **Adam**'s transgression, not a benediction, but a curse: *for dust you are and to dust you will return.*

40   Though kin to **The Fool** of medieval Tarot, **The Joker** is an American newcomer, not appearing in standard decks until the **1860s** as "best bower" for Euchre, though **Walkman**™ **G**, whose undergrad procrastinations were steeped in endless hands of cigarettes & Euchre, never saw use of a **Joker**.****

41   From *Guys & Dolls*, sung in the film adaptation by **Marlon Brando** as bad boy gambler, Sky Masterson, at which **WG** still can't help but swoon.

42   Previously known as **Trump** & Triumph, the trick-taking **game** dominates centuries of European & US card play, forbearer to Bridge, Spades, **Euchre** & Oh Hell.

43   Though not, despite **Hoyle**'s association w/its rules & etiquette, Poker. Poker: skill at which **WG** has made men pay & pay attention. Think she's bluffing?

---

* Major Tom: **astronaut** & alter ego of **Bowie**'s 1969 "Space Oddity" released days before the **Apollo** 11 moon landing.

** Most expensive to date—August 1, 1980—a year to the day before the launch of **MTV**.

*** What happens when an **iconoclast** becomes an **icon**? Is that what it is to be a **rockstar** (rock as in shake the fundament, **star** as in luminous fusion—single hydrogen atoms copulating to beget **helium** in a celestial porno? Do **rockstars** experience something akin to the nebulous **Overview Effect** of **astronaut** transcendence, epiphanies of a **pilgrim** soul tethered to a craft adrift, as the cobalt marble, down unlit hall, rolls away? Is returning to Earth a disappointment, like that of an expat? Do **rockstars** never want their old self back? Is love like that?

**** *See also* **Joker** (2019), origin story of the **Batman** nemesis. Tale of a failed **clown** (**incel**) who **dreams** of being a **star**. Starring **Joaquin Phoenix**, brother to River, star of *My Own Private Idaho* (1991) dead by overdose at 23, like **Heath Ledger** at 28, whose inspired **"Joker"** in *The Dark Knight* (2008) garnered an Oscar he did not live to see.

photographs...back then they were objects,[44] booty,[45] a **ghost**[46] caper o'er precious-metal-laced paper, in chaperoned light kissed,[47] bathed in chemicals.[48] They were flammable. Floodable. By many means woundable. No **cloud** to save them from rainy days. What you got: seldom what you thought you paid. Till the Quick Print reveal they were a mystery, a glossy present from the past, a past you never saw, but hoped to keep,[49] kept to steep—except sometimes, quite commonly, they stank. The ribbon squirreled into its light tight cave[50] had been promising, promising was the canister's plastic click. But half were blurry, overexposed, a pool of ink—wrong film, wrong flash, wrong aperture to shutter speed & the clear ones caught the blink, the grimace, passers by, a sudden gust—whole roll a bust, so whatever you hoped happened—hoped, like a leprechaun, to capture—is gone, poof! swallowed by a lone eyed Kodak **wolf**[51]...too bad you ordered **doubles**.

---

44 With mass! That take up space! Weighting file folders & envelopes **licked** w/half a book of stamps, grossing padded albums to rattle & split their cellophane seals, tucked in travel trunks*, the jewelry box, coffins that bore new shoes—precious little fireproof—choking attics, basements, wallets, adorning lockets & desktops, staining the **glass** of wooden/pewter/gilded frames, back scrawled w/names, dates, nothing, to dust the walls, plaster the fridge, to be hid (under bed, floorboards, w/the last cigar, the recipe tin)—

In baptism, the body drowned is saved.

45 A) n., stolen goods, plunder, the spoils of war; B) n., buttocks, especially of humans, especially w/r/t **sex** appeal; C) adj., disappointing.

46 A) the animating principal of humans, the soul; B) the presence of one who once lived; C) the essence of **god**; D) an evil spirit; E) an optic illusion; F) the writer who crafts a first-person narrative on behalf of another; G) the severance of communication initiated by one party, often w/no explication or warning.

47 O precious! O so sensitive!

48 **WG** recalls the red bulb basement, dim & damp, darkroom enlargers, plastic vats, the acrid scent of liquids—developer, stopper, fixer—to summon some unseen thing, long since fled.

49 *Photography makes the world seem more available than it is.* Susan Sontag**

50 Like the windowless gay bar where, mired in election grief, **WG** hoped to *dance herself clean**** in a river of other sweaty **pilgrims**. Instead, like bees or a **bird** bewildered by **glass**, dancers thrashed against the **mirrors** (WG too has been spelled by mirrors)—or worse, vogued on the floor just long enough to snap a quiver of selfies**** (*see* "**Vogue**"*****, *see* ***Vogue***,*6 *see* **Right Said Fred***7).

51 *All the better to see you with my dear*...says **Wolf** to Little Red from the bed of Red's partly digested Gran. And if, as **Sontag** says, *there is an aggression implicit in every use of the* **camera*** what of **selfies**—how are they, which surely limit experience *to the search for the photogenic*** like & not like cutting? As in, *my what big teeth you have?*

---

* E.g. in the 1960s, a high school photo of would be poet Carolyn (C.D.) Wright adorned a footlocker in Vietnam belonging to her enlisted fiancé that she may be looked upon when he lifted the lid (even after she returned the diamond).

** From her essay "In **Plato's Cave**" published as "Photography" a year before **W-Girl's** birth & in the 1977 collection ***On Photography***, gifted **WG** by poet & cinema aficionado, A. Van Jordan.

*** *See* opening track of **LCD Soundsystem's** 3rd studio album, ***This Is Happening***, 2010.

**** Again Sontag: **camera** as means of possessing "space in which [one] is insecure."

***** Madonna triple-platinum, 1990. *See* the video on which ***Fight Club***8 director **David Fincher** cut his teeth.

*6 Before social media, influencers were magazines. We poured through, porous.

*7 *I'm too **sexy** for your party...no way I'm disco dancing...from Up,* 1991.*9

*8 Another core text of **incels**, the **manosphere**, the **red pilled**.

*9 As opposed to **Ross Gay** w/Patrick Rosal in "Went Free: Dancing the 11th Incitement", *Inciting Joy*, 2022.

Speaking of "truth in advertising," bred in the Swiss & Italian Alps for rescue work, the **Saint Bernard** is frequently depicted w/a barrel of brandy around its neck to warm avalanche victims, but the monks of St Bernard Hospice deny this was ever practice. They trace the myth to an 1820 oil painting by **Edwin Landseer**,[52] "Alpine Mastiffs Reanimating a Distressed Traveler;" a painting recast as replicable and widely disseminated engraving in 1831. If a picture is worth a thousand words, how much are a thousand pictures?

medicinal...think Margaret[53] from *9 to 5*, the hit film-turned-musical, chronicling the revenge of three harassed secretaries (**Jane Fonda**, Dolly Parton, Lily Tomlin), who kidnap their ***sexist egotistical lying hypocritical bigot*** of a boss & reform the workplace.[54] Inspired by a true story.[55] Second highest grossing film in 1980.[56]

---

52   Best known for the bronze* Barbary **lions**** at the base of Nelson's Column*** in Trafalgar's Square. Renowned as a painter, **Landseer** took on the lions after sculptor John Graham Lough rejected the commission for untenable work conditions & the full-scale models Thomas Milnes cut of sandstone were dismissed for insufficient grandeur. The effigies were further delayed when Landseer—whose frequent depictions of Victoria's critters gave him full reign of her majesty's zoo—requested a live (dead) model, procurement of which took years. When at last he obtained a corpse (sources conflict on the method of procurement), its rate of decay exceeded the painter's progress, causing anatomical "discrepancies" in the final trophies.

53   The "lush" coworker played by Peggy Pope, catch phrase *atta girl*. *See also* the 1984 space adventure, ***The Last Starfighter******* in which Pope plays "Elvira", our hero's cranky neighbor. The **hero**, a handsome, down-on-his luck adolescent misses a weekend frolic w/his girlfriend when a power outage threatens Elvira's daily soaps.*****

54   Truth be told, until drafting these leaves, **Walkman**™ **G** knew nothing of the progressive origins of her girlhood fav & **fairytale** ending notwithstanding, the film seeded a strong aversion to clerical work.*6

55   In 1970s Boston, the grassroots organization, *9to5*, spurred national reform in the clerical sector, then 12% of the U.S. workforce, predominately women. Co-founded by **Karen Nussbaum** & other anti-war*7 activists working in humiliating conditions for shit pay, the organization began w/a newspaper they distributed to thousands of women in their daily commutes, broadcasting stories of workplace malfeasance & opportunities to join the resistance.

56   In a related story, that year's *highest* grossing film, *The Empire Strikes Back*, chronicles the misadventures of grassroots organizers who, after blowing up a fascist government building in the first installment of the **Star Wars**™ franchise,*8 face fierce retribution. *See also* 1980s conservative backlash. *See* POTUS 45/47.

---

* From melted down cannons. Duh.

Also known as North African **Lion, Atlas Lion & Egyptian Lion, the largest (perhaps) of the big **cats**, hunted to **extinction**. Last shot in Morocco's High Atlas Mountains, 1942, though sightings in Morocco & Algeria carried into the '60s. The line continues in captivity. Brits have kept Barbarys since 1280 when—in concert w/prisoners, the mint, the armory & other beasts of menagerie—their growls choked London Tower. As given to live, we called them prides.

***To honor Vice-Admiral Horatio Nelson, among the GOATs, evidenced by battles won, especially the last, to his death. *See also* MGM™ mascot, Leo the **Lion**. *See also* big **game**.

****In which the kid from the trailer park, whose college loan has just been rejected, bests a coin-op arcade, thus drawing the gaze of bellicose aliens & is highjacked to end their intergalactic war.

*****Aka ***soap opera***, a serial drama for daytime radio & tv traditionally catering to unemployed White women. "Soap" from the cleaning products whose commercial dollars sponsored the show. *Opera* as critique of low brow, femme melodrama, tongue in cheek.

*6 Despite which in her late thirties, after a decade as president of a design-build construction company, **WG**, mid career shift, briefly worked as secretary to a ***sex**ist egotistical, lying, hypocritical...*

*7 Through **Vietnam War** protests, **Nussbaum** became friends w/**Jane Fonda**, who, regaled by Nussbaum's stories of workplace atrocities, convinced **Hollywood** producers there was not only a story, but an audience to deliver on **Hollywood** investment.

*8 Estimated worth as of April 2025 between 65-70 billion dollars, w/10 billion in box office sales, a distant second to the Marvel™ cinema franchise, whose **hero** conglomerate grossed over 31 billion (box office) as of April 2025.

Doris Day...Famed singer & film **star**[57] of the 50s & 60s. Her **Hollywood** launch? ***Romance on the High Seas.*** Shared screen w/**Jimmy Stewart, Cary Grant,** James Cagney, **Rock Hudson,** Clark Gable, Jack Lemmon, **Frank Sinatra.** *See also* **Hitchcock's** ***The Man Who Knew Too Much.*** Not just "the girl next door" & "American's sweetheart,"[58] but "world's oldest **virgin**" & "the all-American middle-aged girl," "wholesome as a bowl of cornflakes and at least as **sexy.**"[59] Retreated from Hollywood after the **sex**ual revolution.[60] No **fairytale** princess: philandering father, divorced mother, a **dream**-shattering vehicular accident,[61] four **marriages,**[62] three divorces & one son[63] she outlived. Perhaps her greatest act was appearing "safe."

---

57 But NOT a **rockstar.** *See **icon,*** not ***iconoclast.***

58 **WG** can't say why she shows up *here*; WG never wanted to be *her*—

59 So sayeth **Dwight McDonald** whose critique of "art" manufactured for the masses,* aka *masscult*, scorns not only the lack of craft, but of personality, "it must be easy... It asks nothing of its audience, for it is 'totally subjected to the **spectator.**' And it gives nothing."

60 And yet, co-**star** James Garner, "I'd rather have Doris than **Liz Taylor,**** Everything **Doris** does turns to box-office gold... I think Doris is a very **sexy** lady who doesn't know how **sexy** she is. That's an integral part of her charm." Garner does not appear in *The Man Who Knew Too Much.*

61 On the eve of the 15-year-old's departure to fufill a **Hollywood** dance contract, while cruising the unlit roads of rural Ohio w/ her brother, their car intercepted a train. Bye-bye dancing.***

62 The first **husband** had schizophrenia, beat her, died by **suicide** post-divorce. The second was a Christian Scientist. Between 2 & 3 she dated b-list co**star, Ronald** (Horndog) **Reagan,** a playboy dem w/political ambitions who planned to propose.**** The third, a director, was happy while it lasted, but postmortem she learned he'd spent all her dough & sentenced her to 5 years of *The Doris Day Show.* The fourth, a maître d', won her heart w/doggie bags & when it was over complained she loved him less than her pets.

63 By the 1st marriage. As an adult, made the hitlist of **iconoclast, Charles** (not-an-**incel**) **Manson,** but died of natural causes.

---

* **McDonald** defines "masses" as the reduction of individuals to statistics in a **cyber**netic loop that renders them "unable to express their human qualities because they are related to each other neither as individuals nor as members of a community. In fact, they are not related *to each other* at all..."

** **Hollywood icon, sex** symbol (*see*: ***Cat on a Hot Tin Roof, Cleopatra, Who's Afraid of Virginia Woolf?***) & confidant of **Rock Hudson.** Used personal & cultural capital to promote research for **HIV/AIDS,** eventually convincing fellow thespian, **Ronald Reagan,** to acknowledge the disease though only after the evangelical vote secured his 2nd presidential term.

*** An injury also ended **WG's** dancing career, but nothing so tragically cinematic. In hindsight, the injury was probably related to then undiagnosed chronic illness, exacerbated by an eating disorder & possibly **sexual** trauma; whoever dubbed hindsight 20/20 never sifted a haystack for the particular straw that broke the camel.

**** Before his eye wandered. In truth, the "over**sex**ed" screen guild president diagnosed himself w/a possibly fatal case of leadingladyitis before b-list actress Nancy Davis won the day. Others who scratched his itch: **Marilyn Monroe,** Susan Hayward & Lana Turner. Fashion designer, Hazel Lee Phillips, told her son (the **Hollywood** reporter), Darwin Porter, that Lana Turner told *her* **Ronnie** was a 40-minute man (as opposed to four-minute **JFK**). **Marilyn Monroe** did not confirm.

the merits of **cats**...apart from their viral video antics, **dog** people claim there are none, especially the ones, to cats,[64] allergic.[65] But w/superior satellite dish ears besting any dogs' auditory range, dear darling, cats *hear* you, they just don't obey.

anchovies...O silver filter feeders no longer skimming the briny **dream**. O scattered **star** twinkles snagged & tucked to snuggly sleep. O **argonauts**. O **astronauts** stacked & shipped in tightly tins. O narrow berth—O communal coffin. O of thine own oils to be born again/made swim again—chewed & swallowed/maw & wallow. Down **rabbit hole**/worm hole/belly of the **whale**/the **wolf**/an intestinal slip/a transcendental **labyrinth**—bone & gill/ scale & fin—converting assets/ liquidating excrement—now through pipe/sewer/waste water treatment—Feeding the furied frenzy till frenzy too to slumber slides/to by & by (O buy & bye)—Blessed be the salted—caught & closeted—feast of the moment's celestial slide.

14   **Double Down.**

Double *Down*: in standard Blackjack, after the initial two cards, to double the bet & receive just one additional card. Often paired w/a split.[66] *Double Down.* In a risky situation, to re**double** commitment & increase risk. *Double Down.* To perform **sex** acts w/more than one person at once or in alternation.

implications of **symmetry**...organization, balance, reciprocity, the scales of justice. That everything's connected. As in Gestalt psychology: the mind's tendency to view **mirroring** objects as one.[67] The pleasure of subdivision.[68] Some say nature's essence: necessary for **bird** flight, dimensional sight, general & special relativity. **Aristotle** says beauty. In biology, approximate, degrading w/age. A disproportionate fascination w/may be symptom of OCD.

overkill...more force than necessary[69] to obliterate the target; American thrasher band formed in 1980.

---

64 *See*: feline wiles, what curiosity killed. *See* at night all be gray. *See* **cat** lady, **sex** kitten, Bastet. Who let the cat out of the bag. Like herding cats, independence, drowning kittens, cat got your tongue, what the cat dragged in, more than one way to skin. *See* Satan's minions. *See* **Catwoman**, cougar, Katherine M. Rogers, *Gray Gardens*. ...*Among the Pigeons*. *See* pussy (coward, vulva, weakling, wimp; intercourse w/a femme); *see also* get some; *see also* whipped. *See* **Artemis, Diana**, Donald Engels. *See* Pussy Riot. *See* Barrison Sisters. *See* where to *grab 'em*. In **hell**'s chance, **hell**cat, no room to swing, who's got the cream, who may look at a **king**. That ate the canary. *See also* scaredy. Catty. Caterwauler. Baby killer. Cat's cradle. Cat's pajamas. *See* Freyja's *purring chariot*. Pussyhat. Pussyfoot. What a cat in gloves catches...in a room of rocking chairs. *See* Li Shou. Witch familiar. *See* Pope Gregory's call to slaughter (Vox in Rama...) along w/their female owners. Tie a bell on it. Alice Maddicott. Agnes Waterhouse. W/all the morals of an alley cat. Wanton kittens make sober cats. Hep cat. Cool Cat. Dead cat bounce. See which way the cat jumps. Having **kittens**. Is it sport to the cat? Might as well ask the cat.

65 E.g. **WG**'s mother, sisters, **husband**.

66 Split: dealt two of a kind, to separate the pair into two autonomous hands, betting on each. *See also* mitosis.

67 The Gestalt Law of Symmetry. *See* sister theories: the Law of Past Experiences, the Law of Closure, the Law of Common Fate.

68 Like a clean blade through an allergen free cupcake.*

69 As a Jedi would never.

---

* Half of which—the half w/a lightly crushed frosting rose, dusty pink—on a clean linen handkerchief, **WG** would offer any gentle soul who reads this.

bodhisattva—in Buddhism, one who seeks enlightenment,[70] or in ***Point Break,***[71] the **nihilist** bank robbing surfer[72] **mask**ed as wildly popular[73] B-list Hollywood **romancer, Ronald Reagan,**[74] whose ex-president conspirators include **Carter, Nixon & Johnson.** In *Point Break*, Bodhisattva/aka Bodhi/aka Ronnie is a disaffected, charismatic, mostly **shirtless** anarchist played by the late A-list boomer **Patrick Swayze**[75] (*see also **Roadhouse**,*[76] *see **Donnie Darko**[77]),

---

70   Or to be "woke"—what some call a **dream.**

71   A surf break formed by land jutting into the sea, creating a long, consistent wave. Limited supply contributes to localism, tribalism & gangs. *See also* **Wolf**pak, Longos & Bra Boys.

A 1991 action/crime/thriller* directed by **Kathryn Bigelow** described by ***Rolling Stone*** as "a wet western," "the greatest female-**gaze** action film ever."** **Cult classic.**

72   Half a century ago, before it was a corporate market, before it was **Olympic,** before generational wealth realized where the bums were having fun, surfing (*water*, not *web*) drew White youth escapists. Before that: a practice of colonial resistance. Before that: Polynesian religion associated w/**Lonos, god** of fertility, going back 15 centuries. Back in the day, no way to predict waves; bad weather recipients "should've been here yesterday." Today associated w/yoga, meditation, the Beats, hippies & anti-capitalist draft dodging. Precursor to skateboarding. In 2014, publicly traded Volcom dropped its tagline "youth against establishment" decades past authenticity. *See also* beach **bunny.**

73   In the red sea of 1980, following a period of economic stagnation, **Reagan** trounced incumbent **Jimmy Carter** w/ 90.9% of the electoral college (50.7% of the popular (!)), only to surpass himself in the 1984 scorch of Mondale*** & Ferraro (first woman on the national ticket) carrying 49 states & 58% of the popular vote.

74   Who debuted in the 1937 sleeper, ***Love is on the Air,*** as Andy McCaine, a corruption-busting radio reporter demoted to a kiddie show, despite which he solves the murder & gets the girl.

As of 2024, **Criminal** indictments for **Reagan**'s "shining city upon a hill" exceeded that of any other president. A wiki chronicle of Reagan scandals lists Iran-Contra, Hud grant rigging, "sewergate", "debategate", Operation Ill Wind & the savings & loan crisis. Not listed: HIV/AIDS negligence. **HIV/AIDS,** known then as "gay plague,"**** 4H disease***** & "nature's justice" yielded 46 thousand reported deaths under Reagan's 8-year reign, 10 thousand in his last year, 10% of which were children.

75   The practicing Buddhist began show-biz at his mother's dance studio in Texas, later training w/the Joffrey Ballet. In his 1987 breakout, ***Dirty Dancing,*** predatory **romance** at a 1960s family resort elicits unintended pregnancy, a botched abortion & certain death until straight-shooting **Swayze** saves the day.

76   B-list **cult classic star**ring a **shirtless Swayze** as wannabe pacifist bouncer fighting to free a saloon owner from the tyrannies of rural organized crime, 1989. Remade in 2024 w/**Jake Gyllenhaal** (*see also Brokeback Mountain*).

77   Set in the 1988 U.S. election, a 2001 **cult classic,** star**ring Jake Gyllenhaal** as a teen trapped in a time warp, suffering from acute perception of adult hypocrisy*[6] & visions of a grotesque, humanoid **rabbit** courting violence.

---

* Top grossing film that year was *Terminator II: Judgement Day* directed by **Bigelow**'s then-**husband** James Cameron. Other earners include *Robin Hood: Prince of Thieves, Sleeping with the Enemy, **My Own Private Idaho** & **JFK.***
** Remade in 2015. *See* "Tough Guys Have Feelings Too: The Power of ***Point Break*"** Robbie Collin, 2016.
*** Who beat out Gary Hart & Jessie Jackson, 2nd Black American to launch a national campaign (after Shirley Chisholm in 1972) for the Democratic nomination.
**** Lowkey, the **Hollywood** pres & first lady had many openly gay & closeted pals, but when his gubernatorial chief of staff was outed, the actor running to end "moral decline" said "you're fired."
***** H for hemophiliacs, **heroin** users, homo**sex**ual men & Haitians.*[7] Not to be confused w/the youth organization (4H for Head, Heart, Hands, Health) whose mission was to prepare rural young people w/rurally useful skills.
*6 E.g. **Patrick Swayze**'s new age hustle as a high school motivational speaker & pedophile.
*7 How did Haitians get it? Systemic poverty inciting widespread prostitution inciting **sex**ual tourism in the 1970s.

who befriends the ex-quarterback G-man Danny Utah played by A-list boomer **Keanu Reeves**[78] (again, w/ *The Matrix*[79]). *See* cameo by equally fuckable Chili Pepper front man Anthony Kiedis—never mind **Walkman**™ G preferred Lori Petty & the **Dead Kennedys**.[80]

does love require suffering?... Quora says *yes, but it's worth it*. Reddit says that Dostoevsky as a Christian would say *yes*. Naty Sin Taboo writes suffering is NOT love. Dappled Things calls it a gift. It's hard to wrap. The bows fall off. What gets us off is often suffered. *Suffer*, says a stiffy, *the shorties unto me, just make sure* (wink wink) *they're 18.*

& see stars... as when struck by a blunt object.[81] Or as in ancient times before we banished night, smogged the sky, decked the lid w/satellites. Or since we fixed the **Hubble**,[82] all the dark that **star** death verified.[83]

*his eyes   all three...*whose foremost revelations are derived from meditation. *See mind's eye/inward eye*, Wordsworth's metaphor for memory. Alas, **WG** has aphantasia.[84]

*a pair of koi...*won't mate for life if given options. What critters will?[85] Red titi **monkeys** & Eurasian **beavers**. Coyotes & black vultures. Cockroaches, too, make loyal lovers. And after a courtship ritual that elevates whirlwind **romance** to cyclonic tango, the four-eyed butterflyfish will only ogle you.

---

78 His first **Hollywood** gig? Gopher on a set filming **martial arts** icon Chuck Norris. Like Chuck, Keanu would be lauded for disciplined sincerity & disarming **symmetry** more than thespian range. But who'd have thought the sweet doofus of *Bill & Ted's Excellent Adventure* could become the dystopian **Christ** of the **Wachowskis'** 1999 smash, *The Matrix*, or the grisly vigilante of *John Wick*—who Tom Lamont describes as "a 50-something man absolutely exhausting himself for our viewing pleasure." But **stars** too take pleasure in views. After the third *Wick*, Reeves** broods, *"I wonder if the Wachowskis have seen it, I wonder if they liked it."*

79 In *The Matrix* only **redpilled** nonconformists get laid **IRL**; the rest are fodder to the **Wasteland**,*** unable to detach from the motherboard & **hero**.

80 Whose name & angst are said to derive from the death of the **American Dream**, emblemized by the assassination of some of its dreamers. In truth, in their hay day, pre-teen **WG** knew nothing of the *Frankenchrist*****rage decrying the hypocrisy of **Reagan's** "moral majority" & if asked (just a kid!) she would have called herself Republican.

81 A cartoon darling—concussed—thence to be dazzled by tweeties absent. E.g. the Looney Tunes™ "**Hollywood** Daffy" in which a fowl stan attempts **IRL** sighting of his favorite leading ladies. *See also* "circling **bird**ies".

82 It took some doing. When the first photos came back fuzzy, the fault was found in the **mirror.**

83 E.g., confirming the existence of **dark energy**—the invisible force that drives asunder (versus **dark *matter***, that beckons & smothers)—through witnessing the near "real time" wreckage of **stars.**

84 Eyes closed, turned inward to the mind's deeps, low or no capacity to conjure a picture.

85 Those w/greater success pair-bonding than w/variety. For some, the behavior is reinforced w/a hormone receptor whereby bonding gives them pleasure, though for these species (prairie voles, bonobos, pigmy chimpanzees, humans) the influence of such a pleasure on individuals (vis-à-vis **monogamy**) varies wildly.

---

* That same year***** the nameless **protagonist**/corporate-castrate of *Fight Club* (Edward Norton), splits to give us the **disaffected voice of his generation**, vis-à-vis his alternate personality/**bully-antagonist** Tyler Durden, played by Brad Pitt. A decade later, the *NYT* dubbed *Fight Club*[*6] the **cult film** that anticipated & shaped the zeitgeist, & by 2025, it's key text of **incels**, Proud Boys, Elon **Musk** & the **manosphere.**

** No relation to the "all-American" icon, **Christopher Reeves.**

*** Dominion of the **Fisher King.**

**** *See also* ***Penis Landscape*** by painter H. R. Giger, the Oscar recipient who conceptualized the alien of *Alien* (1979), known also for airbrushed human-machine entanglements.

***** The year **WG** & **husband** sweet—w/whom early courtship involved drunken wrestling—are **married**. Also the year congress removes the Depression-era barrier between investment & commercial banking precipitating the 2008 recession, nearly leading to **WG** & family bankruptcy & inciting the **suicides** of several associates in the construction industry.

*6 That anti-corporate, anti-capitalist, anti-snowflake **meme** darling, who's famed, "first rule of Fight Club..." nails self-actualization to **anonymity**: anonymity: the bastion of outsiders. And as director **David Fincher**, champion of White outsider **heroes** proclaims, "who doesn't think they're an outsider?" *See also* **branding.**

abyss...from the Latin translation of the Greek translation of the Hebrew signifier of bottomless, fathomless depths; the primordial chaos whence creation. Whence also **hell**. In **heraldry**, the center of an escutcheon.[86] Modern usage:[87] an unfathomable chasm where fathom refers both to physical dimension (naval : 2 yards) & intellectual/moral/spiritual comprehension. Ie. the unmapped regions of the ocean or of space. Ie. the dark night of the soul; the gulf between us. An icky sitch. *See also abyssal zone.*[88] *See also* Gulf of America.

to visit neither outer space/nor lower depths... **Nevermind** that "we are all astronauts,"[89] **nevermind** the epiphanic sublimity of **the overview**.[90]

some nights you don't come back from/ even with air to spare...though if you ever want to fly again, dear **astronaut**, you better not share...[91]

---

86   A shield adorned w/coat of arms; emblem by which one proclaims identity/allegiance; a defense. *See* **heraldry**.

87   *Google ngrams*, a tool for tracking word usage over time via **datafied*** texts, reveals modern usage of *abyss* peaked w/the **Romantics** from 1800-1848, then sharply fell, bottoming out between 1910-1980; but since 1980 has risen acutely. *See also* **Ronald Reagan**.

88   The unmapped regions of the ocean. Less than 25% have been charted w/high resolution technology... as opposed to the moon & **Mars** each fully mapped. Of course what's out there, even far away, may be easier to see than what's w/in.

89   As proclaimed by R. Buckminster Fuller in his 1969 treatise *Operating Manual for Spaceship Earth*.** Fuller went on to argue that off world colonization technologies (*see also* nationalist military contest) should be used to augment life on our own planet. Accordingly, innovations in off-world technologies have verily enhanced nuclear fallout shelters.

90   An epiphanic effect theorized by **Frank White** based on astronaut claims*** that glimpsing the "blue marble" from space recontextualizes Earthly difference & instills a powerful sense of shared fate.**** White interprets these revelations as cosmic messages indicating human significance. *See also* **manifest destiny**.

91   In astronaut culture, fear, anxiety, & sadness are perceived as vulnerabilities; **astronauts** seeking redeployment cannot display weakness, thus cannot display fear, anxiety, or sadness. *See* "born to ride", "lie to fly". *See* **Superman**.

---

* **Datafication:***** the translation &/or conversion of "all aspects of life" into quantifiable data that can be mined & analyzed (& sold & resorted & resold & resorted & resold...) to make predictions, decisions, money. A "non-rivalrous good" value-enhanced by advances in "big data" processing.*6 *See also* **surveillance** capitalism.

The earliest articulations of the concept of **Spaceship Earth are by political economist George Henry, who believed that natural resources including land should belong to all, "It is a well-provisioned ship, this on which we sail through space," (*Progress and Poverty*, 1879) & by **Walt Whitman**:

> *One thought ever at the fore—*
> *That at the Divine Ship, the World, breasting Time and Space,*
> *All peoples of the globe together sail, sail the same voyage, are bound to the same destination.*
> Old Age Echoes, 1897

*** "Despite the fact that the first **astronaut** in space, Alan Shepard, described the experience as "disorienting", the Earth appearing small & insignificant. Understanding his part in the play, in official reports the space **hero** waxed poetic. *See also* **hyperreal**. *See* **fraud**.

**** Jordan Bimm & others note **White**'s theory is based on self-reporting in a military culture so intolerant to weakness psychologists have developed computerized mental health therapies for **astronauts** to access in space w/absolute **anonymity** as otherwise they deny themselves treatment.

***** Not to be confused w/*digitization*, the gigabyting of libraries.

*6 **WG** would swear the voice reading the audio book *Big **Data**: A Revolution That Will Transform How We Live, Work, and Think* by Viktor Mayer-Schönberger & Kenneth Cukier is computer generated. A canned beneficent that wants to be called *Uncle*, each syllable a smiling assurance *all is well*. Is it better or worse to know the sycophant is human?

sealed/submerged & assailed...as opposed to *signed, sealed, delivered...*[92] closer to *bewitched, bothered and bewildered...*[93]

the guardian of her dearly beloved's solitude...See **Rilke**,[94] "a good **marriage** is one in which each partner appoints the other to be the guardian of his solitude" from his correspondence w/aspiring poet Franz Kappus 1903-1908,[95] edited & published in 1929, shortly after Rilke's death at **50**. The guru began his epistolary mentorship at the ripe age of 27, not two years into a marriage that would be over in three.[96]

---

92 From the 1970 hit by Motown icon **Stevie Wonder*** swearing fealty to his baby after roaming. *See also* "The Tears of a **Clown**". *See* ***Innervisions***.** *See* ***Jungle Fever***.***

93 Tune from the Rogers & Hart musical, ***Pal Joey*** (1940) about a nightclub performer who seduces a married socialite into bankrolling him. **Gene Kelly****** riles Broadway critics w/his amoral "Joey." But in **Hollywood**'s redo, **Frank Sinatra**'s portrayal of the hustler charms, while Rita Hayworth as doting sugar mama plummets from victim to cloying villain hussy.

See also **Hays Code**, *Great American Song Book*, **Doris Day** & **Ella Fitzgerald**.*****

94 **Rainer Maria Rilke** (1875-1926) born René Maria Rilke, Austrian-German poet & contemporary self-help guru,*6 who rues the doting mother who made him an effeminate dress up surrogate for his dead sister. In his early twenties, at the behest of his first great love & life-long confident, **Lou Andreas-Salomé**,*7 René changed his name to Rainer, the latter (she said) being more forceful & masculine.

95 Or not. Despite numerous attributions to ***Letters to a Young Poet***, **WG** can't find the **marital** dictum therein. Worse than useless, **AI** proliferates the lie,*8 fueled, of course, by pre-AI error. For example, in his 1994 anthology, *Rilke on Love and Other Difficulties*, translator John Moody offers a fifteen-page assemblage from unspecified epistles including, "I hold this to be the highest task of a bond between two people: that each should stand guard over the solitude of the other" but Moody offers no indication when, to whom, or from what context the precept emanates. Of course the fault *here* lies in **WG**'s failure to attend Rilke's greater body of letters—ideally in the original German. However complicit, let her bear witness to the replicating virus evincing Rainer's erasure. And again, **Rich**, what we see/we see/and seeing is changing.*9

96 To sculptor Clare Westhoff w/whom a son. The couple split after a few years, but by Catholic law remained **married**. Apart from his lifelong friendship w/sometime lover, **Lou Andreas-Salomé**, Rilke's longest **romantic** partnership was 6 years. Not that it's a contest. Still, at **50** years old, half of them **married**,*10 **WG** agrees a good partner values (the illusion of) solitude but finds it's also helpful to—w/the other—like hanging out.

---

* Aka Little Stevie, signed at age 11, navigating the world sans outer sight since infancy.

Among the GOATs, 1973, groundbreaking. Born in the same waters as **hip hop & the fall of **Nixon**, **Wonder**'s 16th studio album **married** funk to R&B, **sampling** street sounds, decrying bigotry & conservative hypocrisies.

*** Spike Lee's homage to **Yusuf Hawkins**, killed by an Italian gang in Brooklyn who wrongly suspected the boy, 16, Black, of a **romance** w/one of their own. Hawkin's murder followed the rape of a White female jogger for which 5 Black teenagers later known as the Central Park Five were wrongly convicted & in their 40s, exonerated. In 2024, the man convicted of killing Hawkins claimed mistaken identity & was granted a hearing. Reader, for whom are you mistaken?

**** *See American in Paris. Singin' in the Rain. See Brigadoon* (swoon). **Baryshnikov**: *no one can dance like* ***Kelly***.

***** Queen of Jazz, First Lady of Song, 1917-1996. Orphaned in Yonkers at 14 or 15 (sources differ), fled to Harlem. Whose perfect pitch, improvisational finesse & dance moves helped her survive homelessness, aka systemic negligence. Debuted in the dawn of amateur night at the **Apollo Theatre**, 1934, a 17-year-old in "raggedy dress & workman's boots" singing "The Object of My Perfection" or "Judy" (sources differ). Stole the show. Though her prize should have included a week performing in the Apollo spotlight, the future **icon** was turned away for her disheveled appearance, a detail you won't find on **Apollo**'s website. Indelible collaborator w/**Louis Armstrong**, **Count Basie** & **Duke Ellington**. Later: 14 Grammys, National Medal of the Arts, inaugural NAACP President's Award, The National Medal of Freedom.

*6 His anxiety, paralyzing depression & flighty **romances** notwithstanding, **Rilke**'s "wisdom" is revered by all manner of seekers: bloggers, scholars, psychologists, **marriage** counselors, life coaches, poetry enthusiasts ad infinitum....

*7 Visionary psychoanalyst, author & **iconoclastic** feminist of unparalleled influence on **Freud, Rilke, Nietzsche***11 & others. Refused numerous proposals before entering an open, **celibate marriage** to linguistics scholar, Friedrich Andreas. First woman to write on female **sexuality**. Notable for her writing on creativity, narcissism & gender, scholars argue her Rilke memoir & proto psychoanalysis of Nietzsche singularly illumine the minds & motivations of the masters.

*8 Consider the optics: the replication not of substance but of a satisfying replacement.

*9 **Adrienne Rich**, "Planetarium."

*10 W/plenty of turbulence.

*11 Including his concepts of eternal return & stellar friendship. Later in *Thus Spake Zarathustra*, **Nietzsche**'s **fantasy** that women, who know only the tyranny & enslavement of love, are incapable of friendship, may have been inversely inspired. After she rejected him in **marriage**, it was **Nietzsche** who could not accept **Salomé**'s offer to be *just friends*.

so few ways to fly...okay okay there's many: private, commercial, first class, economy. As cargo, payload, medivac patient. By helicopter, hang glider, sling shot, magic carpet. Hot air balloon. Enchanted broom. Tardis.[97] Chocolate. The Good Year dirigible.[98] *See also* blimp. Grand jeté,[99] jet packs, motorcross, swings. *See Chitty Chitty Bang Bang. See* **The General Lee.**[100] Skydiving. Base jumping. All manner of drugs. **Sex** acts, assorted. As **superhero** or, to **hero**, attached. Dragons, Pegasus, Falkor,[101] **dreams.** Telekenisis, surfboards, horses, skis. From bullies, exes, home, the police. As overlord of underworlds. By avatar,[102] an **astronaut.** *See* cinema, bronco **bulls**, music, fiction. To eighth circle by Geryon.[103] *See also* from Eden. To shilly shally, hem haw, or delude to escape. *See* transcendental meditation. *See also* psychotic break.

sympathetic nervous system...responsible for increasing heart rate, dilating pupils, relaxing lungs...in preparation for fight or flight...

---

97   *See Dr. Who.*

98   Frequent sight of **WG**'s childhood—that daily commute to Houston for dance class—a blip in blue between billboards—before the fields of **stars.**

99   In the nomenclature of classical ballet, great leap. *See also* numerous variations.

100   Named for Robert E. Lee, the Confederate striped '69 Charger from ***The Dukes of Hazzard**** (1979-1985). **The General** appears in each episode aiding & abetting Bo & Luke Duke** & their cut-off clad sister*** & moonshining Pa, flying through fields & backroads, o'er craigs, creeks & other cars all to escape the long arm of the law.**** Generals & replicas (w/440 Magnum V8 & Dixie tooting horn (*oh I wish I was in the land of cotton*)) are money. As many as 300 Generals were killed in the making of *Dukes of Hazzard.*

101   A luck dragon in 1984's, ***The NeverEnding Story*** (think flying serpent meets fluffy **Shih Tzu**) who aids the **hero**, a **bullied, motherless boy** bibliophile-turned-warrior-in-a-**fantasy**-reality to save the princess & defeat the Nothing.

102   Avatar: a digital representation, often idealized or fictionalized to **fantasize**. In Hinduism, a deity incarnate.

103   Infernal monster of deception *that infects all the world.* A winged serpent w/a man's face, a **lion**'s paws & a scorpion's tail, who delivers **Dante** & his trusty guide, **Virgil**, from the cliffs of the 7th circle (violence), down the Phlegethon falls to the rims of the 8th circle (**fraud**). No relation to the three-headed grandson of Medusa.

---

* Grade school fav of **WG** who did not, at 8, recognize the unbridled racism & misogyny.
** *Just a good old boys/never meaning no harm/beats all you never saw*...goes the **Waylon Jennings** song.
*** *See* Daisy Duke, a name synonymous w/denim revelations.
**** Or the short arm of Boss Hog (white suit, 10-gallon hat) & **minions**, Rosco & Cletus.

22   **OK Look.**

*Seldom is scrubbing linoleum selfie terrain...*though the field is wide: consider the shelfie,[104] the belfie,[105] the helfie,[106] the smize,[107] the pelfie,[108] the felfie,[109] the suglie,[110] the squinch.[111] The groufie, the usie (see! I have friends!), the welfie (*see* gym rat, six-pack, sun-steeped asana, *see* paddling rapids, *see* marathon exhaustion), beach feet brag, family brag, fancy pants, protest. Dog made a mess. Toasting success (look! my next book!). Wedding, ailing, birthday, Christmas. Self-incriminating selfie. Selfie-transcendence.[112] [113] [114]

25   **A Lap or Three Around the Rosary.**

*rosary...*literally *rose garden*, refers both to the object & the practice, the ritual & accessory affixed w/ crucifix). A pre-literacy mnemonic.[115] Psalter for the poor. Prayer abacus. Early forms: jar of seeds, knotted rope, heap of stones. *See also* mala beads, Misbaha beads, Komboloi, worry. Flourished after Mary's visit to St. Dominic,[116] 13th century (*Hail Mary*). Or so claims Alan de la Rouche in his rosary campaign of the 15th century. Early cantillations the *Our Father* didn't take.[117] Weapon against heresy, seduction,[118]communism, modernity.[119] Domain of crones, mothers, the barren, **virgins**.[120] Weapon of **gun culture**.[121] Of dailiness, counting, ordinals, murmur. Liberation of repetition. Mystery parsing algorithm. Quantitative sentence of devotion (*see also* sentence reduction). *See* Madonna, souvenir, boho chic, goth irony.

---

104   w/bookshelf.

105   w/booty.

106   w/good hair

107   like Mona Lisa.

108   w/pet.

109   whilst farming.

110   looking "ugly".

111   w/scowl.

112   ...

113   As opposed to *self-transcendence*, a trait coined by Viktor Frankl & Abraham Maslow depicting the dissolution of the selfish self for increased connection to other humans, philosophical truths, etc. Some use self-transcendence as a measure of spiritual health & others as a pathology for mood & psychotic disorders. *See also* **overview effect**.

114   "Photographs alter and enlarge our notions of what is worth looking at and what we have a right to observe.* They are a grammar and, even more importantly, an ethics of seeing." **Susan Sontag**, "Plato's Cave."

115   Proto app?

116   Patron saint of scientists & astronomers.

117   Michael P. Carroll links recursive, obsessive aspects of the rosary (53 recitations of the Hail Mary while passing beads between thumb & forefinger) to anal erotic** fixation. *See Journal for the Scientific Study of Religion*, Dec. 1987.

118   *See* **Dante**, Eight Circle, **Fraud**.

119   *See also* Legion of Mary, organization of Catholic laypeople 10 million strong, for deployment in battles of faith. *See also Legion of Mary*, a short-lived rock band formed by Jerry Garcia of the *Grateful Dead*, from July to July, 1974 to 1975, anno domini, first year of **Walkman**™ **girl's** life.

120   "In its way, then, the Rosary is subversive; undercutting the metanarrative of the bodiless male by an insistence on the necessity of the body as full partner in the Incarnate mystery" Mary Gordon's rosary as feminist meditation.

121   *See* "How Extremist **Gun Culture** is Trying to Co-opt the Rosary," Daniel Panneton, *The Atlantic*, Aug 14, 2022

---

* or...flaunt?

** anal erotic: the early developmental stage described by **Freud** as the seat of neurosis, wherein a child derives pleasure from shitting & playing w/shit, the latter of which any good mother prohibits/redirects (*see* mud pies, sandbox, playdough, marbles); the former, she teaches to regulate. *Hail Mary, full of grace, the Lord art w/ thee.*

*if it weren't for that blasted cross...*what **Christ** said.[122]

26   **Dream Wedding.**

my word is my **bondage** *said the corpse...s'nuff said?*[123]

handcuffs[124]...as ubiquitous in **sex** play as in "security" going back to the ancient Greeks.[125] [126] *See also kink.*[127] Speaking of **gun culture**, Smith & Wesson[128] dominates the market w/numerous models & accoutrements. "When the second cuff is locked," says a retired officer, "the suspect calms."

*red felted letters/ ironed onto his tee...*all the rage for personalizing threads mid-(last)-century.[129]

wedding *rings...*of equally ancient & multifarious history. The outward sign & testament. A warning in translation. As on poisonous creatures, aposematic coloration, a flash of red. Easy enough to take off unless constructed to fall apart.[130] Easy to wear for show. Like security **cameras** to nothing plugged. Battery-less fire alarms. Contrarywise, many **married** can't wear them for what else they do w/their hands—even light **bondage** can be dangerous.[131]

---

122   Not really. *See* **superhero**. *See* **sacrifice**. *See* **rockstar**. *See* the musical. *See* the light. Find grace. Beg forgiveness.

123   *See* **John** 1:1. *See* **Elaine Scarry**, "achieving an understanding of political justice may require that we first arrive at an understanding of making and unmaking," **The Body in Pain**, 1985.

124   From "hand*cop*", *cop* meaning *to catch*.

125   The **epic** poet **Virgil** sings of the binding of Proteus to prevent his shape-shifting **escape**.

126   Though it is unlikely **BDSM** in ancient Greece was defined by **consent**.

127   *See* **Kinky Boots**, Tony Award winning* musical composed by 80s popstar, Cindi Lauper.** Based on a British film based on a true story about a man who inherits his father's failing boot factory & collaborates w/a drag queen to revision the mission. *See* blue collar men in hard times. *See* drag queens as light. *See* quirk, *see* **kink** as endearment. Witness salvation.

128   Which, along w/Winchester **Repeat**ing Arms Co, was the offspring of the Volcanic **Repeat**ing Arms founded by Horace Smith & Daniel Wesson, who, w/Oliver Winchester, made beaucoup bucks off the **Civil War**, through arms that replicate a particular action in quick succession, i.e. make instant copies*** of a hurling bullet, a missile projection, though receipts are invariably distinct.

129   Consider Mr. Kaminsky, **WG**'s ancient & beloved dance teacher whose dazzling array of plaid polyester bellbottoms & groovy tees**** gave him time traveler mystique which combined w/ his arthritic port de bras & beguiling disparagements won him pre-teen bunhead devotion.

130   E.g. puzzle rings.

131   One winter, another beloved teacher—a pianist—hiking alone in deep drifts of snow—tangled w/a half-buried chain-link fence, steel snagging his band of gold—& lost three fingers.

---

* Best musical score, 2013, marking Lauper the first woman to win solo.
** *See also* The Goonies.
*** *See also* printing press. *See* Enlightenment. *See* Industrial Revolution. *See* Pete & **Repeat** sitting on a fence; Pete falls off so who's left? **Repeat**. Pete & **Repeat** sitting on a fence; Pete falls off so who's left? **Repeat**. Pete & **Repeat** sitting on a fence; Pete falls off so who's left?
**** **WG's** fav: *you toucha da shirt/I breaka you face.*

*After **Rilke**...*after **Rodin**. The lauded **sonnet**, also ekphrastic, "Archaic Torso of **Apollo**" opens the Austrian's *New Poems, Vol. II*,[132] dedicated to the Parisian **rockstar**, the father of modern sculpture.[133] Though the poem responds to a decapitated bust of antiquity,[134] its insights derive from Rodin's advice to fanboy: find your **muse** at the zoo. There the poet stares into the eyes of what beast looks back until he perceives the animal's vision of himself,[135] an imaginative act he dubs *einschen* or *inseeing*—a **marriage** of vision—the beholder to the beheld.[136]

O Apollo—what good is the god of mind headless? No... *the eyes like ripening fruit*—& yet, writes Rilke: **here** *there is no place that does not see you...*

As indeed **here**, amid the barrage of lovelorn trivia, the catalog of creatures caught & captioned, arcade of savage salvage, shades from **virtual** obsolescence, fixed by lens, by **gaze**, by app, by **gaze**, by **algorithm**, **gaze**, watercolor, **gaze**, by verse, by page,[137] bound each to unknown inmates, cubicled artifacts of the **muse**um, the mausoleum, the menagerie...dear Reader, your trusty fellow voyeur wonders, do you feel, do you feel here seen?

Must you—as **WG**—

dein Leben ändern—

                           change your life[138]

---

132 **Rilke** drafted *New Poems, Vol I & II* in the same period as the epistles that became ***Letters to a Young Poet.***

133 Auguste Rodin, Scorpio,* 1840-1917, Rilke's elder, employer & informal mentor. *See The Thinker*, first titled, *The Poet* (after **Dante**), that crowns ***The Gates of Hell*** (after **Dante**), the poet at once tortured & free. *See also The Kiss.* Failed seducer of the modern dancer, Isadora Duncan, otherwise no **incel**. Got his sculpting chops as a mass producer of objets d'art. Rebuffed for unflinching realism, many of his now renowned sculptures were never—in his lifetime—cast. On the other hand, his unparalleled command got him dubbed a cheat. Once accused of *surmoulage*,*** the **rockstar** scaled work larger than life as proof of **virtue**. Believed body manifests character.**** Subject to forgeries.

134 Which **Apollo**nian hunk modelled for **Rilke** remains unknown, for as w/these truncated portraits, there are many. Of course busts of antiquity are oft decapitated by conflict or accident, but Rodin viewed anatomical parts as wholes, even his own studies for larger works. To wit, some "parts" got **married**. *See* Frankenstein masterpiece, ***The Walking Man***, in which legs from one statuette buttress the battered torso of another, w/no attempt to dissemble the suture. *See* Rilke: *he has the power to bestow on any part the independence and completeness of a whole.*

135 "...unlike objects, animals look back. The two-way **gaze** tethers these separate lives together and fulfills the "beholder's involvement," which the Austrian art historian Alois Riegl argued was a necessary component in a successful work of art." *You Must Change Your Life: The Story of Rainer Maria **Rilke** & Auguste **Rodin***, Rachel Corbett, 2016.

136 By extension, **WG** wonders if being *seen* depends on how one beholds others? Dear reader, did you ever read the encyclopedia?

137 Set upon the masticated bones of trees—the mill's wet dust, the slab wood pulped—stewed w/yester's broadcast dispatch, the rag to ribbons, bleached.

138 As in **WG**'s midlife return to grad school, amid Deb Albery's opening lecture...**WG:** *In dark—the middle sleep/the—from sleep—//twisting.*

---

* Like many men dear to **WG** (**husband**, father, brother...**husband**'s father), said to be loyal, passionate, intense, aloof & secretive. No comment.
** The commissioned portal to a museum that was never built.
*** The practice of casting plaster molds directly atop live (or dead) models.
**** And knew how much to reveal. The maestro funded artistic rebellions via the wealthy's proto-**selfies**....He knew them w/means will pay (heaps) to be seen (as **sexy**).

a contagion/of hides half-cocked... where are the male supermodels? They came (quick) & went.[139] Didn't stay the night let **alone** for breakfast. Seems buyers & sellers of menswear *prefer* their models **anonymous**. The genteel genius of **everyman Adonis**.[140]

There are exceptions. In a new campaign for the souls of men, Calvin Klein enlists **Bruce Weber**[141] & a hunky **Olympian**. It's 1982,[142] an underwear shoot w/(shit you not) *pole vaulter,* **Tom Hintnaus**.[143] In two weeks Bloomingdales sells 65K (over 200K today) in tighty whities. After that any fine specimen will do, disposable as tissue, till the brand needs a facelift. In 1992[144] that's Marky Mark grabbing his junk; in 2024, **Jeremy Allen White**,[145] otherwise hunks modeling Klein (& Ralph Lauren, Marc Jacobs, Gianni Versace, Georgio Armani, Raf Simons, Rick Owens, Tommy Hilfiger, Teddy Santis, Michael Kors, Tom Ford, Christian Dior, Virgil Abloh, Pierre Cardin...) are mostly nameless. Disposable **chameleons**.[146] For **anonymous**-in-the-flesh, *see* **Abercrombie & Fitch**.[147]

---

139 Fashion journalist, Tim Blanks, claims the **myth** of the male **supermodel** never manifested, but came closest via **Bruce Weber**'s vision **quest**.

140 **Adonis**—beautiful & fluid. Bedfellow of **Aphrodite, Persephone** & sometimes **Apollo**. (All 4 for a porno.)

141 "**Weber** proposed a different kind of male ideal—ambiguous, submissive, sensuous—and the unabashed homoeroticism of this proposal flipped the lid on the hidebound way men were depicted in the media. Man as **sex**ualized object was the linchpin of gay **porn**, not mass culture. Weber legitimized the notion for the mainstream, amplifying narcissism as the soul of male **sex**uality, gay or straight." Tim Blanks, "The History of the Male **Supermodel**," 2007.

142 Peak gym culture, nascent **looksmaxxing**,** aided & commodified by indie lifestyle tech: Sony **Walkman**™.

143 Not just hunk, but **hero**. Favored to win the 1980 **Olympics** in Moscow,*** the Brazilian American could have vaulted for Brazil. Instead he joined the boycott & w/fellow U.S. Olympians received a Congressional Gold Medal.

144 But **WG** thinks, really, how could a male Cindy**** or Christie***** stand a chance amid the culture swing of the 90s—i.e. *Right Said Fred*s **supermodel** satire busting the charts w/"I'm Too **Sexy**."*6

145 *The Bear*, sure, but also *Shameless*.

146 Raf Simons once described **David Bowie** as a chameleon, "able to reinvent himself...More than a man—an idea." *See* **rockstar**. Super*hero* not **supermodel**.

147 Beginning in the mid aughts, **Abercrombie & Fitch** CEO, **Michael Jeffries**, commanded a legion of (mostly White) hunks to man his stores **shirtless**,*7 a campaign that ran over a decade. Racist hiring practices & other abuse led to Jeffries stepping down in 2014. As of March 2025, over 40 men have accused Jeffries of drugging, raping & **sex**ually abusing them during his reign at A&F; Jeffries, out on bail, is charged w/**sex** trafficking & prostitution as well as numerous civil suits though a dementia diagnosis may render him unfit to stand trial.

---

* At which time subversion flipped from Glam to Grunge.
** The practice of making oneself as attractive as possible via softmaxxing (skincare, exercise, fashion) &/or hardmaxxing (plastic surgery, hair transplants, steroids)*8 though it will be 30 years before the term enters the vernacular on **incel** message boards & another decade to proliferate mainstream Tik Tok.
*** Protesting its 1979 invasion of Afghanistan, along w/60 other countries.
**** Crawford, **supermodel**, household name of 80s & 90s.
***** Brinkley, **supermodel**, household name late 70s & early 80s.
*6 Brainchild of Richard Fairbrass (former bass player for Boy George), who owned a London gym w/his brother & soon to be bandmate, Fred. One day, fed up w/"narcissistic" gym posing, Richard half-stripped & began serenading the **mirror**, *I'm too **sexy** for my shirt...too **sexy** for my shirt so **sexy** it hurts.....* The 1991 single (*Right!?* said Fred) topped charts in 7 countries & was listed among the greatest pop songs of all time in 2023. The video features the **shirtless** bros mobbed by **camera** wielding femme bikini models.
*7 The models, subject to strict rules of dress & grooming, unsolicited groping & endless **selfies**, report a range of feelings.
*8 *See also* sadomasochism.

*some sun **god blunder**...See also* **blunder into wonder**. *See* **Kennedy**'s moonshot, **Project Apollo**.[148] *See* **Ella Fitzgerald** at the **Apollo Theatre**.[149] *See* **Apollo Creed**. Apollo may also refer to: a rescue **dog**, racehorse, pet parrot, record label, numerous songs, albums, characters, corporate entities, magazines, two bays, a beach, an astroid, a lunar crater, a junior high, a group of astroids, ridges, a peak, military vessels, cities, the make of numerous automobiles, a system of subaquatic cables spanning the Atlantic... *See* the **blunders** of each, should they exist, as singularities.

hypotonia...diminished or undeveloped muscle tone.

---

148 Amid the space race* of 1960s **Camelot**,** the quest to first light on the moon, thence safely return.*** *See* **Kennedy Space Center**—base that launched a dozen **Apollos**—now contested spoils in the billionaire space race twixt Bezos/Musk/Branson**** (Blue Origin*****/Space X/**Virgin** Galactic). But—though lawsuits & tweets suggest brutal rivalry—the pirates **bully** the pulpit lowkey united: *Stand with* **Crypto**! *Stand with Doge!* (*See* X, *see The Washington Post*). *See also* **Gilded Age**. *See* **Bone Wars**.

149 The neoclassical theatre*6 at 125th Street, Harlem, that amped the mics of **Ella Fitzgerald**, Gladys Knight, and Lead Belly Ledbetter, began as a 1913 burlesque*7 for White audiences. In **1934**, under new ownership, was re-visioned as a family-friendly venue for growing Black communities in Harlem. After the god of music & prophecy, **The Apollo** spotlit artists banned from elsewhere & rewrote culture the world over (*see* **Jazz**, **Blues**, Beebop, Swing, Rock-n-roll, R&B, Gospel, Soul, **Funk**, **Hip Hop**...).*8 Amateur Night, a nonagenarian tradition whereby prescient audiences (known to boo off dim lights) discover **stars**. *See* **The Jackson 5**, Lena Horne, Billie Holiday, Dionne Warwick, Smokey Robinson, Sarah Vaughan, Sammy Davis Jr., Frankie Lymon, The Ronettes, The Isley Brothers, **James Brown** (took twice) & Luther Vandross (booed off 4 times).

Who else? Bessie Smith, **B.B. King**, Stan Getz, Little Richard, **Aretha Franklin**, Dizzy Gillespie, Duke Ellington, Miles Davis, Thelonious Monk, Patti LaBelle, Lil' Wayne, Drake, John Coltrane, Michael Jackson,*9 Otis Redding, Richard Pryor, Ben Harper, Buddy Holly, Lou Rawls, Sam Cooke, Lauryn Hill, **Nat King Cole**, Ice Cube, Gorillaz, Josephine Baker, Tina Turner, Count Basie, Eddie Murphey, Lenny Kravitz, Nina Simone, Bob Marley, Prince, War, Bill Cosby, Cab Calloway, Redd Foxx, Moms Mabley, Parliment-Funkadelic, L.L. Cool J, Chuck Berry...

In **July 2024**, age 90, **The Apollo** became the first cultural institution to receive a **Kennedy Center** Honors Award.

---

* A product of the Cold War between the U.S. & the Soviet Union beginning w/US plans to launch a satellite into outer space & ending w/the dissolution of the USSR in 1991. Media & government agencies depicted the **space race** as a matter of national security linked to nuclear missile proliferation & satellite reconnaissance. The competition fortified nationalism & American exceptionalism, lending optimism to an era otherwise marked by fear of nuclear annihilation.

** In the wake of her **husband**'s murder, Onassis likened the war **hero**'s presidency to the fabled court of **King Arthur**. W/**star** power rivaling her husband's, Onassis' portrait cast Kennedy as soul of progressive **virtue**, glossing extramarital affairs & other flaws. In the shock of collective grief, the myth of **Camelot** stuck.*10 *See* **Marilyn Monroe** as **Lancelot**?

*** On the 5th anniversary of the moonwalkers' return, **WG** born.

**** Who made *his* bones w/**Virgin** Records. *See* **Eurythmics**, **David Bowie**, **LCD Soundsystem**, Gorillaz, **George Michael**, Janet Jackson, Tina Turner, **Lenny Kravitz**, Ben Harper, **Courtney Love**...

***** While **Musk** may lead the way in **data** theft & government takeovers, you got to give it to **Bezos** for brand ethos; w/vessels christened New Glenn, New Armstrong & New Shepherd, he honors (commodifies) astro-**heroes** of yore in the tradition of colonial namesakes: New York, New Hampshire, New England, Georgia. *See also* **branding**.

*6 Neoclassical architecture **echoes** Greek ideals via **symmetry**, geometry & form as an articulation of social function. In contrast to the naturalistic ornamentation of Rococo, it emphasizes the wall over the chiaroscuro.

*7 American burlesque, derived from the **Victorians**, gained popularity in the 1860s, postbellum. Initially an absurdist parody, featuring minstrel acts & risqué dancers, by the late 1920s the striptease eclipsed all else; what "acts" remained were prelude to the commodified **gaze** on White femmes, by White eyes only. But, as The Depression took hold, the reform factions championing the **Hayes Code** also banned Girlie shows, supported in NYC by Mayor LaGuardia & later by Uncle Sam's call for **heroes**. W/war igniting The Greatest Generation's sense of purpose, appetites shifted & burlesque went under...What popped back up a generation later was seedier.

*8 **Elvis Presley**, Mick Jagger, The Beatles, **David Bowie**, Bill Clinton & all took inspiration from **The Apollo**.

*9 Originator of "the moonwalk" an impossibly smooth, impossibly cool perambulation adored the world over w/almost no resemblance to the slo mo bubble-headed bounds of actual lunar pedestrians.

*10 *See also*: **Camelot**, a **Broadway** musical released the year **Kennedy** won the presidency, written by his Harvard classmate (Alan Jay) tunes from which, Jackie claimed, the young president loved to play.

The history of Euro **dic. pics** is long & crooked. Ancient Greeks enjoyed the organ's **pageant** as symbol of **sex &** beauty incarnate, favoring (for display) a small, flaccid *package.*[150] Roman love of phallus equated *size* w/strength & *might* w/*right* as evidenced by numerous obelisks plundered from Egypt.[151] In their winner-take-all society,[152] young males of status donned **penis** pendants[153] to mark them off-limits to brutes who'd otherwise subject them to "the female experience."[154] Then Rome falls, the church ascends & the popes claim flesh be devil. Bedeviled **members** go to ground[155] or to the comic relief of marginalia. Or galvanize, **lion**ize, to higher purpose transform, hammered to swords, steeples, monuments...rockets.

Fast forward to the early aughts when phone **cameras** augment **sex**ting & online dating & ***dick pic*** enters the lexis, soon demonized for images sent w/o **consent.**[156] By 2016, 49% of women in the US report receiving an unsolicited photo of men's genitalia w/the overwhelming majority describing the experience as disagreeable.[157] Though most men claim to send unsolicited photos in naïve appeal to reciprocity, woman & girls also report receiving pics after refusing **romantic** overtures.[158]

A friend of **WG**, a man, sees the watercolors, reads the poems, sighs. Says it's a **shame** men can't compete w/nipples & breasts—says there's no hetero male equivalent to the wet t-shirt contest[159]—as if embarrassed, as if it really is a **shame**—& she thinks, *oh,* **boner**[160] as projection...*I want you to want me. I need you to need me. I'd love you to love me. I'm begging you...to...me...me....*[161] [162]

---

150 Not a euphemism. The Greeks preferred their **members** groomed & *bundled.*

151 Going so far as to award military promotions based on a man's measure.

152 *See* Roman Empire, **Roman Circus**; *see* Ridley Scott's turn of century *Gladiator.* * *See* 2024 provided a sequel.

153 An amulet known as *fascinum,* often depicted w/wings. Cousin to *fascinate*: draw the **gaze**, inspire awe.**

154 Of penetration. Seed to soil, incisor to muscle, needle to leather, saw to sternum, S.W.A.T to periphery, product to market, porcupine quill to **wolf** snout, inspector general to predatory lender, PI to mystery, **Big Brother** to closet.

155 *See* the flex & flux of underground societies; *see also* **sex** trafficking, **porno**graphy, prostitution; *see* [dark web].

156 A practice widespread & growing, prompting new legislation. Researchers agree: no female equivalent.

157 Women report disgust & **shame**, whereas homo**sex**ual men report feeling aroused, flattered or curious.***

158 A 2019 study of over a thousand hetero**sex**ual men found that while a significant minority (17%) sent pics to cause a negative response,**** 82% hoped to positively excite the recipient & 50% hoped to make them feel attractive. The study hypothesized that male over-estimation of female reception may be due to the more favorable response men have to visual **sex**ual stimuli, coupled w/ perceived normalization of the practice. It was further supposed that some men send pics because hard as they may be, words are harder.

159 Her first thought: why would you *want* to compete as meat? Next thought— no equivalent? *Really?* Brigade of **shirtless peacocks**, notwithstanding? **Cock**fighting the world over back to antiquity notwithstanding?...*really?*

160 *See also* "**boner**" crimes performed by the **Joker** in *Batman* #66, 1951, w/lines like "So! They laugh at my **boner** will they? I'll show them," & "stunned by his **boner**, Joker lashes out," back when ***boner*** meant ***blunder.***

161 ***Cheap Trick***'s signature song, a 1977 pop parody turned classic, off their second studio album, *In Color.*

162 *The world's oldest profession,* the first **mirror**?

---

* In which a Roman General (penetrator) falls from favor (is penetrated, along w/**wife** & son) until he penetrates everything in the Arena. *Are you not entertained?* jabs the **rockstar** as Scott & Crowe take home Oscars (& the villain **Joaquin**? merely nominated.)
** Awe: the result of a sight that obfuscates seeing, before which—terror, trembling.
*** Is this because homo**sex**ual men better perceive the gesture as intended? Or because, as men, they respond more favorably to **sex**ual images? Or because they find the organ more appealing? Again, our fascination w/**mirror**ing...?
**** To shock, disgust, or dominate via virility. Also to punish feminists for perceived **misandry**. The study revealed **narcissists** are **dick pic** prolific, but no correlation between digital package traffickers & **IRL** exhibitionists.

Titania...elven Queen of **Midsummer Night's Dream.**[164] Oberon's estranged boo, potioned[165] to fall in love w/an ass.

roofied...passive, *to be given a roofie*, like Rohypnol[166] or other autonomy-diminishing chemical.

the ass/hat Bottom...Nick Bottom, self-aggrandizing weaver, transfigured by **Puck** to humiliate Titania.

the Jack...as opposed to Jill. The guy. The dude. Also jackass. A means to lift. To steal. The lowest face card. What's it gonna be, Jack? Kerouac. **Kennedy**. Nicholson. Nicklaus. Black. White. Dempsey. Dorsey. Palance. Lemmon. The Ripper?

beards...a decoy spouse or beau, a guise broadcasting hetero**sex**uality.

Bard...a poet; *the* poet of quivering spear.[167]

wildlife refuge...a kind of **fantasy**—like Disney—in which legendary creatures dwell in alt reality? *See* Rodin, "Nothing, really, is more moving than the maddened beast, dying from unfulfilled desire..."[168]

sweet **lion** *among/the ladies*...from Act III, scene i, in which Bottom, Quince & other *mechanics*[169] rehearse their play[170] of **star**-crossed lovers. Concerned their play-violence will distress ladies in attendance, Bottom proposes the player's face be made visible through the neck of his **lion** suit.

Big O...**Oberon**, elven **King**, roofie orchestrator.

---

163 Elven trickster & Oberon henchman à la **Midsummer Summer Night's Dream**, not the hockey projectile.

164 Written in 1595 or 96, a **fantasy** romcom in which the fates of human & fairy lovers tangle in a moonlit topsy-turvy reality.* From the early-mid period, following the smash hit, *Romeo & Juliet*, written, perhaps for a wedding.

165   In ancient Greece & medieval Europe, love potions containing mandrake & other nightshades w/hallucinogen properties were popular, though they were far more efficacious as plot device.

166 Illicit use of the odorless, colorless **pill** began in the 1970s & peaked in the late 90s & early aughts. Since 2015 such usage in the US is rare, replaced w/alcohol & other benzodiazepine drugs.

167 Who too loved men & thus for whom *all the world...* stage.

168 Alternatively, what is more tragic than photographs of the last black rhino,** guarded by men w/automated weapons, pacing the perimeter of his mateless pasture.

169 The troop of laborers (carpenter, weaver, tinker, tailor, joiner, bellow's mender) who, seeking noble recognition, moonlight as actors in an inadvertently comic rendition of the tragedy of *Pyramus & Thisbe*.***

170 *See play w/in the play*...a convention that winks at art's charade, tipping the **mask** to reveal an identifiable face. *See also* film w/in a film, e.g. snippets of 50-year-old *Captain Blood* (1935)**** in the basement scenes of *The Goonies* (1985), or self-referential **Tarantino** positing clips from his previous films on the screens animating subsequent projects. *See also*, again, **infinity mirror**.

---

* *See* **rabbit hole.**
** Casualty of poachers seeking the horn—an ingredient in many Chinese remedies, though not, as commonly believed, for aphrodisia. Today the horn is sought as symbol of wealth & power. Conversely, rhino hunters live well below subsistence.
*** From Ovid's *Metamorphosis*, inspiration to the bard's acclaimed *Romeo & Juliet*. *See* **self-referential?**
**** In which Her Majesty's privateer (read pirate), played by **Errol Flynn**, works to disrupt the evil Spanish armada & **romance** the heart of a Spanish loyalist. *See also In Like Flynn.*****
***** A childhood consumer of Golden era Hollywood, **WG** confesses to numerous girlhood **fantasies star**ring the suave swashbuckler, followed by betrayal informed heartbreak when she learned the namesake's idiom & origin. *See* 17-year-old Errol, rabble-rouser, whose mother dubbed him Tasmanian devil, possibly abused, expelled from an elite Australian boy's school, hopping a ship to New Guinea. *See* the boy man boat captain/diamond smuggler/**bird**-trapper/pearl diver/plantation managing/gigolo who may or may not have killed a man. *See* ocean-skipping-con to Hollywood. *See* him con **Hollywood**. *See* heart throb of the silver screen, raging parties, raging alcoholic. *See* oranges injected w/vodka, *see* **heroin** drips. *See* a labyrinthian mansion outfitted w/peepholes & two-way **mirrors**. *See* **sex**ual assault. *See* minors. *See* case dismissed. *See* the posthumously published autobiography, "they were asking for it."

Inferno...is a midlife crisis poem[171]...not unlike revenge **porn**, if you sub *porn* for *horror*.[172] Dear **Dante**.[173] Gross luminary. Justice warrior.[174] No love for Emperors. No love for Popes sans jurisdictional limits. But his party lost! To the curb he was kicked! To **hell** in a handbasket.

O dead Beatrice...Dante's **muse**. Believed to be **Beatrice** Portanari who bewitched the poet one May Day Festival[175] when she was 8 & he 9. Imagine a girl in white, wreathed in flowers, amid a sea of ribbons & petals, waves sweeping the young, motherless boy into her aura.[176] They may have met only twice in person & married other people,[177] yet **Dante** practiced a *courtly* devotion[178] re**doubl**ed by her death at 24. In ***La Vita Nuova***,[179] Beatrice appears semi-divine & in *The Divine Comedy*, like the **Virgin Mary**, she intercedes from heaven to ameliorate his journey.

---

171   But one doesn't need to read a book to figure this out. One could simply find oneself in the middle of the woods in midlife, listening to **Caroline Bergvall's** "VIA", the recursive fusion of 4 dozen attempts to English* **Dante**...

> *Along the journey of our life half way*
> *I found myself again in a dark wood*
> *wherein the straight path no longer lay.* Dale, 1996.

...& realize, shit. The only way on is down.**

172   For some a negligible substitution. Reader, what (horror/**porn**) would you circumscribe in a Venn diagram?

173   **Dante** Alighieri (1265-1321): **Gemini,***** father of four, White Guelph warrior, Florentine exile, **epic** poet after whom they fixed the tongue. Father of horror.****

174   By sword, stealth & rhetoric (folio as medieval social media?)...however ineffective.

175   Though May Days of 13th century Florence honored Floria, the Roman goddess of flowers, not (yet) the **Virgin** Mother, Marion devotions flourished via numerous shrines inciting pilgrimage to Dante's province. Devotions in which a motherless boy under Dominican tutelage perhaps took comfort?

176   The poet's mother died when he was 6. Those formative years—a grief. Hard not to hypothosize the girl caught in May's phosphorescence as **fantasy** transference. A longing turned symphonic when, like his mother, probably also in her 20s, **Beatrice** died. *See **The NeverEnding Story***. *See* the **Rosary**.

177   **Dante** is betrothed to Gemma Donati at 12, marries her at 20, consummates 4 children, yet she never appears in his poetry. Why?!*****

178   Some describe ***courtly love****6 as rhetorical practice, lyric gaming, a **fantasy** to entertain nobility; others describe it as a vehicle for spiritual/erotic/humanist exploration; still others as useless neologism. In 1883 Gaston Paris catalogued 4 requirements: 1) illegitimate **romance**, e.g. adultery, 2) the author (man) unworthy of the beloved (woman), 3) quests undertaken by author (man) in the beloved's (woman's) name, 4) deferment to honor/propriety (adulterous longing notwithstanding). *See **The Fisher King***. *See* **Dungeons** & Dragons™.*7

179   ***La Vita Nuova***, in which the poet attempts to transcend the self-aggrandizing legacy of **courtly love** & address love's essence. A book of **sonnets** coupled w/contextualizing autobiographical commentary. *See* **self-referential**. Ahem. *See* me.

---

* And were we to consider translation as **self-portrait**, or were we to assemble **portraits** of the translators, what would we see?

** Again **Rilke**... *no place/that does not see you...*

*** The **twins**. *See* duality, **symmetry**, schism. Also **WG's stars** ascending.

**** *See* 1001 video **game** references.

***** Perhaps he didn't like her. Found her simple. Mediocre. Cruel. She was petty. He feared her powerful family. Knew too well the flaws to make of her perfection. Shuddered to utter in what nether circle he'd put her. She was shy. Hated poetry, begged him not to. Or, *he* was private. Dubbed the **marriage** sacrosanct. Refused to conscribe her to pedestal, reduce her to symbol/**Virgin**-surrogate/plot-implement.

*6 Not to be confused w/**Courtney Love, rockstar**, grunge punk frontwoman of *Hole*, sidelined for side-eyeing **Harvey Weinstein**. *See Hole Studies*, Hilary Plum, 2022.

*7 A role playing **game** facilitated by an **IRL** storyteller (DM, aka *dungeon master*), in which players construct personas & undertake a **quest** (aka *campaign*) in a co-created **fantasy**. Like **hip hop**, Converse™ & **WG**, just turned 50.

their slant symmetry…See **rhyme**:[180] slant, flat, perfect, internal, end, eye. *See* **rhyming action**.[181] *See* Emily Dickinson.[182] *See* **mirror symmetry**.[183] Symbiosis. Simulation.

---

180 *See also* **Echo***. Ditto. Magpie. Shadow. Clone. *See* mimicry. Other cheek. Knock knock. Carbon copy. Pastiche. *See* neurosis. *See* callback. Hollerback. Copy**cat**. Déjà vu. Contrapasso.** *See* refrain. **Parrot**. Monkey see **monkey** do. Humbert Humbert.*** *See* uniforms. Mass art. Spare parts. Counterparts. **Doppelgangers**. Stunt **doubles**. Twins. **Memes**.**** Redundancies. Covers. Earworms. Earthworm hearts.

181 *The stories that poets have always liked to tell tend to be somewhat hypnotic and mesmerizing. One of the reasons for that is that poets have often attended to what I would call narrative* **echo**-*effects. The narrative* **echo**-*effect is itself an almost subvocal denial of historical progression.* **Charles Baxter**, "**Rhyming Action**." *See also* **fairytales**.

182 The (**virgin**?) mother of modern poetry who renders one & each *Nobody!*

183 A phenomenon in which objects that appear different are equivalent in the extra dimensions of **string theory**.***** *See also* super**symmetry**.

---

* Mountain nymph, cursed decoy, lover unrequited, doomed empath besotted w/a **narcissist**.
** **Dante's** theory of equivalencies.

*** Anti**hero** of **Nabokov's** *Lolita*, nymphet*6 lover.

WG has known men like **Humbert Humbert**.

For starters, the ballet master at her high school. Who rescued the newly driving **virgin** from the snowstorm. Who offered her shelter w/ he & his **wife** overnight, their cabin nearby. He did not say his **wife** worked nights.

As it was happening, **deer** in the headlights, **WG** did not—could not?—speak to stop it. Did not—could not?—move to stop him.

The first man to make her come.

But after…perhaps because she had not been *groomed* it was easier to tell the truth, easier than for her friend who'd invested in private lessons…

It came out the young **teacher** had been hosting secret parties, plying the boarding school kids w/booze.

And in Men's Class—instead of teaching the boys to leap like **Baryshnikov**—he lectured in the proto **manosphere** arts of female seduction, emotional manipulation & **roofies**.

She told her parents. She told the dean. She told the police.

He tried to reverse her testimony.

WG was home when he rang the bell. Behind the **glass**, a wavering **shadow**. A *misunderstanding*, he tried on her father, lawyer, church deacon, who replied if he ever saw the **teacher** again he'd kill him. Then bought a sidearm.

The **teacher** was fired. Quietly.

No trial.

No public record.

Because 16 was the age of **consent**? Or to keep it out of the papers?

Back then records were kept, stories spread, on paper.

The analog body.

Just ducky.

The age of **consent** & yet—whether to press charges—**WG** does not recall being asked.

Had she been asked?

Was she, in fact, relieved not to press charges? Not to testify

in open court....to describe....publicly...

Relieved it had been decided for her? As if it could not have been otherwise?

And what of his **wife**—who had once been his student—**did** she leave him?
She did not. Not then.

A 2025 search revealed that **José Anibal Macedo**—b. June 6, 1961, boomer, **Gemini**, 125 lbs, 5' 3",[*7] owner of Advanced Dance Academy outside of Baltimore—was arrested (2002) , tried & convicted (2003, 2004) on multiple counts of **sexual** child abuse, attempted **rape** & related **sexual** offenses.

Records indicate the abuse for which he was publicly accused began in 2000, a decade after his quiet dismissal from a fine arts boarding school in northern Michigan.

Records indicate his accusers were between 11 & 13 when the abuse began.
Those private lessons again. And went on for years.

The Sun[*8] does not identify victims of **sexual** assault.

What does it mean for the first **sexual** encounters to be violation. To violate. Isolate. Not that kind of secret.

These are not questions.

Sentences, Steinorth. Try again.

Is this what it is to be? A... body?

FIRST TRIAL. June, 2003. Summer break. The court room packed w/students. Students proclaiming their **teacher**'s innocence. Packed w/parents. Engaged parents who love their children. Who proclaim the surrogate caregiver's innocence. Parents contributing substantial funds to his defense. Their presence a defense.

Against which a girl not yet old enough to drive, to go to war, to vote, to drink alcohol, details violations that went on behind closed doors. For years. In a room packed w/peers who don't believe her. After two days of testimony & many hours of deliberation, 8 men & 4 women deadlock.

Mistrial. Go again.

As to reset a badly mended bone. To break again.

SECOND TRIAL: July, 2003. Same lawyers, judge, venue. New jury. In an effort to discredit the fifteen-year-old accuser, the defense moves to subpoena her school records to demonstrate she did not satisfactorily complete the 8th grade. Should not, therefore, be trusted. Is denied. The girl testifies again to abuse going back three years, to a courtroom packed w/former friends & their parents.

On July 16th, 2003, 6 men & 6 women convict **José Anibal Macedo** on all counts of **sex**ual child abuse, attempted **rape** & related charges.

The Sun[*8] does not identify victims of **sex**ual assault.

The foreman reads the verdict as the **teacher's wife**, his former student, mother of their two young children, clutching her Bible, weeps.

WG's therapist says *belief* can be a survival strategy.

FIRST SENTENCING. October 2003. A new team of lawyers funded by parents of **Macedo**'s students move to appeal. The new team produces a polygraph that "proves" zero deception. The polygraph bester*[9] is sentenced to 6 years in prison & 5 years' probation. He must register as a **sex** offender.

It's true classical ballet is the domain of **fantasy**. Of **fairytale**. Damsels & **heroes**. Tall tales. Royal **weddings**. *See* pink satin. Tulle & toile. Bloody slippers.

At **WG**'s school Macedo set *Sleeping Beauty*.*[10] And lured **WG**'s friend w/promises of performing Giselle in *Giselle*.

Giselle. In which, deceived by the man she loves, driven to madness, our **heroine** dies in anguish, dies, but instead of exacting revenge via the the Wilis, those wrathful spirits of maligned women, Giselle takes pity on her betrayer, lets him live.

In classical ballet, even the gruesome is pretty.

THIRD TRIAL. April 2004. Charges on behalf of a second accuser are tried before a new judge in a new venue to prevent any semblance of prejudice. The defense attempts to have charges dismissed based on the prosecutor's failure to present evidence establishing that the defendant, then 42, was at least 4 years older than the victim, then 14, when the abuse began.

As if the difference twixt 42 & 14 or 39 & 11, or 39 & 12—same difference—could ever not be decades.

To perform as in a **Roman circus**.

In the third trial, the pedophile's **wife** & supporters continued to populate the courtroom, though slightly less so. The girl testifies in detail. Her peers & their parents testify against her.

What does it mean that for injustice to be met w/justice, the private must be made public?

I mean. In the body. What does it mean?

WG wonders if the three accusers became friends. If they were friends before this. If they ever held hands.

Perhaps the girls were not permitted to speak to one another.

No. Let them be friends. But if then friends, how long thereafter? Are they still in touch? Did any keep dancing? Did any after let men touch them? Did any after need men to touch them? Are any of them therapists? Any of them mothers?

WG did not speak of it w/her friend or anyone after it was over. It was over. No big deal. No big deal, she said, more or less, for 35 years.

Making things small, said her therapist, is another means of survival.

SECOND SENTENCING. September 2004. Only his lawyers w/him in the courtroom. 6 more years in prison, consecutive sentences.

FOURTH TRIAL. Charges on behalf of a third accuser were indefinitely suspended, backup in the event of overturned convictions. And perhaps 12 years was sufficient (*see* a 5' 3" pedophile in the pen).

But not hard to wonder if the third accuser was okay w/this. At 14, the eldest when the abuse began, 17 when it might have been tried—unable to vote or go to war, but old enough to **consent**—**WG** hopes she was asked.

WG was 50, when she googled her assaulter, read how he'd harmed others. W/in hours her back went out. A seizure. For several days she could not move, for two weeks she could not sit. Could not drive. On her back could not roll over. Call out.

She called her friend for help. Then a therapist.

So old, the badly mended bone. A body protects maligned bones.

To not break again.

Break again.

For the girls who might have been spared. For their parents. For the pedophile's children. All he'd trained. Whole communities deceived. Gaslit. His **wife**, also a victim, also complicit. For what didn't survive him. For him. What he suffered to become this. For what was surely done to him in prison.

For the women those girls became.
For the girl she is.

WG wishes she could thank the ones who stopped him. The girls who spoke & those who believed them, who devoted years to stopping him.

How did it come to light? It is something to know how an invisible thing, call it **dark matter**, is discovered. How tempered **glass** is shattered.

A parent of one of the girls witnessed a change in her daughter, or her daughter, **suicidal**, asked for help. The mother took her to a counselor. The girl told the counselor what she could not tell her mother. What the **teacher** had done to her. The counselor, following the law, reported it to the police. The police investigated. Sussed out other girls harmed. Each girl had to speak. Had to break again. Silence. Had to describe what was done to them. Others had to hear. What they did not want to hear. Had to believe them. Had to ask them to speak again to break again. The girls had to articulate many times in many ways what had been done to them for the man to be named. To be stopped. To be put away. They had to produce evidence of breaking. The violations had to be clear. The violations were clear. Still, it was their word against his. No bruises. No **rape** kit. Nothing to see but the girls themselves. Nothing but words in their mouths to tell.

<hr>

How many didn't tell. Weren't believed. How many—too old, too brown, too poor
too promiscuous—to convince a jury of his peers.

As of March 2025, **José Anibal Macedo** is a registered **sex** offender living in Baltimore. He served time in prison, though **WG** cannot say how long.

Is fine not knowing.

In a parallel story, twenty-five years after **Macedo** assaulted her, **WG** encountered another predator at the same institution, though it took years for her to recognize him.

It took comparing stories w/other women to recognize him.

Even then, she did not know the half of it until, soon after he left the institution, a young woman, not old enough to drink when the abuse began, confided what he'd done to her when she worked under him. How her boss, old enough to be her father, had **sex**ually harassed, abused & assaulted her. **WG** listened to the woman, and encouraged her to report what he had done to her. At the institution that had quietly fired her assaulter decades prior. **WG** encouraged the young woman to report him. To their institution. And the next institution that hired him. The woman did. The next institution quietly fired him. Another one hired him. He may soon be up for tenure.

**** A unit of culture. Coined by **Richard Dawkins** in *The Selfish Gene*, 1976, w/applied **Darwin**. *See also **memetics***.

***** An attempt to reconcile differences. The micro & macro of physics. The theory of relativity w/quantum mechanics. **String** because it's no good binding apples & oranges w/a stapler.

*6 Pre-teen girls.

*7 Could **WG**, 5' 4¾", have overpowered him? Her **teacher**? In his home. Middle of the night. Middle of a snowstorm…?

*8 ***The Baltimore Sun***, largest general-circulation newspaper in MD, established in 1837, purchased by the Sinclair Broadcast Group[11] in 2024. Also, the nineteenth card of the **Tarot**'s major arcana.[12]

*9 *See also* **fraud**, 8th circle.

*10 A whole **king**dom put to sleep, till true love's kiss….what other **fairytales** did those girls believe.

*11 A conservative, pro-**Trump**, telecommunications conglomerate that as of Jan 2025 owns or operates 193 television stations in over 100 markets covering 40% of American households. A 2019 study demonstrates that after purchase by Sinclair group, local political reporting decreases, national political reporting increases & becomes increasingly conservative, requiring reporters to read pre-scripted pro-**Trump** content. *See also* John Oliver.

*12 The sun shines on a naked child, nothing to hide, astride a horse. The sun indicates, among other things, the lessons & knowledge of the subconscious made conscious, integrated. Success, health, happiness, a good **marriage**, liberation.

delusion[184] *is an egregious sin*...by **Dante**'s account to **mask**, twist, or hinder truth is the penultimate plummet—drop you 8 of 9 **dungeons**—worse than heresy, lust, sodomy & murder...*See also* seducers, flatterers, false prophets, hypocrites, authors of **fantasy** & speculation.[185] *See* fallen **heroes: Jason**,[186] **Ulysses**,[187] Pope Nicholas III,[188] **Elon Musk**.[189] Then the word became fiction, flesh—a doctored image[190]—& walked among us.

---

184   Would it could be penetrated by flashlight

185   Does Dante count himself in this lot?...w/just cause...?

186   The **argonaut**. Cursed for the seduction & abandonment of Medea & progeny. *See also* **Diane Wakoski**, who describes herself as Jason's progeny. Who made a trade of articulating betrayal.* *See* Wakoski's "Archeology of Movies & Books", especially ***Argonaut Rose***, especially the 1st three poems of "Medea, the Argonaut Rose" in which the acclaimed poet draws imagery & narrative from a student's poems** thus offering, perhaps inadvertently, commentary on the student's love life. In 1998 the student will find the newly released book on a round wooden table in a small bookstore in Ithaca where she'd moved after college to live w/her boyfriend. Her boyfriend, she'd recently discovered, was for years unfaithful. The student, alone now & heartbroken in Ithaca, shocked & delighted to find in a tiny bookstore, front & center, the newly minted verse of her mentor, will open it to a poem depicting the student & her (now ex) boyfriend. Her boyfriend who "doesn't really love her very much...." Had she world & time to keep it up, the younger poet's nails would still be blue.

187   **Homer's hero**, by Athena blessed, who so brutally dispatches w/**Penelope**'s handmaidens...

188   Best crony a would-be Pope/dictator could hope for...who traded sacred offices for $, favors & loyalty.

189   Is technocracy the new papacy? *See also* ***musk***.***

190   **Dr. Williams** said *Its abuse is apparent.* Sic.****

---

* *See **The Motorcycle Betrayal Poems**, 1971, first book of a prolific poet of the Silent Generation, dedicated (the poet proclaims, not in the interior, but on *the cover*) to all those men who betrayed me at one time or another, may they fall off their motorcycles & break their necks. A pseudo-reckoning w/the disconnect between real & **fantasy** men, the book begins w/"Learning to Live with My Face."
** Poems shared in **private lessons**, aka independent studies. Having exhausted all undergraduate & graduate course offerings w/her mentor, the young poet lept at the elder's invitation. *See* **WG**'s **"We Were Just Going for Smokes,"******* in which the younger poet recollects what a man in mock crucifixion tells her it takes to be a man. *See* **DW**'s **"Blue Nails"** in which the elder poet mourns the youngster's failure to juggle more than one lover & critiques 90s hippie-grunge aesthetics. Compare.
*** Glandular secretions from animals (*see* civets, bred that their asses be daily scraped; *see* **musk deer**, the shy, nearly extinct Himalayans, so like our own dear **deer**, but miniature; *see* **beavers**, who mark their industries via castoreum that mellows to spiced leather, for which a little slaughter; *see* ambergris, coveted furballs of **sperm whales**, notes of wood, moss & amber; *see* **musk**rats, kissing cousin to the **beaver**, population near collapse, whose inimitable scent complexities have perfumed & fattened **cats** for a millennium).
**** ***Spring & All***.
***** Written autumn, 1996. Collected in ***Forking the Swift***, 2010.

*Huxley said six **monkeys**...* Astrophysicist **James Jeans** wrongly attributes the **Infinite Monkey Theorem**,[191] to **Henry Huxley** in his 1930[192] pop-sci text, ***The Mysterious Universe***,[193] "It was, I think, Huxley[194] who said that six monkeys, set to strum unintelligently on typewriters for millions of millions of years, would be bound in time to write all the books of the British Museum," an inaccuracy proliferated by **Richard Dawkins**[195] in his 2008 anthology ***The Oxford Book of Modern Science Writing***. In **IMT**—the proposition that given time & world enough anything that can happen *almost surely*[196] will—"**monkey**" serves as stunt double for any thoughtless entity punching random keys, versus our actual kissing cousin who, like us, plays favorites & may be less given to depressing letters than defecating on the machine.

---

191 In his 1939 essay, "**The Total Library,**" **Jorge Borges** traces the origins of **Infinite Monkey Theorem** back to **Aristotle**, then uses the concept to populate a fictional reality. In "**The Library of Babel**"* (1941) the universe is a vast, possibly infinite series hexagonal rooms affixed like honeycomb, each wall lined w/identical shelves, each shelf filled w/identically bound books, each book filled w/a different permutation of 25 characters. The orderly structures are counterposed by text that is almost entirely nonsensical, nevertheless inhabitants search for meaning. Their pursuits produce limitless dimensions of hope & despair, the likes of which drive the speaker nearing his end to lament, *"Methodical writing distracts me from the present condition of men. But the certainty that everything has been already written nullifies or makes phantoms of us all."*

Love child of **fantasy** & probability notwithstanding (*see also* **String Theory**), **IMT** is most certainly a practical & mathematical impossibility & rejected by both scientists & aesthetes. Like **fraud**, embezzlement & first-degree murder, art, we tend to think, requires intent.

192 **Nevermind** Wikipedia's 1931 inaccuracy.

193 Which **Dawkins** describes as prose poetry, e.g. "We find the universe terrifying because of its vast meaningless distances, terrifying because of its inconceivably long vistas of time which dwarf human history to the twinkling of an eye, terrifying because of our extreme **loneliness**..." **James Jeans**, *The Mysterious Universe*.

194 **Thomas Henry Huxley** (1825-1895), biologist, anthropologist, self-taught comparative anatomist, aka "**Darwin's Bulldog**." Huxley's famed debate w/Bishop Wilberforce (Oxford, 1860) is credited w/accelerating acceptance of evolutionary theory, though surviving accounts, some of which recollect **Infinite Monkey Theory** as supporting evidence, are believed to be fictitious.**

195 The zoologist father of **memetics** uses **IMT** in his own argument, ***The Blind Watchmaker***, a 1986 defense of evolutionary complexity arising from random mutations. *See also methinks it is like a **weasel**.****

196 In probability theory a probability of 1. *See also almost never. See also almost everywhere.* Nothing is no problem except in the infinite set. *See **Everything Everywhere All at Once*** (2022).**** *See* **Joy Division.***** Fall almost apart.

---

* Whose *Ficciones*, **WG** twice received from one dear artist crony.

** *See* the evolution of story. *See* also **meme**. *See* **Dawkins**.

*** Some versions of **IMT** sub "the entire works of **Shakespeare**" for "all the books of the British Museum." For the purposes of *his* argument, **Dawkins**, an evangelical atheist, simplifies the goal to reproducing a single line from ***Hamlet***, "me thinks it is like a **weasel**." A line not chosen at random. In the referential scene, aware others think him delusional, Hamlet toys w/hierophantic **Polonius** by describing what he sees in the **clouds**: a camel, a **weasel**, a whale. Dawkins uses the scene to discuss human propensity to perceive "intelligent design" where none exists. Intelligent Design advocate, Jonathan Witt, points out that in the larger context of the play, it's sycophantic **Polonius** who fails to see signs of (malicious) design (the artful murder of the **King**) & gaslit Hamlet who accurately reads "clouds" & divines the cause. The Bard's designs, of course, are not on trial.

**** A comic, absurdist, genre-bending **epic** traversing parallel universes to save Joy, the world & myriad humanities from the bagel of doom. *See* **string theory**. *See also* **The Nothing** in *The NeverEnding Story*.

***** An English, post-punk band formed in 1976, known for the hit "**Love Will Tear Us Apart**",*6 posthumously released after guitarist/lyricist Ian Curtis, who suffered from depression, a failed **marriage** & epilepsy, committed **suicide** on the eve of their North American tour. The band was named for a term given to Nazi concentration camp brothels, whose **sex** workers were enslaved girls & women. *See also* the Nazi youth appearing on their 1st album, *An Ideal for Living. See* Nazi nouveau as post-punk, anti-establishment, shock darling, heralding serial killers, medical horrors, & anarchy. After Curtis' death, the remainders +1 became New Order.

*6 Until recently, **WG**, long obsessed w/**Joy Division**'s smash hit, knew almost nothing of the band which came & went before she was 6. She has also loved New Order.

*don't be a square...*said Uma Thurman as Mia Wallace[197] to John Travolta as Vincent Vega[198] in the cherry Malibu convertible of **Pulp Fiction.**[199] Square: someone priggish, prudish, or old-fashioned, as opposed to *hip*. A fuddy-duddy. The quality of conventionality. 1944: first use of *square*[200] as jab: in reference to one who failed to appreciate **jazz.** *Square*: a conductor's gestural translation of 4/4 time. *Square*: **SpongeBob's** pants.

44   **OK ~~Angel~~ *Go Fish.*[201]**

Angels[202] & angelfish, *both* ambush **predators**, use wispy, fringe elements to disappear. In the wild, the fish form **mono**gamous pairs, seldom replacing their mate even after death. In captivity,[203] semi-aggressive. May tolerate more of the same. May tolerate a **sucker.**

---

197 Modeled after Anna Karina, **iconoclastic** actress, director & co-creator of **French New Wave** film.*

198 Brother to Vic Vega, aka Mr. Blonde, played by Michael Madsen in *Reservoir Dogs*** (1992), first film both written & directed by **Quentin Tarantino.**

199 A 1994 nonlinear, **self-referential, cult classic** known for long **mono**logues, unabashed violence, comic, anti-social **heroes** & pastiche. Tri-**Star** passed on the screenplay which, along w/Tarantino's **True Romance** & *Natural Born Killers*, were derived from an unfinished script by **Roger Avary.** Thank Miramax à la **Harvey Weinstein,**[***] **Tarantino's** great champion,**** for the manifest.

200 As opposed to *fair & square*, what Cub Scouts swear, a square deal, *The* Square Deal,***** "Hip to Be Square."*6

201 A **game** in which players seek mates.

202 To whom, **Rilke** said, we cannot turn—our cries in the eternal current indistinguishable. *See* "First Elegy."

203 Keeping **fish** as ornament originated in ancient China where breeding for "gold" dates to the Tang Dynasty, 7th century. In Europe, a thousand years later, **husbands** gifted their wives gold**fish** as a symbol of luck & fortune on their first anniversary. Then English chemist, Robert Warington, published his aquarium how-to (1850) & craze ensued. O for an undistorted, unrestricted view. Window as container to capture...imagination. Imagine!---the puckered kissers ubiquitous! Step right up—toss a penny—win a guppy! These days, carnival winnings dispatched swimmingly (or belly up) are mostly banned, but **WG** recalls the fist of plastic bag, the gulping, giddy. Influencers & celebrities notwithstanding, a **fish**bowl lifesucks & luck kept dies.

---

* **Iconoclastic** genre of the late 50s & early 60s, known for absurdist/existential themes & anti-realist techniques, e.g. **camera** work that disrupts the panoramic axis, bucks audience expectations & undermines the naiveté of the **gaze.** *See also* fourth wall breaks, long tracking shots & an overthrow of plot.

** Taken together **Tarantino's** films create a reflexive universe, w/character relationships crossing seemingly disparate narratives. Unlike the **fantasy** universes of Narnia, **Neverland,** Asgard or Middle Earth, Tarantino's world world **masquerades** as our own. Like **French New Wave,** the artifice struts less in the world-building than in the telling.

*** From 1966-2016, Academy Award winners thanked **Harvey Weinstein** as many times as **God.** In 2017, over 80 women filed complaints of **sex**ual abuse, instances of which went back 30 years. Some who spoke out prior to 2017, including **Courtney Love,** credit Weinstein w/ career annihilation. Convicted of **sex**ual assault, **rape** & **sex**ual battery in both NY & CA, the producer was exiled from his company & the Academy, then stripped of his honorary title, Commander of the Order of the British Empire. In April of 2024, Weinstein appealed three NY convictions. The 2025 retrial yield: 1 guilty, 1 not-guilty, 1 mistrial.

**** Following **Weinstein's** numerous convictions, **Tarantino,** whose partnership w/Weinstein included co-directing Miramax & The Weinstein Company for two decades, admitted to knowing about his champion's misdeeds...for decades. The **icon** concedes numerous reports from respected colleagues, dismissed as isolated instances of mischief & hopes his own legacy won't be affected.

***** The Domestic policy of progressive republican, **Teddy Roosevelt,** whose "square deal for every man" was said to thread the needle.

*6 Huey Lewis & the News, 1986, widely interpreted as a pro-square anthem (*see* Nancy Reagan "Just Say No") though Lewis denies this intent. In **American Psycho** (another two-tiered **manosphere** opus), both the 1991 novel & turn of the century film adaptation star*ring Christian Bale as **villain protagonist Patrick Bateman***7) "Hip to Be Square" features prominently in one of Bateman's anti-social tirades.

*7 The **unreliable narrator, sigma male, serial killer** wannabe appears in several Bret Easton Ellis novels. Ellis claimed he based Bateman on his abusive father, then claimed he wrote what he saw in the **mirror.**

surely the father of lies[204]...See **John** 8:44:

> *Ye are of your father*[205] *the devil, and the lusts of your father ye will do. He was a murderer from the beginning,*[206] *and abode not in the truth, because there is no truth in him. When he speaketh a lie, he speaketh of his own: for he is a liar, and the father of it.* KJV

*recirculating tank...*as opposed to open circuit scuba which wastes unmetabolized oxygen, recirculating tanks, aka rebreathers, recycle exhales for dives that are longer & deeper. Preferred by the military for the bubblelessness that keeps frogmen **anonymous.**

47   **OK Switch.**[207]

open corkscrew in her hands... For demonstration of an "open corkscrew" defense, *see* ***True Romance,***[208] "Alabama vs Virgil", wherein our smells-like-a-peach heroine (played by Patricia Arquette) defends life, love & **booty** from plug-ugly hitman (à la James Gandolfini[209] who goes by the name **Virgil**).[210]

---

204 *See also* **Hero**dotus, 5th century BCE, famed orator, researcher & author, hailed by Cicero as the Father of History, by others as Father of Lies for integrating the folklore & tall tales gathered in his research travels alongside the "true" history. Also critiqued (by Thucydides, the rhetorician) for digressions which undermined (or disguised?) authorial control. Scholars agree *Histories** contains inaccuracies but remains, nevertheless, the earliest Greek prose to survive intact & the result of painstaking note-taking the known world over, "to prevent the traces of human events from being erased."

205 One might also consider a word from mother **Emily:** *The truth must dazzle gradually/Or every man be blind.*

206 *See also* **John** 1:1, *In the beginning was the word and the word was with God and the word was* ***God****.* Word.

207 In **BDSM** terminology, someone who takes on different roles—top & bottom, dominant & submissive—depending on partner, context, etc. *See also* switch hitter.

208 1993 film directed by Tony Scott, written by **Quentin Tarantino****...after the (uncredited) story by **Roger Avary.** In *True Romance,* Clarence Worley (Christian Slater), a **comics** store clerk turned vigilante, navigates a criminal underworld counseled by a gold-blazered **Elvis** who appears in bathroom **mirrors.** Under Elvis-advisement, Worley saves his just-met girlfriend by killing her pimp.*** X-country odyssey ensues, leads them to **paradise** by way of a trailer park & a brutal shootout in **Hollywood. Cult classic.**

209 Best known for Tony Soprano, "family man" & New Jersey nobility in the 21st century underworld of *The Sopranos* (1999-2007). Toxic masculinity vis-à-vis a mob boss in therapy—a role G won after powers on high witnessed his *True Romance* slaughter.

210 Three cheers for the wayward **villain** named for a hoary Roman poet—maestro of **epic** & pastoral—**rockstar** blazing the dark medieval—not to mention, **Dante**'s pilot through **hell.**

---

* An ennealogy: each book named for one of the nine **muses:** the inspiration of **Theresa Hak Kyung Cha**'s genre-bending novel, ***Dictee*** (1982), described by poet Juliana Spahr as, "part autobiography, part biography, part personal diary, part ethnography, part auto-ethnography, part translation... presented with an intertextual mix of photographs, quotations, translations, and language so as to create a history," *College Literature*, 1996. Published a month before Cha was **raped** & murdered by a guard at her **husband**'s Manhattan office.

** Who, like his **hero** Clarence, is **Elvis** obsessed & indebted. As the **icon** oft relates, a walk-on bit as an **Elvis Impersonator** in a syndicated *Golden Girls* episode helped finance *Reservoir Dogs*, the 1992 darling of Sundance & Cannes (later picked up by **Weinstein**'s Miramax (pronounced *mirror Macs*). **Cult classic.** *See also* **Tarantino** as asylum attendant #2 in *Eddie Presley* (1992), a dramedy about a down on his luck **Elvis**-impersonator.

*** Drexl Spivey, fan favorite, played by chameleon, Gary Oldman, ever **anonymous.**

To pan is to pivot: door on a hinge, wrench on a bolt, spotlight to blind, liar on a dime. In cinema *see* panorama, the lateral sweep, may establish spatial relationships, convey distance. A slow pan builds suspense. Quick makes chaos. We're talking **magic**. Sleight of hand. We're bringing **sexy** back.[211] *See also* the cloven prancing beguiler **Pan**.[212]

linkless cuffs...mean less incriminating evidence.

we call it **heroin**...*heroin*—from the German, *heroisch*, strong, heroic, from the Greek *hērōs*, protector or in feminine form, *heras*, for **Hera**,[213] sister-**wife** to Zeus—*heroin* for the elysian veil that descends, reality's rift, painlessness, **god** sans limbs, bliss, rhapsody,[214] **paradise, cloud** nine,[215] seventh heaven.[216] The rapture.[217] **Nirvana**.[218] Ironically *illicit*. *See also* laudanum, codeine, morphine (but not ecstasy)...back to 16th century. *See Euphoria. Rush. Requiem for a Dream. See Traffic. See Trainspotting.*

---

211   Compare **Right Said Fred**'s *too sexy* mockery to **Justin Timberlake**'s "SexyBack"* 15 years later. To wit, DJs thought the latter a joke, till JT macked them w/the video: #1 on US charts for 7 weeks. The video—a black&white, cloak&dagger, smoke&**mirror** shot in Barcelona—features espionage **spy**ware but JT swears he's not a creeper.

212   Wild & pastoral. Improvisational flutist. Nymph consort. Goat-man halvsies. Hybrid deity. All **sex**. Will also play his *pipe* solo, a trick he taught the shepherds. Progeny of **Penelope** &....? Some say **Hermes**, some Mercury, some **Apollo**. Some credit w/ complex paternity, the upshot of 108 suitors through the house of **Ulysses**, the Megaron door swinging nearly off its hinges.... Hand it to **Homer**.

213   But really, who wants to be **Hera**? Not **WG**. Always scorned. Always pissed.** The rueful, rulekeeper of **marriage**. The protector, never protected. Honestly, who but gay men want to be *queen*.***

214   *See* Queen's Bohemian, 1975. **Icon/iconoclast**. Whose wildly successful pre-**MTV** video presaged the practice.

215   A phase en route to Buddhist enlightenment, of joy & peace. Or, from the 1896 **Cloud** Atlas, big white fluffy cumulonimbus. Or the uppermost of *Paradiso* nearest to **God**, by way of **Dante**.

216   From ancient Mesopotamia, referring to the seven domes that enclose Earth, where dwell the **gods**. The seven heavens of the Jewish Talmud & seven celestial spheres in Islam's Quran may each be traced to Babylon. *See also* **echoes**. *See* serendipity, *rhyme*.

217   From the Latin to seize, to carry off. An eschatological forecast inferred from Paul's first epistle to **Thessalonians** (4:16-17) a possible future in which the faithful, like spoils of war, are stolen away at the second coming... believers like **booty** plundered **into wonder**.

218   *Come as you are*, sang the nineties, sang **Kurt Cobain**, sang **nihilism**. As if it cared? It's a particular look. It's not not **Looksmaxxing**. When is not not not caring a defense strategy? When is singing not belonging? *See also* kids see, kids, see? *See also Rage Against the Machine.*

---

*Inspired by **David Bowie**'s "Rebel Rebel" written to piss off Mick Jagger, released when **WG** was in utero: *you've got your mother in a whirl/ she's not sure if you're a boy or a girl*...which was true.
** **WG**'s **husband** says *petty*.
*** Even the one played by Cate Blanchet, **hero**.

*he's turned the **gaze** back on her...*it might be scopophilia;[220] it might be scopophobia;[221] a flex;[222] a defense;[223] *there is no spoon,*[224] said **boy wonder** to **boy wonder,**[225] **mirror** to hypnotist, the being & nothingness. It's fine. Not fine! The lens internalized.

*she wears **glasses**...*accessory to the crime of reading from the days of **Dante.**[226] Like other disability adaptations, glasses aspired to invisibility till Theodore Roosevelt[227] made them manly, Siegel & Shuster veiled their **hero**[228] & four eyed[229] **Buddy Holly** broadcast **sexy.** Whoever said love is blind hasn't seen social media, **nevermind** the **game** show. Warby Parker™ claims to be the love child of Jack Kerouac,[230] no relation to **Dorothy.**[231]

---

219   A term coined by British philosopher Gilbert Ryle to illustrate Cartesian dualism's a logical fallacy. According to Ryle the mind is but a figment of self-consciousness arising from particular cognizance. Also applied to emerging **AI,** but **Walkman**™ **G**'s rage against the machine predates that travesty.

220   Pleasure, especially **sex**ually, from looking at a person/object, especially **anonymously** or in secret. PSA to clear your browser history.

221   Fear of being looked at, seen in public, ogled. Anxiety related to disembodied self-seeing. *See also schizophrenia.*

222   *See* **Berger:** *The principal **protagonist** is never painted. He is **spectator.** *

223   *See* **Berger:** The ***surveyed** is female.*

224   Or woundable body; *see* **Elaine Scarry.** From ***The Matrix,*** visiting the Oracle, wunderkind to wunderkind.

225   But also the Bat's mentee, naïve accomplice, alt conscience. Whose **blunders** make of **Bat** a surrogate father.

226   Also born in central Italy, possibly Florence, late 13th century.

227   Trust-busting, rough riding, Harvard intellectual, **cowboy,** widower. First U.S. citizen to win Nobel Peace Prize. Authored **The Square Deal.** Inspired the much beloved plushy.*

228   As **Clark Kent.** That **Lois** can't see the **Super** through the **specs** is testament.

229   Rock n Roll **icon,** 1936-1959. Dead by plane*** at 22, not 6 months **married.** Survived by **Waylon Jennings** who swapped seats w/ J.P Richardson, otherwise destined to take the bus when "The Big Bopper" came down w/a nasty flu. *See* **"Love is Strange"** a posthumous release & **WG** fav from ***Dirty Dancing.***

230   The **spectacles**' namesakes, legend has it, were discovered in the beatnik's archives, a couple of characters, Warby Pepper & Zagg Parker. Moreover, it's company policy, all Warby Parker employees get *Dharma Bums* on day one.

231   Poet **Dorothy Parker** (1893-1967), *Men seldom make passes/At girls who wear **glasses**.* News Item: that's the whole damn poem. High key **DP** trouncing **WG** w/ *the soul of wit.*****

---

* **WG** once loved an artist who refused art as Trojans should have the **horse***** or in *The Body Snatchers,* those nefarious spores.*6 *See* **Eliot**'s "Tradition." *See* Bloom's *Anxiety of Influence.* Quarter century later, the artist was much the same. *See* **Dorian Gray.**

As the story goes, on a bear hunt in Mississippi, last in the company to trophy, **Roosevelt was gifted w/a black bear tied to a tree. Teddy refused the victory, but asked that the creature, hounded then bludgeoned into submission, be put out of its misery. The statesman's disgust was captured by numerous cartoon journalists w/early depictions portraying a man-sized black bear noosed to a domineering (White) hunter, while later iterations depict a cuddly, trembling cub. If he'd trademarked his **meme**-spurred stuffy, the first teddy-maker would've made a killing. *See also* "The Teddy Bears Picnic," a 45 found w/her father's records at grandma's, that **WG** played repeatedly.

*** Along w/Ritchie Valens & J.P Richardson, Feb 9, 1959, The Day the Music Died. *See* "La Bamba" (1958). *See* "Chantilly Lace" (1958). *See* Don Mclean's **"American Pie"** (1971), which for better or worse, **WG** knows by heart.

**** You again, **Polonius?**—*and tediousness the limbs & outward flourishes.* Sigh.

***** **WG** was nearly **50** when she realized the horse was myth or metaphor, the physics **virtually** impossible.

*6 A 1954 serial sci-fi written by Jack Finney wherein **alien** spores adrift replace sleeping **Earthlings** w/vegetable lookalikes. Reproduced in **Hollywood** in 1956 & 1978*7 & 1993 & 2007. *See* communism. McCarthyism. Consumerism. Pop-psychiatry. *See* self-help malarkey. *See* woke.

*7 "Validates the entire concept of remakes..." *Variety.*

limbo: a liminal space, indeterminate, twixt & tween,[232] post & pre, the porch, portico, foyer, lobby, the shuffle/deal/ante,[233] on deck, standby, timeout, detention, in holding, refugee, in the wings, in suspense, intermission, the Casablanca of *Casablanca*, the changeover,[234] long volta,[235] a realm this side of **hell** postulated by Bishops to address paradoxical "certainties," where a poet on the brink of becoming **mono**ymous joins himself to **epic** company,[236] a dancing contest that favors the bendy, the haunting, monochromatic single-player **quest**[237] of a virtual boy who wakes in the woods at **hell**'s brink & dies many deaths searching for his sister.

52 *the* **Sears Catalog**...Speaking of "truth in advertising", the purveyor's "Book of Bargains" goes back to its post **Civil War** origins, "a **mirror** of our times, recording for future historians our desires, habits, customs, and mode of living."[238] *See also* the Christmas Edition, aka "Wish Book"[239] purveyor of Mattel's™ 1965 hit, **Mystery Date**™.

cavalier...From Late Latin for **horse**man, Vulgar Latin for **horse**. *See* mounted. *See* high **horse**. *See* various moods of that long-faced beast between the thighs.

to MacGyver...v., to resourcefully negotiate bad situations like the genius **protagonist** of the 1985 tv series, i.e. escaping a locked, windowless room w/a roll of duct tape, pack of mints & a Swiss Army Knife™. The unlikely 80s **hero** practiced nonviolence,[240] half a dozen languages & applied physics to save "the little guy" (farm workers, deaf children, the Black Rhinoceros[241]) from **bullies**. First name unknown.

---

232 In adolescence: the swift, shaleshifty riverbed of double digits, before the bramblewood teens.

233 A gambling rollcall. *See also* Antecedent. Antenuptial. Antebellum. Antemortem.

234 "....this is a moment in which the aesthetics of both the photograph and **the virtual** are characterized by liminality*... at some point in the future, people will have forgotten celluloid and the indexical image, and this particularly contemporary consciousness of displacement from one medium to another." **Laura Mulvey**, from an interview by Rebecca Sassatelli in *Theory, Culture & Society*, 2011.

235 Some turn on a dime, others take lines, pages, all night, months in therapy, decades, lifetimes. *See also* universe.

236 Again, **Dante**. Who, in the **Limbo** of his speculative memoir, confers w/his **rockstar heroes**—Ovid, Horace, **Homer**, Lucan, **Virgil**—thus writing himself into their company—mechanics at his pitstop, gurus to his vengeance, roadies on his infernal tour. Authorial arrogance? Or desperation? O what reinvention comes of exile.

237 Via a video **game** some call poetry, w/German expressionist overtones, released by Playdead™ in 2011.

238 According to a 1943 Sears News Graphic. Selling everything from house kits to hair tonic, Sears' success—a mail order Amazon— was hitched to railroads, **manifest destiny** & the U.S. Postal Service.

239 **WG** dogeared the glossy, Bible thin leaves, a 300+ page **amuse bouche**. Window shopping a virtual cart.

240 Wiki authors describe his emotional intelligence, mood congruence & refusal to carry a gun notable for the era (1985-1992); **WG** postures the Wiki authors invested in the 2016 reboot.

241 Now extinct.

---

* Here is **Gen X**, named for the variable, splitting the difference.

*every **marriage** falls/ into misery*...years back, sure it was over, no visible future tolerable, **WG**'s friend[242] offered her counsel. Said, if you're lucky enough to be married long enough, every **marriage** [every **marriage**] [every **marriage**] traverses....or collapses...in **hell**. Said, *you know this.* Unshakable couples suddenly split. Or remain in misery, bound to it. A few fall in, bushwack through, come away new the other side. **WG** cried. Threw up her hands. Could not imagine the other side. But some dark thinned. Some brick to cloth. A **double**-bolted door unlocked. And across the pitch, months to years, a light in the distance blossomed.

a path//less wood...how it always begins.[243] Even when, retelling—we think we know the way.

*leopards & she-**wolves***...in the Comedy, these beasts associated w/lust & avarice[244] are no less dangerous for their Earthly habitat. To survive them, **Dante** must descend & bear witness to the consequences exacted by infernal denizens.

55   *...the seven new Goldilocks[245] planets*...those lands far away, lately discovered[246] replete w/beds, chairs, bowls of porridge. *See also* breaking & entering. *See* colonists. *See* Vikings.

---

242 Clinical social worker, grief counselor & stellar poet, Melissa Fournier.

243 *See* **Inferno**, the get go. Or again **Caroline Bergvall's "Via: 48 Translations of Dante."**

244 *See* **Jeremiah** 5:6—which, like **Dante** also speaks of the **lion** (pride)— **WG**'s sign, here acquitted.

245 Because, in the end, we're all little blonde girls (raised by **wolves**?) traipsing about the woods, **blundering** into other folks' homes. *See also* **Karens.***

246 Or..."lately." In 2017 a NASA telescope discovered a red dwarf **star**, Trappist-1, 40 light years away, w/7 Earth-sized planets, 3 of which, TRAPPIST 1B, 1C, 1D, suggest water, if water there be, neither frozen nor vaporous. In 2024, another NASA lens caught a possible **Earthling** habitat 137 light years away. The planet, TOI-701 b, not yet properly named, presumably to avoid emotional attachment.

---

* A White, cry-**wolf surveyor** of Black men. *See* Becky. Permit Patty. Cornerstone Caroline. *See* Miss Ann. **Crocodile** tears. Asymmetrical haircut. **Femme fatale**** sans **sex** appeal. *See* Hays Code,*** Plankton's **WIFE**. *See* meme.****

** Associated w/**film noir** the concept of a woman weaponizing vulnerability & **sexual** appeal to manipulate men is ancient. Of course, unlike **femme fatale**, a creation of hegemony, **Karen** arises from Black experience of White women's maintainance of White supremacy. Contrarywise, **femme fatale** as a **villain** construct, flatters the dominant (male/**hero**) gaze.

*** A decency "Formula" outlined by Presbyterian **Will H. Hays**, consequential to the Supreme Court's 1915 decision not to apply *free speech* to motion pictures. Though Hays intended the formula to be self-regulated, **Hollywood** didn't & by the early 1930s,***** American Catholics organized for enforcement. Depictions of homo**sexuality**, interracial **romance**, illegal drug trafficking, nudity (actual or in silhouette) & blasphemy were strictly prohibited. Also prohibited: *Willful offenses to any nation, race or creed.**6 Extramarital **sex**, if suggested, must be lurid. Crime punished. Authorities respected. Under no circumstances could clergy be ridiculed. Depictions of the flag, arson, burglary, smuggling, sympathetic criminals, "a woman selling her virtue,"*7 governmental institutions, kissing, men & women in bed, "third-degree methods,"*8 "first night scenes,"*9 **rape**, surgery, childbirth & **branding** must be treated w/extreme caution. Institutional corruption depicted only as the exception. Not yet satisfied, the Catholic Legion of Decency, later dubbed the National Legion of Decency, further codified films as "harmless" or "condemned". Condemnation, of course, a boon for ticket sales.

**** From the French, **meme**, meaning *same*. Or *me* x2. *See* **Dawkins**. *See* **infinity mirror.**

***** Pre-**code Hollywood**—those films produced between the first "talkies" in the late 1920s & mid 30s & **Hays Code** enforcement—was racy, profane, subverse, progressive & fabulous, besotted w/gangsters & **sexually** liberated women. *See...see...see...*

*6 E.g. racism. Though who defined "willful offense"? You guessed it.

*7 Aka prostitution.

*8 Aka torture.

*9 Aka **marriage** consummation/conjugal **sex**.

keyhole...an aperture for peeping. Or when **Bob Hope** plays detective,[247] a means of documenting creeps.[248] Or the **surveillance** by which power monitors reputation across social media—a big **data** peek at group think.

*where's **big brother** now*...not the reality **game** show launched in the Netherlands in 1999 w/franchises in 63 countries & regions, but the Orwellian eye from 1949's *1984* that inspired it. Both mean business. In the game show, "houseguests" cohabitate in tight quarters under constant **surveillance**,[249] isolated from outside society[250] in an *each against all*[251] contest of social manipulation **Big Brother**™ wins.

57   **Self-Portrait as Slag Heap[252] for Data/Gratification[253]**

cloud[254]...a visible aerosol of liquid...[255] harbinger of rain, storm, blindness...an *elastic pool of... physical or virtual*[256] *resources...see also* fog computing...cloud sandbox (byo bucket) **nevermind** the mass gathering on the horizon...

---

247   *See* the 1947 **noir*** parody, ***My Favorite Brunette*,**** in which **Bob Hope***** plays Ronnie Jackson, baby photographer & aspiring man of action 'til Dorothy Lamour as Baroness Carlotta**** (his *femme fatale?*) mistakes him for his neighbor, a private **dick**.

248   The plot hinges on a "keyhole **camera**," the photographer's invention, to document nefarious secrets, *see also* nanny cam.

249   Though producers edit content to create "shows" adhering to a prescribed narrative, subscribers have access to round the clock feed from myriad **cameras**, a spectacular **choose your own adventure**.

250   TV, internet, radio, books & writing materials are strictly prohibited. Contestants *become* rather than *consume* media.

251   A common translation of Hobbes' state of nature, *bellum omnium contra omnes*, though considering the role of the spectator/consumer/media corporation, *a war of all against each*, might be more accurate.

252   Waste product of coal mining. *See also spoil tip, boney pile, culm bank, waste tip, gob pile, mine dump, bing.*

253   **Dat**afication: the conversion of anything & everything into **data** for mining.

254   From old English, *clud* or *clod*, a hill or mass of stone. As metaphor for mounded vapors, 13th century.

255   In contemporary meteorology, **clouds**, like life forms, are characterized by genus & species, according to atmospheric level, shape & stability. Ancient Akkadians believed them the breasts of Antu, her milk, the rain. In China, a symbol of luck & happiness. A guide for ancient Jews through the desert. A 14th century gnostic text, ***The Cloud of Unknowing***, acknowledges the shortfall of human intellect & advocates for spiritual enlightenment via solitary meditation; it didn't go viral. In the Aristophanes comedy, **clouds** are deities, **muses** & **mirrors** that reveal the nature of whoever sees them, an early example of *pareidolia*.*****

256   Almost or nearly. Approaching but not exactly. By **virtue** unrecognized. Good as. Really not really. Sorry not sorry. A simulation. **Fantasy**. In digital realms vs **IRL**.*6 May also be defined as no less real. **Virtually** everything. *See also* literally. From Latin: virtutem: moral strength, goodness, courage, valor, manliness, worth.

---

* A retrospective classification of ongoing debate marked by moral ambiguity & the moody aesthetics of German expressionism. Informed by depression era crime fic in pulp mags like *The Black Mask*, classic **Noir** of the 40s & 50s features low-key lighting, liminal settings, flashbacks, quasi-documentary narratives, smoking, night-for-night shooting & shots angled through **mirrors**, windows & other **glass** distortions. **Protagonists** are cynics, stoics & fall guys, morally flawed & semi-antisocial, **antiheroes** w/a soft spot for the vulnerable. **Noir** women stretch ethical boundaries & per **Hays Code** are punished. Offshoots—neo-noir, neon noir, tech noir, space noir, etc.—are **self-referential**.

** A girlhood fav, beloved for its campy melodrama, dopey one-liners & slapstick **blunders into wonder**. **Hitchcock** loved it too, stealing scenes for his **everyman spy fantasy**, *North by Northwest*, 1959. Another case of mistaken identity w/**Cary Grant** as **Cary Grant***7 & Eva Marie Saint*8 as **femme-fatale?** Eve Kendall.

*** **Lesley Townes Hope** (1903-2003), English-American comedian, whose anxious, self-deprecating personas inspired **Woody Allen**.*9

**** Namesake of a papier-mâché cow that took first at the Houston Livestock Show & **Rodeo** circa 1988.

***** The human tendency*10 to find meaning where none exists. *See also apophenia. See* **Borges**. *See* **Dawkins**.

*6 In real life. Now a necessary designation.

*7 *See* **Cary Grant** as **Cary Grant**, wishing he was **Cary Grant** in *Cary Grant: A Brilliant Disguise*, Scott Eyman, 2020.

*8 Real name! Born July 4, 1924, happily married most of her life & as of Jan 2025, still alive.

*9 No comment.

*10 Though rhesus **monkeys** have also fallen prey. *See* ocelli, nature's trompe l'oeil, survival by design.

*war gamed...See **WarGames**,* the 1983 techno thriller in which nuclear disaster is threatened then averted by a high school **hacker** who teaches **AI** that nuclear proliferation is stupid.

at sufficient scale/every brain's a universe   looks/the same... Consider **rockstar Isaac Newton**'s cosmic claim[257] that viewed from far enough away...it's all milkshake, humus, a fine carrot puree. Or machete hack a dozen coconuts[258] w/the force of a headsman's axe, what spills will splash.

*these faceless suitors/ are mostly White...*a conversation w/the artist revealed that though the **anonymous portraits** *herein*[259] indicate suitors of predominately White-European ethnicity,[260] this homogeneity is atypical of her matches generally. While the artist did not include every anonymous pic in her **survey**, she believes her sample was representative, suggesting...*what*...about White men & **anonymity**?

58   **OK Super.**

Bestselling **hero** in American **comics** up to the 1980s.[261] Enforcer of *truth, justice & the American way.*[262] *See also* **Big Blue Boy Scout.**

Contrarywise, despite the **mask**, there's zero **Bats**. So what's the 21st century appeal of a mild-mannered man of steel?

---

257   Vis-à-vis The Cosmological Principal, 1687: *viewed on a sufficiently large scale, the properties of the universe are the same for all observers.*

According The Cosmological Principal,* not to be confused w/ the Cosmological Argument,** scientists project 85% of matter & 68% of energy is **dark**.*** That is—*invisible, unobservable*—only evidenced by their effects: the inexplicably bent light. *The revolution will not be televised.*****

258   Though the machete technique of opening coconuts (& beheading opponents) varies widely. *See **Survivor**.******

259   And in **Walton**'s larger work, ***Match/Enemy***, cataloging over 200 **portraits**.

260   In so far as ethnicity is visibly suggested.

261   Albeit most popular during the Golden Age of American **comics** (1938-1956) which began w/the launch of ***Superman*** & ended w/the moral panic incited by **Fredrick Wertham**'s junk science*6 manifest, ***The Seduction of the Innocent*** (1954). After the television broadcast of his testimony to the Senate Subcommittee on Juvenile Delinquency comparing the comic book industry to Adolf Hitler, 15 publishers went out of business & Wertham ran for president.

262   As opposed to **Batman** who subverts authorized corruption, **Superman** works *with* law enforcement. Nevermind the brawny*7 patriot is also an illegal immigrant, a bonified *alien**8—his farm boy/reporter act, a **mask**.*9

---

* Critiqued by Karl Popper for making ignorance a principal of knowledge.
** Which makes the case for God.
*** **Dark matter**, like love, holds galaxies together; **dark energy**, Love, rips asunder. O longing, O long division, **Joy Division**, collective collapse, supernova—a ripple glancing light's distortion—the rest amass, loadbearing, laugh at our maps.
**** Initially responding to a lyric by *The Last Poets*, "When the revolution comes some of us will probably catch it on TV," **Gil Scott-Heron**'s spoken word rebuttal (1970, 1971, 1974) clocks dozens of fault lines, including **heroin**, **Nixon**, **Hollywood stars**, police brutality, Xerox, the Watts riots, **soap operas**, folk singers, commercial campaigns & **re-runs.**
***** A reality tv **gameshow** born in late 1990s Britain, played in over 40 countries, simulating a survival of the "fittest" contest of strangers marooned on a deserted island. Like ***Big Brother, Survivor*** is a game of social strategy, though players also contend w/natural elements & may win advantages via physical & intellectual dominance.
*6 A 2011 study demonstrates **Wertham**, a trained psychiatrist, "manipulated, overstated, compromised, and fabricated evidence" for example falsifying the size of his "sample population" which was in fact a small group of troubled adolescents w/a previous history of behavior issues.
*7 Whereas the most popular **villains** (**Lex Luther, Brainiac**) were known not for strength, but intellect.
*8 In early rejected drafts he was the infant son of the Last Man, sent back in time from future Earth on the brink of collapse, **Nietzsche**'s Übermensch....
*9 *See also* **code** switching.

Husband says...duh, **Bat**'s just a rich guy w/gadgets & a lair—but **Superman**'s invincible:[263] strength, speed, flight, bulletproof skin, X-ray vision, laser eyes, fortress.[264]

swole suits...aka muscle suit. Like a fat suit,[265] but different.

shrapnel vests...*see also* flak jacket, armor, chain mail...superfluous for the man of steel.

scurvy knave... among the Capulet nurse's many jousting pivots. *See **Romeo & Juliet**.*

sperm banks....regulating (or not) deposit & withdrawal since 1964. These days would be parents can **survey** a **data**base replete w/photographs, Myers-Briggs & IQ. Whether doners can remain **anonymous**, varies.[266] To diversify the species & decrease the odds of consanguinity,[267] the ASRM recommends no more than 25 kids per donor per community of 800K, but enforcement is nada. *See* survival of the fittest, contestants on *ice*. Motivations for donation include altruism, financial gain,[268] desire to propagate & to test virility. *See also* Ice Follies, Ice Capades, & The **Lion King** *on Ice*.

supersonic...In dry air at sea level, quicker than 343.2 meters/second...faster than thunder!..aka Mach 1. *Every* (milli) *second counts!*[269] Speeds > Mach 5 = Hypersonic. *See also* hyperactive. Mediums are elastic; supersonic's slower when mediums are thicker, thus, *super* is relative. On some planets Einstein's a dolt.

---

263 But not invulnerable. *See* mind manipulation...**magic**...witchcraft...**Krypto**currency.

264 Ah, the Fortress of Solitude. *See also* **Rilke**. Here our **hero** discovers...himself. Birthname, parents, planet of origin, Earthly purpose. Of course, the den for the man w/everything but a girlfriend is made of ice. It also protects his diary, super workout equipment, robot **doppelgangers** & when they need some R&R, his Super Friends.

265 Whose effectiveness, to portray a character* or to experience difference, lies in invisibility. Lies in invisibility.

266 Colorado has recently banned **anonymous sperm** donation, as has Portugal & other nations.

267 *See The Man with a Thousand Kids* (2024) based on the prolific deeds of Jonathan Meijer, a Dutchman,** whose **sperm bank** offspring handily span 4 digits, at least two of whom, half-siblings, *matched* (though did not *hook-up*) on Tinder.

*Wow, a real-life **Starbuck******, said **WG**'s son, of Vince Vaughn's 2013 comedy, *Delivery Man*, a shot-for-shot remake of acclaimed Canadian flick, *Starbuck* (2011), named for the seed slinging **hero**, father of hundreds. Or rather, named for the **hero**'s alias. Can we presume he takes his alias, not from the steadfast first mate of ***Moby Dick***, but the sci-fi swashbuckler—space pilot & ace shooter—of ***Battlestar Galactica***—1970s version, not the 21st century reboot in which Starbuck is female & spoiler alert, cylon? Maybe. But note the monster **Melville** writ was a **sperm whale**.****

268 Some say it's not much, but there are worse ways for a healthy buck to make a buck.

269 Catch phrase of culinary artist, Carmy Berzatto (**Jeremy Allen White**, *see also* ***Shameless***), perpetually caught in the crosshairs twixt quantitative vs qualitative assessment. Ever ***The Bear***, 2022.

---

* Most often for comic effect. *See* "Fat Bastard" in *Austin Powers* & "Sherman Klump" in *The Nutty Professor*.
** *See also* Flying Dutchman: a **ghost** ship doomed to sail the deeps forever, harbored never.
*** In addition to ***Battlestar Galactica***, ***Moby Dick***, *see* Dana Scully as a kid, plus the Canadian wrestler & of course the coffee **mono**poly.
**** In fact, dear Reader, neither propositions is true. According to Wiki, **Starbuck**'s alias honors a Holstein steer, Hanover Starbuck, who sired several hundred thousand, milk-makers from which nearly every dairy **cow** today is descended.

On Earth, man's been sonic booming for the last 158,468,400,000 seconds[270] via **bullwhips**,[271] though it's possible Apatosaurus[272] beat us to it. *See also* popped **balloon.** *See also* speeding bullet.[273]

*single dads...*Ooh la la!...is there anything **sex**ier? Infinitely more attractive to women[274] than single mothers are to men.[275] O paragon of manhood, o **hero.**[276]

solo....see spotlit **rockstar.** *See* **cowboy.** *See* Han.[277]

---

270 Math check? Experimental **AI** claims the **bullwhip**, among the oldest human tool, dates to ancient China & ancient Egypt 3000 BCE. *Wonderopolis.com* claims a year has 31,536,000,000 seconds... x 1000 x 5 + (31,536,000,000 x 25) = ...

271 A pastoral tool fashioned of the hide of creatures it's meant to corral. The braided length, known as the thong, contains one or more bellies, beyond which *the fall*, bridge to *the cracker*, whence the clap. In managing **cattle**, used less to strike (& mar) than to steer via sonic bite. Known to have other uses. *See* cracker. *See also* Indiana Jones,* "antiquities" **cowboy**, his preferred weapon for rustling "lost" treasures. *See also* **pirate.** O how we love to make **heroes** of thieves.

272 "Deceptive lizard" of the Late Jurassic. Herbivore w/a whip smart tail. First discovered by a Colorado miner & his investor pal. Initial fossils were mixed w/those of the *dubious species*** Atlantosaurus, first dino identified in the **Bone Wars*** Gilded Age****** when reason, ethics, financial prudence & scientific method were **sacrificed** for glory. *See also* **Ahab, Conquistadors, Billionaire Space Race, Trump.**

273 You can't, unless you're **Neo.** *See* Neo **limbo.** *See* Neo stop them bullets in their tracks. *See* Neo rewrite the Matrix.

274 *See also: The Sound of Music; Corrina, Corrina; Love Actually; Three Men & A Baby; What Women Want; Safe Haven; The Game Plan; Holiday; Sleepless in Seattle; Jersey Girl; Overboard; We Bought A Zoo...*Moreover, children encourage fathers to pursue **romance** more than mothers. Psychologist, writer & former **sex** worker, Elicia Jane attributes this phenomenon to 1) the children's desire for surrogate maternal care, 2) the jealousy children of single mothers have for a mother's attention & 3) their fear of another man's potential to harm.

275 Is it ego? Or biology? Variances of evolutionary altruism? Or convenience? If you dress a newborn orphaned lamb in the carcass of a stillborn lamb, the mother of the dead will take the living as her own.

276 Organizations for the advocacy of paternal rights claim children of single fathers are 5x's less likely to commit **suicide,** 9x's less likely to drop out of school, 10x's less likely to abuse drugs, 14x's less likely to **rape,** 20x's less likely to go to prison & 32x's less likely to run away from home. Elicia Jane further posits that single dads & their motherless kids are more likely to illicit sympathy resulting in surrogate maternal care via **romantic** partners, family & other females in the community, while single mothers are less likely to partner/re-partner or to receive aid.

277 The space **cowboy**, outlaw smuggler & **anti-hero** of *Star Wars* that made Harrison Ford **Harrison Ford.** *See also* Indiana Jones. *See* **Harrison Ford** now as a crotchety therapist w/a degenerative disease (*Shrinking*).

---

* Whose swagger inspired an upsurge in competitive **whip**-cracking & other "Western performance arts."

** A scientific classification to denote doubt w/r/t scientific classification, aka *nomen dubium.*

*** Between Edward Drinker Cope of the Academy of Natural Sciences in Philadelphia & Othniel Charles Marsh of the Peabody Museum of Natural History at Yale, a friendship that quickly devolved into a cutthroat rivalry deploying bribery, sabotage, theft, slander & destruction of evidence. The men discovered 136 species of dinosaur, but their rash methods set the field back decades & left their reputations & finances in ruins. Sometimes referred to as The Great Dinosaur Rush.

**** Between the Reconstruction & the Progressive Eras, late 1870s to late 1890s, marked by rapid economic growth, material excess & political corruption, retroactively named for Mark Twain & Charles Warner's collaborative novel, *The Gilded Age: A Tale of Today*—a tale of *today.*

In their hay days, **cowboys**[279] held low social & economic status (despite exacting skills required) & were considered untrustworthy, possibly criminal.[280] The **romance** of a rugged loner abiding by a Cowboy **code**[281] arose only after the frontier ended. Cue **Hollywood**. Cue **Rodeo**.[282] Rhinestones. Cue fringe.[283] Cue the Marlboro Man ™.[284] Guns-n-Roses.[285]

---

278   Days of the open range & **epic** drives* along the **Chisholm Trail** to Abilene** loom large in American mythology but lasted only a few decades beginning w/the meat packing boom in Chicago after the **Civil War** & ending w/the proliferation of railways & barbed wire in the 1890s.

279   Aka **cow**poke, **cow**hand, **cow**puncher & *buckaroo*...by way of *vaquero* (horse-mounted)...by way of Spain.***

280   *See* The **Cowboys**, a gang of outlaw smugglers. *See* copy**cat** bandits. *See* **cowboy** diplomacy.****

281   Proselytized by country crooner, Gene Autrey. *See* Buffalo Bill's (White-washed) **Wild West**.***** *See* eagle-eyed Annie Oakley.*6 *See* chivalry. *True Grit.*7 *You calling me a liar? See* spaghetti. *Yippee ki-yay, motherfucker.*8 *See* "The Gambler." *The Red Headed Stranger*9 "My **Hero**es Have Always Been **Cowboys**." Copland's *Rodeo.*10

282   Akin to gladiator sports of the **Roman circus**, a ritual contest between mastery & wilderness, **rodeo**, Spanish for **roundup**, dates to **bull** wrestling of ancient Crete, thence to Spain, thence Mexico, where steer wrestling, *Charreada*, is the national sport. *See also* medieval tournament.

Some say July 4, 1883 was the first U.S. **rodeo**, organized by **cock**sure hands for bragging rights. **Pageantry** increased over the 20th century & in the 1970s, a boom legitimized rodeo performer as profession (of almost exclusively White men)...lucrative enough that by 1985, half of **rodeo** performers had never worked a ranch. *See all hat, no **cattle**.*

283   *See* **peacock**. *See* **pageantry**.

284 1954-1999, R.I.P. Among the most brilliant marketing campaigns in history, rebranding a woman's cigarette, *mild as May*, in a matter of months. As health hazards emerged in the early 50s, research revealed men would choose filtered cigarettes if they weren't viewed as feminine. While other brands promoted (false) claims that filters were safer, Philip Morris turned to Chicago marketing guru, Leo Burnett, who ditched the health pitch for ethos. The Marlboro™ campaign would feature men of various manly occupations: war correspondent, sea captain, weightlifter, construction worker, but **cowboy** was first & stuck. *See* 5 o'clock shadow. Rugged individual. *See* **hero**.

285 **WG** *hates* Guns-n-Roses.

---

* One herd (3000 head) necessitated 9 skilled hands plus a cook (who **doubled** as a nurse) & 30-40 **horses**.*11 The **cows** required 24-hour **surveillance** over several long months & to maintain weight, the future burger could not be rushed.
** Kansas. Thence by train to Chicago.
*** In arid regions of Spain inhospitable to farming, **husband**ry thrived for centuries, with vast grazing tracts managed by **horse**back. In Spanish colonies runaway success led to feral herds... *See* American born Long Horn. *See* Mustang.
**** George W Bush's foreign policy.
***** 15-25% of professional **cowboys** in the late 19th century were Black & 15-30% of Mexican descent. A few were indigenous. In **Wild West Shows**, **cowboys** were White & Native Americans, their "savage" adversaries, a flattery.
*6 The highest paid performer, next to Wild Bill, whose feats included shooting a playing card "on edge". In **Wild West** limelight, **cowgirls** came into their own—until a bronc riding accident killed Bonnie McCarroll at the Oregon **Roundup** in 1929. Some attribute her death to tied stirrups, a double standard purported to aid women riders, put them at greater risk. After McCarroll's death, women were barred from men's events*12 & women's contests radically limited.*13
*7 **Hollywood** blockbuster of 1969 & 2010. *See* anti-**hero** Rooster Cogburn help Mattie Ross (girl w/grit) get justice.
*8 *See Die Hard II, 1988. See **cowboy**ish* Bruce Willis as John McClane **rhyme** w/John Wayne.
*9 Consummate road trip soundtrack of **WG**'s childhood, **Willie Nelson**'s 18th studio album, an extended ballad about a man on the lam after murdering his **wife** & her lover (*You can't hang a man for killing a woman/who's trying to steal your **horse**...*) went platinum many times over. This to spite the **fools** at Columbia who called the concept album "a piece of shit" & "underproduced." An iron-clad contract granting "complete creative liberty" secured the 1975 release & Willy's **outlaw** legacy—light of a nonagenarian **rockstar** who once kissed **WG**'s cheek.
*10 Aaron Copeland, 1942. Written for ballet. A sliver of the hymnal bit **WG** choreographed & performed as a kid, in Texas circa 1986.
*11 During **roundup**, the tax season of cowboy accountants, handlers required 3-4 fresh, cutting **horses***14 daily.
*12 Death & injuries to men & animals continue, especially in *rough stock* events, despite which contestants forgo **helmets**.
*13 Among the remaining: barrel-racing. **WG**'s second cousin, Rhonda, was a national champion.
*14 **Horses** specially trained for the precise work of sorting **cattle** from the herd.

home home...on the range... goes the unofficial anthem of the West written in the late 19th century & spread by **cowboy** campfire along the **Chisholm Trail**.[286] Bing Crosby's[287] recording in 1933 caused a plagiarism ruckus between Kansans Dr. Brewster Highley of Smith County & Emma Race of Raceburgh. Doc won, of course. *See also* **Boys Don't Cry**.[288]

***branded** skin*...to indicate possession of animals & humans in ancient Egypt, 2700 BCE; as punishment for treason, criminal activity & escape from captivity, 1600-1860s, North America; a present day mark of forced prostitution; an indication of membership in criminal organizations, prison groups, fraternities, sororities & other gangs; used by **BDSM** participants as body art[289] *slash* sign of allegiance *slash* initiation; unlike tattoos, cannot be removed. In open range grazing, allows variously owned animals to co-mingle. Despite prevalence, prohibited by **Hays Code**.

check the box...hop a boxcar. Flip the box spring. Change the litter box. Like a box of **birds**.[290] There's a prize at the bottom.[291] Safety deposit. A box of chocolates.[292] Black box. Black box.[293] Pop goes the **weasel**.[294] Cue the music box. Jack in the box. Check the glove box, toolbox, tackle box, suggestion. Stuff the ballot box.[295] Try a juice box, Otter Box™, DropBox™, kick boxing. Put it in the mailbox. Use your soap box, voice box, boom box, brain. Shadow box.[296] X box. Hot box[297] w/ *Fox in Socks*.[298] Feed the juke box. Ditch the pine box. Bring your lunch box, cash box, **magic**

---

286 Encompassing a pathway established by Lenape trapper Se-ket-tu-may-qua (Black Beaver) in 1861 & a wagon trail established by Jesse Chisholm in 1864, the route allowed ranchers to drive **cattle** from Southern Texas across the Red River through "Indian territory" to the railhead at Abilene.

287 Crooner: a style of singing characterized by low, smooth vocalizations implying intimacy, first popular in the 1940s, made possible by the advancing mic technologies.

288 British pop band whose 1986 one-hit wonder "I Wanna Be A Cowboy" became the unofficial anthem of Oklahoma State University (home of the **Cowboys***). Despite **MTV** VJ's strong aversion, the video—featuring the cowboy **fantasy** of a dude** in a clawfoot tub w/nods to Spaghetti Westerns, silent movies, **comic books**, 1960s live-action **Batman**, colonial **fantasy** (conflating early **Hollywood** "Indians" w/ Asian Indians), saving a bound damsel & generally *looking like a **hero***—was frequently requested.

289 *See also* **peacock**.

290 Happy.

291 The **magic** decoding ring in your corn flakes. *See also* **Spy**.

292 *You never know what you're going to get. See Forrest Gump, 1994 (I love you, Jenny).*

293 1) A recording device to assist tragedy diagnostics. 2) A performance space originating w/early 20th century Avant Garde, characterized by lack of permanent stage structure & seating. 3) An opaque system which can be monitored according to inputs & outputs, w/o knowledge of inner workings. May also refer to a transistor, engine, **algorithm**, the human brain, a government or institution.

294 English tune, from the 1850s, soon a popular social dance. The lyrics note the ebbs & flows of living hand to mouth. Or refer to the pop of a spinner's **weasel**. And insinuate male arousal. And arousal's relief. A melody given to children's toys & ice cream trucks.

295 Cheat.

296 To mime boxing. Or a box for display, e.g. the frames emblazoning **Trump** hotels w/ *Time* magazine covers trumpeting T as "Man of the Year" years before it happened in 2024. *See* deep fake meet **self-fulfilling prophecy**.

297 To smoke pot or hashish in a small unvented space

298 A Dr. Seuss tongue-twister & **WG** fav.

---

* & meet cute of **WG**'s parents.
** Dude: a guy who knows nothing of ranch life. (Dude's an 80s urban Brit. (Dude gets it.))

box, **dick in a box.**[™][299] **Box & cox.**[300] Think outside the...match, shoe, letter, bread, cracker, batter's, window, red, pizza, tick... Get 'er done.[301] Duke it out. Dumb as rocks. Boxed in. Box pleat. *You put your weed in it.*[302] "The Boxer".[303] Canine pedigree. Big box store. Box & tow. Boxed ears. Witness, donation, confession, Pandora's. Cornell box,[304] press box, chatter, **sonnet.**[305] Box & whisker. Box the compass.[306] Box clever.[307] Idiot Box. HBO. Box seats, box elder, turtle, wine. Lock box, toy box, **sex**-box, boxwood, box tops, jewelry, penalty, ice, cutter.

burrs...a **cowboy** stowaway. Somehow both prickly & clingy.

loner...**Waylon & Willie** warn "Mamas Don't Let Your Babies Grow Up To Be **Cowboys**"[308] *cause they're always alone*...but are they? The work seems collaborative. The Lone Ranger certainly wasn't...& what about all those **cows & horses**...**WG** wonders...if **incels** had creatures to care for... & an endless horizon... a fellow or two to jaw w/'round a campfire...or a harmonica...would life be less painful?

---

299 For the 2006 Christmas episode of *Saturday Night Live*, hosted by **Justin Timberlake**, some gift-giving advice to boyfriends hoping to wow their boo. **Dick** went viral w/28 million views by the following October & won a Primetime Emmy for original music.*

300 A mid 19th century vaudeville farce by James Morton; two people that share the same resources at different times, w/ or w/o knowledge of the either; in alternating turns. *See also* **double down.**

301 *Git R Dun*...catch phrase of the American comedian known as Larry the Cable Guy, aka Daniel Lawrence Whitney, of the *Blue Collar Comedy Tour*. Cringe.

302 From *SNL* skit "Out of Africa", w/creator Rob Schneider as import/export stoner, like **WG** in 1993.

303 Paul Simon for *Simon & Garfunkel*, 1969. 1st person lament & melancholy portrait of poverty & loneliness. Covered by everybody.

304 **Joseph Cornell** (1903-1972). Obsessive collector. White **magic**ian. Penny lonesome. Voyeur. Who caught flight behind **glass** in his mother's basement. Who flew his mother's coop never. *See* Utopia Parkway. *See Utopia Parkway.* Whose *Rose Hobart*** made Dali tantrum w/envy. **Incel** who knew *everyone.**** Architect of desire's arcade.

305 **Nate Mickelson** unpacks it.**** In **WG**'s copy of "**Sonnets** and/as Boxes..." she underscores, "involve ourselves in the 'near distances,'"***** "that emerge between their components"*6 & "as containers, frames, shrines, **games**, and puzzles." She highlights, "defining liminal spaces" & "proliferate rather than resolving into articulable wholes." She stars "peep show" & "The possibility of breaking from sequential reading emerges." She circles, "associative entanglement".

306 Reverse course.

307 To act w/cunning.

308 By Ed & Patsy Bruce, 1975. Made iconic by Outlaw Country **rockstars, Willie Nelson** & **Waylon Jennings.**

---

* Writers include The Lonely Island comedy trio, Andy Samberg, Akiva Schaffer & Jorma Taccone. Also **Justin Timberlake**, SNL musical director Katreese Barnes & musician Asa Taccone.
** **Cornell**'s 1936 film made by splicing clips of a 1931 adventure **romance**, named for the actress on whom the lens lingers. *See also Nymphlight*, 1957.
***...Marcel Duchamp, Andre Breton, **Susan Sontag**, Lee Miller, Marianne Moore, Andy Warhol, Lee Bontecou, **Robert Rauschenberg**, Dorthea Tanning, Yayoi Kusama, Willem de Kooning, Yoko Ono, Tamara Toumanova...
**** "**Sonnets** and/as Boxes: Ken Taylor, **Joseph Cornell**, and the New Lyric Studies" in *The American Sonnet*, 2023.
***** Last words of "Joseph Cornell," Frank O'Hara's sonnet/homage, which opens, "Into the sweeping meticulously-/detailed disaster"...
*6 & in the margin: *think of my personal /snippets as "near distances"/ intimacy in* **data** *absent/the violet sinewed conglomerate*

Sex appeal is **sex** appeal. Not every costume conceals. Some **masks** reveal the bonny interior. Imagine a frictionless slide into third base, home plate. Umpire shouts *safe!* ***Game!*** Everyone wins.

*the lesser-known plight of **peahens***[309]...ahhhh the terrible burden of choice! Which **cock**'s waddle most invigorates, which shimmer shines most opulent, whose train (like a bride's!) longest & w/most dazzling eyes endowed? The dun **peahen**, practically dressed, practically tailless, decides,[310] then goes for a ride.

Darwin viewed the cock's train-rattling[311]...The case of the **peacock**,[312] whose ostentatious florescence incommodes defensive evasion, boggled **Darwin** for years, a stick in the eye of natural selection,[313] eventually forcing him to contend w/a concept he abhorred: the female power of choice.[314] "I suspect that the male will pair with any female, and that the females select the most victorious or most beautiful **cock**..."[315]

such/ brazen vulnerability/ to what end...not actually **Darwin**'s words, though he did say, *a feather in a **peacock**'s tail, whenever I **gaze** at it, it makes me sick.*[316]

---

309 Speaking of **anonymous**, ever heard of a **peahen**? Until a student cited a study & despite frequent encounters w/their baroque suitors at the Houston Zoo & elsewhere, in 49 years, **WG** hadn't.*

310 Some **peahens** don't so much choose as narrow down to a few & alternate. *See also* **Box & Cox.**

311 A dance cocks begin to rehearse as chicks. In mating season adult **cocks** gather into leks to perform their elaborate shimmies, orienting their tails to 45° of the sun to capture the greatest iridescence.

312 Whose wanton ornament, some said, evidenced the divine hand.

313 For why would **birds** w/more cumbersome (if fabulous) trains, easier upon to prey, be superior mates?

314 **Darwin**'s frustration leads to his greatest contribution to evolutionary theory, the distinction between natural & **sexual** selection—the drive to survive vs. the drive to procreate w/best possible mate.***

315 **Darwin**, 1859. By way of Evelleen Richardson's reviewing Elle Hunt's ***Darwin** and the Making of **Sexual** Selection.*

316 In a letter to Asa Gray, April 3, 1860. *See **Darwin** Correspondence Project.*

---

* What did she think? They were all blokes?

** Whose 1997 retrospective at the Guggenheim (uptown & down) altered **WG**'s relationship to visual art.

*** In **incel** communities, a source of despair **coded** as the **80/20 rule**: the belief that 80% of women angle for 20% of men. In the **manosphere**, this codified despair also takes the form of an elaborate **pill** dispensary. For example, while the Red Pill indicates general initiates, the Black **Pill** indicates one who has given up efforts to improve SMV (**sexual market value**) through **looksmaxxing** or via financial/emo appeal, having lost all hope of finding a mate. In this state, the "black **pill**ed," are considered more susceptible to radicalized Rape**pill**ing & Seige**pill**ing, which mean just what you think.

a train wails...e.g. from **Sing Sing**[319] in Ossining[320] to the Apple core & back. Tick, tick, tickets, please! A daily commute. A sentence reduced. Here we go down & up the river.

tick tock!...goes the clock, the mortal meter's essence. *See also* solar, circadian, ovarian, candle, grandfather, astronomical, astrological, kitchen timer, atomic, analog, sundial, clepsydra,[321] hour**glass**, pendulum, oil lamp, noon cannon,[322] church bells, obelisk, cuckoo, pyramid,[323] digital, seasonal, liturgical, incense,[324] time ball,[325] merkhet,[326] rolling ball,[327] tower, lunar, doomsday,[328] **cat** eye lake,[329] **crocodile.**[330]

---

317 Don't tell **Tinkerbell, Peter Pan**'s** moody pixie pal.*** According to **Neverland**** founder **J. M. Barrie**, the nymph's power is tied to our *belief.*

318 Whereas unlike Tinkerbell, **Captain James Hook**—***** cutthroat & capable, **hero**ically handsome & eloquent, w/ eyes of forget-me-not blue—needs no such faith to actualize. Perhaps **Pan**'s dread of becoming his elder, a renewable resource the world over, sustains him. *See boomer* as insult. *See* **plunder** sans **wonder.** *See* **Dorian Gray.**

319 The infamous prison, 30 miles from Manhatten, up the Hudson, considered a model prison when it opened in 1826, because it turned a profit. The first warden & construction overseer, retired Army Captain, Elan Lynds enforced absolute silence w/whipping for 15 years. Also home to "Old Sparky" in whose arms 614 men & women died including numerous members of Murder, Inc.,*6 several serial killers*7 & Ethel & Julius Rosenberg, sentenced as **spies**. *See also* Peter Sewally/Mary Jones,*8 "Lucky" Luciano*9 & Ferdinand Ward.*10 *See* **Hollywood.***11

320 Ossining, a village in Westchester County, previously **Sing Sing**, of the Sinck Sinck tribe (also Sintsink) from whom Frederick Phiipse purportedly purchased the land in 1685. *Sinck sinck* translates to *stone upon stone.*

321 Or water clock, by which the flow of water chronicles.

322 *See* Cape Town.

323 E.g. Chichén Itzá, Mayan calendar & megaphone.

324 *See* Song Dynasty (960-1279).

325 *See* Times Square, annually, wear a diaper. *See* Royal Observatory, Greenwich, daily.

326 Replacing sundials at night w/a bar & plumbline to clock **star** swings.

327 Aka a Congreve Clock. Wherein a falling ball zigzags an oscillating path. Contraption of William Congreve, 1808.

328 A metaphoric clock kept by the Bulletin of Atomic Scientists to broadcast projected proximity to apocalypse.

329 According to Eliot Singer, the Odawa*11 people expressed daytime relative to the dilation of a **Cat**'s pupils, w/the eye jelly depicted as bodies of water, thus a literal translation of noon: *the cat has midday eye waters.*

330 The most reliable way of telling time in **Neverland**, on account of a clock the **croc** swallowed whose alarm goes off on the hour. Also the consumer of **Hook**'s hand. The croc-clock, appetite whet & Hook, who wants revenge, are conversely obsessed. A tragic **romance**, inspired by **Melville's Ahab**. Time w/teeth coming for all of us.

---

* The boy w/the detachable shadow, *betwixt & between*, w/all his "first teeth," dressed in cobwebs & leaves, unable to distinguish real from make believe. Unable to recall the past, anticipate consequence. **Fool** hardy AND emotionally unavailable. For whom flying means never needing to grow up. W/whom (of course) the girls—**Wendy, Tink, Tiger Lily**, Mary Darling—fall in love.

** First manic pixie **dream** girl? (If only he'd love her back). Poor Tink. Brief lightening. Incapable of emo complexity.

*** A realm which lacks for nothing but a mother to tell stories. Cue Wendy. Mary. Jane.... *See also* Scheherazade.

**** As **Barrie** tells it, **Hook** is based on **IRL** infamy, "...not his true name. To reveal who he really was would even at this date set the country in a blaze." *Peter and Wendy. See also* Dread **Pirate** Roberts. *See* Q of **QANON**?

***** Prohibition era alliance of the Jewish Mob & the Italian American Mafia based in Rosie Gold's candy store in Brooklyn. Hitmen received a regular salary, plus $1K-5K per pop & family benefits. Between 400-1000 offed.

*6 Including the **Lonely Hearts Killers**, a couple who lured women by responding to Lonely Hearts personal ads.

*7 A transgendered person of the early 19th century, multiple times imprisoned for fleecing wealthy White men as a Black woman, amid cunningly devised intercourse during which victims may or not have realized the whole of her anatomy.

*8 Of the Genovese crime family, convicted of 62 counts of compulsory prostitution.

*9 **Gilded Age** swindler & Best Hated man in the U.S., whose NY investment firm w/Ulysses S. Grant, Jr., a Ponzi scheme, financially ruined President Grant, Thomas Nast & numerous others.

*10 *See **Sing Sing**,* 2023. *See* the **pre-Code** drama *20000 Years in **Sing Sing*** w/Bette Davis & Spencer Tracy, 1932.

*11 An indigenous tribe of the ceded lands known also as northern lower Michigan, where **WG** raised her family.

Never Never...tsk, tsk—a warning. Also, moniker for the Aussie Outback, the namesake of **J. M. Barrie's**[331] beloved habitat. Realm of **Lost Boys**,[332] fairies, friendly indigenous Americans,[333] semi-hostile mermaids,[334] enemy **pirates & Peter Pan**. Possibly an island, easily traversed but limitless. Liminal: the many suns & moons rendering time unquantifiable. Where death is play & love unimaginable. A commutable flight to London. Aka Never Never Land, **Neverland**, the Neverlands & Peter's Never Never Never Land.[335]

Nevermind...an album by **Nirvana**. A **Gen X** mantra. *See also* **rockstar**.

---

331 Scotsman playwright & novelist, whose famed **fantasy** was flanked by tragedy. Whose mother never recovered from the young adolescent death of his elder brother. Partial to penny dreadfuls—precursor to horror **comics**. His one brief **marriage** said to be unconsummated. Adopted 5 boys by sleight of hand* when their parents died three years apart—Nico, Michael, Peter, John & George, ages 6-17 for whom the fantasy. The 2 eldest died in their early 20s, one by war, one accidental drowning. A third, 40 years later lost to lung disease & 7 months after, a fourth by **suicide**. Only Nico, too young for a **Peter Pan** namesake, outlived the author.

332 **Pan's** cohort. Boys who fell from their strollers & were never claimed. *See also* ***The Lost Boys***, a 1987 horror **fantasy** about a single mom & sons who uproot to a California beach town, overrun by adolescent vampires. Like their **Neverland** counterparts, the blood**suckers** will never grow up; they nest in the ruins of a hotel** built on a fault line, replete w/shrine to **lost boy**, Jim Morrison.*** Elain Showater calls the vampire portrayal "a metaphor for the kind of mythic male bonding that resists growing up, commitment, and especially **marriage**." **Cult classic**. *See also* ***Wedding*** *Crashers*, etc, etc...

333 Unlike the **Lost Boys, Pan** can fly & return to the mainland whenever he likes. He prefers the island, the **fantasy**. So did **Barrie**. The "redskins" of his "Piccaninny" tribe, **Wild West** stereotypes, noble savages grunt pidgin English & call Peter "the Great White Father." The princess, **Tiger Lily**, casts off suitors from her tribe because she fancies aloof Peter, who, when she is kidnapped, only rescues her to fuck w/his nemesis.

334 By **Barrie's** account all female, nameless, mysterious. On good terms w/**Peter** but vain, frivolous & like the female fairies, temperamental.

335 **Fantasy** or reality: despite **Peter's** dearth of empathy & maturity or anything resembling love, **Wendy, Tink** & **Tiger Lily** hopelessly crush—?

---

* Altering their mother's will.
** Homage to *The Eagles'* 1976 "Hotel California"?
*** "American Poet." **Rockstar**. *The Doors* frontman. Cause of death at 27 uncertain.

O **Cupid**, perpetual infant, progeny of **Mars** & **Venus**. O brassy bowmen. Quick prick. Venomed **licks**. O **Puck**. Plucky. Delirium. Diaperless squirt. Little shit. Bedeviling wingman.

In an earlier guise, **Eros** mated in Tartarus w/Chaos & begat us. A cosmic force. Invincible warrior. **Sex** machine.[336] *Strumming my pain w/his finger*[337] Apex **predator.**

now algorithms figure prison sentences.... Speaking of the **dark** (**energy...matter...arts...**), for all our epistemological scurries, all neuro & cognitive science appliance, we still don't understand how the human machina makes, stores, integrates & accesses knowledge. In a related story, *humans built the **algorithm** but somewhere along the way we lost the ability to explain it.*[338]

---

336   *See* "Get Up (I Feel Like Being a) **Sex** Machine" by James Brown & Bobby Byrd, 1970. *See* **James Brown**, Godfather of Funk, Soul Brother No. 1, Mr. Please, Please, Mr. Dynamite, Hardest Working Man in Showbusiness, Minister of the New New Super Heavy Funk...born in a Georgia shack, dropped out in middle school for lack of clothes, shined shoes, buck danced for **WWII** troops, paroled from Juvie to sing Gospel, inventor of funk, the drum break, the rhythm shift, who made his band wear full tuxes, grease their shoes & when he turned his back to the audience for a long slide—fingertips up as if taking the celestial pulse —was covertly berating a foul note slacker, the digits raised indicating the penalty to be docked from the offender's pay. The most sampled artist in history, *see also* **sampling,*** the "ultimate idol" of **Michael Jackson,** aka **superhero**; **hero** also of Sly & the Family Stone, Funkadelic, Booker T & the M.G's, Public Enemy's Chuck D, M.C. Hammer, The Temptations, Tom Waits, Charles Wright, Lenny Kravitz, Mic Jagger, Jay-Z, Dr. Dre, **David Bowie**...Whose knee-bruising cape act borrowed from Gorgeous George upstaged The Rolling Stones, whose shout-talk drawn from Gospel & field songs preceded rap, who backed **John F Kennedy**, Lyndon Johnson, Hubert Humphrey, Richard Nixon & the Vietnam War (then **doubled**-back), Jimmy Carter, **Ronald Reagan** & Dixiecrat Strom Thurmond, whose televised concert after the assassination of MLK maybe "saved Boston," maybe "**narcotized dysfunction.**" *See also* the **Apollo Theatre, Apollo Creed.** Who had a thing for PCP. Who beat up women, *see* accusations of **sexual** harassment, **sexual** assault, **rape.** Who upon release from prison received a Lifetime Achievement at the Grammys.** Who died on Christmas, memorial processions fit for a **King**, presided over by onetime mentee Rev. Al Sharpton. No 7 on the *Rolling Stone* 100 Greatest Artists of All Time. *See also* the Colorado bridge (*can we take it to the bridge*) "James Brown Soul Center of the Universe Bridge" in Steamboat Springs. **Rockstar.**

337   *See* Roberta Flack's 1973 smash "Killing Me Softly with His Song". *See* the Lauren Hill/Fugees 1996 revival go viral. Don't forget Lori Lieberman whose managers tried to erase her.

338   Lara Zielin, "Hey Siri...Are We Cool?" *LSA Magazine*, 2024.

---

* A sonic cut & paste, smash & grab, slash-n-burn (one down, w/desire, burnin' & lootin'). A foundation of **hip-hop** w/roots in Jamaican dub reggae of the 1960s. *See also* the sound collages of *musique concrète* (Pierre Schaeffer, John Cage). *See* Fairlight sample **Stravinski.** *See* **Stevie Wonder**'s 1979 *Journey Through the Secret Life of Plants. See also* breakdance. *See* The Turtles sue De La Soul. *See* Paul's Boutique. *See* de minimis. *See* quilting. Makeshift v. make do. Pick up sticks. Remix.

** **WG** learned to get down w/the Godfather, **hip hop** & techno, simultaneously; **James Brown**'s "**Sex** Machine," *C+C Music Factory's* & *L.A. Style's* "**James Brown** is Dead" spinning at the same dance parties. It's 1991 just after The Hardest Working Man's parole from prison. Just after the ballet master didn't go to prison. Papa's gotta new bag everywhere. *See* the *Living in America* pay-per-view w/Ice-T, M.C. Hammer, Heavy D, Tone Loc, Kool Moe Dee, Quincy Jones, C+C & En Vogue...*See* the Soul Brother bestow his "blessing" on Hammer's *Too Legit* throw down to **Michael Jackson. WG** didn't know what he'd done, didn't care to. Besides, back then to get the news you had to watch the news, read the paper...(flashes of war...**Rodney King**...)... social media was *the Real World*, was **MTV**. No internet to **rabbit hole** *why* Papa got sent up the river & anyway, hadn't he done the time? She still shines those shoes. Wanna see **WG** get down? Play **James Brown.**

homophily...The social theory that like attracts like, **birds** of a feather & what not. Central tenant of network science. Coined by fathers of modern empirical sociology,[339] **Paul Lazarsfeld**[340] & **Robert Merton**[341] after studies at an unsegregated housing project in Pittsburg, 1947. Retrospective examinations[342] of their research demonstrate their conclusion—that **homophily** is a natural state vs socially conditioned—was based on flawed analysis of a flawed study. But the **genie** is out of the bottle. Homophily-as-human-condition remains the ipso facto **algorithm** of civil engineering: shaping neighborhoods, cities, social & digital networks. *See also* **self-fulfilling prophecy.**[343]

winedark sea... appears 5xs in the *Iliad*, 12 in the *Odyssey*; they say **Homer** had no word for blue. We have at least 22. They say in the beginning the word spoke & there were two, spoke & unspoke, seen & unseen, light & dark, a binary. Now we've infinite ways to name the infinite hues, still are dumbstruck by the **abyss** &, as in garment washing, lump all the darks together—**dark matter, dark energy, dark web, dark arts**—when there might be a whole spectrum. Perhaps future historians will exalt the visionaries reading auras.[344]

---

339 Whose 1948 essay, "Mass Communication, Popular Taste and Organized Social Action," canonical to contemporary media studies, identifies 3 functions of mass media: 1) to spotlight issues, people, organizations & movements; 2) to enforce social norms; & 3) to "**narcotize dysfunction**," deterring citizens from acting in their own interest because of media FOMO. *See also* **heroin.**

On the influence of capital, i.e., money, on mass media, **Lazarsfeld** & **Merton** agree "who pays the piper calls the tune" but nevertheless suggest, "media may not affect our society so profoundly as is widely supposed." But they died a while ago.

340 **Paul Felix Lazarsfeld**, Austrian-American sociologist & mathematician, 1901-1976, whose integration of quantitative research to social theory shaped the field. Co-founder of mathematical sociology. Founder of Columbia's School of Applied Social Research, w/a goal "to produce Paul Lazarsfelds." Created an academic business plan for the creation of knowledge via studies funded by corporations & capitally endowed entities including the military. Inventor of the "Little Annie" two button device for quantifiably tracking media focus groups.* Downplayed the effects of media on individuals despite evidence to the contrary. His contributions to **data** analysis are so influential as to now seem self-evident. *See also* obliteration by incorporation.**

341 **Robert King Merton**, born Meyer Robert Schkolnick, 1910-2003, changed his name for his late adolescent **magic** act. Founding father of modern sociology specializing in criminology. Argued social deviance was less the result of personal pathology than a consequence of disconnect between socially dictated goals & the means to achieve them. I.e. the **American Dream.** I.e. **marriage**, or at the very least a "**happy ending**". In Merton's rubric, **incels** & other socially unrealized individuals will innovate,*** ritualize,**** retreat,***** or rebel.

342 *See* "**Homophily**: The Urban History of an **Algorithm**." Laura Kurgan, Dare Brawley, Brian House, Jia Zhang, and Wendy Hui Kyong Chun. *e flux architecture*, October 2019.

343 The now ubiquitous term coined by **Robert Merton***6 to illuminate racial prejudice. Merton claims bigots fail to recognize the 'facts' that they "observe" are their own creation.

344 On a birthday in her early 20s **WG** received W.E. Butler's *How to Read the Aura*, in which, "A veteran occultist explains several ways by which auric sight may be developed." The author also explains false auras, etheric leakage, orbicular wounds & psychic vampirism.*7 A slim handbook that occasionally resurfaces, but which **WG** has only ever integrated via osmosis.

---

* Which gave rise to social media's ubiquitous "LIKE" button, which feeds the **homophily algorithms.**
** When a concept is so popularized its inventor is forgotten, coined by **Robert Merton.**
*** W/new goal-seeking behaviors for example via crime.
**** Modeling societal behaviors but giving up the goals (e.g. **sexual** intimacy).
***** *See also* escapism.
*6 *See also role model, role strain & unintended consequences*, all coined by **Merton.** *See* obliteration by incorporation.
*7 Who's there? Is that me or you, Reader?

*white **whale dreams***[345]...obsessive pursuit of a goal. Or compulsive reenactment of a survival strategy? *See* **Captain Ahab**, obviously.[346] *See also* **plankton**,[347] the byproduct of which is 50% of the planet's oxygen.

Mystery Date...by Milton Bradley, 1965. A board **game** marketed to girls 6-14 w/ the objective to acquire a desirable date & avoid the *dud*.[348] Step one: assemble a cohesive 3-piece outfit. Step two: open the mystery door to reveal your date. He may be dressed for...a Formal, Picnic, Ski Date, Beach Party, or slovenly (that's the dud). He will be White. If your fits fit, you win! Reissued in 1970, 1999, 2005.

*apex **predators***... these are the creatures we kill to see: **lions**, tigers, **orcas**, **king** cobras, **wolves**, great whites, gators, **crocodiles**, grizzlies.... On the other hand, no one's paying big bucks to sit on a crowded boat, listen to the eco-guide make jokes, just to see some **plankton**.[349] We want the **rockstars**. Top feeders. We want to look in the **mirror**.

---

345   Though *sunsigns.org* says a **whale** in your **dreams** is a sign of inner peace.

346   Whaling Captain of the Pequod,* whose leg, lust, life & ship are lost to the **sperm whale, Moby Dick**.** Megalomaniac. Revenge seeker. Prosthesis: an ivory scream. By white lightning streaked—an asymmetrical bifurcation down face, neck & below to the cloaked **abyss**. Who made a killing flensing silk. White **mirror** to a frothing sea. *Grand, ungodly, god*—w/co-morbidity.*** Who betrays his **god** Commerce w/a gold doubloon. *See* **King** Ahab. *See* **Narcissus**. Prometheus. *See* Oedipus. *See* **King** Lear. **Hook.** Kurtz. **Plankton. Bezos. Musk. Trump.**

347   From the Greek *planktos*, meaning drifting or wandering,**** a diverse collection of organisms lacking self-propulsion, subject to the currents.***** In the animated series ***SpongeBob SquarePants*,*6 the show's brainy, cyclopic, megalomaniac.*7 Owner of a failing restaurant, ever conniving to steal the Krabby Patty recipe from the Krusty Krab, aided by his **WIFE Karen**, a waterproof supercomputer.*8

348   Hmmm...like firecrackers, grenades & missiles, does a desirable date...shoot off?

349   Political scientist Joseph Foy describes **SpongeBob's antagonist** as the "unsung **hero**" of Bikini Bottom, a **Nietzschean Übermensch** utilizing his superior wit to transcend circumstance (though *plankton*, by definition cannot circumnavigate the currents), tragically thwarted by, **SpongeBob**, dolt of convention & his haphazard **blunders into wonder**.

---

* The hunting ship named for a decimated tribe, bedazzled w/the bones of his kills. The American ship of state that goes down w/its Captain. A loused up vessel, like its captain, fitted w/replacement parts. *See also* Reaver ships of the space western, *Firefly*.
** **Herman Melville's epic** American novel/prophecy, 1851. Described in its day as, "an ill-compounded mixture of **romance** and matter-of-fact." Ahem.
*** *Be sure of this, O young Ambition, all mortal greatness is but disease.* **Melville**, Ch 16.
**** Though not all who wander are **plankton**.
***** E.g. algae, protozoa, jelly fish, fungi...or by air, spores, pollen, wind-born seeds...
*6 The creation of marine science educator, Stephen Hillenburg, launched to critical acclaim shortly after the conception of **WG**'s eldest son. The protagonist, a sea **sponge** modeled after a kitchen **sponge**, a nerdy, naïve, happy-go-lucky adult innocent (not an apex **predator**) lives in a pineapple, works as a fry cook & aspires to getting his boating license. *See also* Pee-wee Herman (1980), Steve Urkel & Bill & Ted (1989), Forrest Gump (1994). Described by TV critic Matt Seitz as "an absurdist masterpiece that Salvador Dali and Groucho Marx would have watched together in their smoking jackets." *TV (The Book)*, 2016. **SpongeBob's** naivety makes him oblivious to **Plankton's** schemes or the disdain of snarky Squidward Tentacles who prefers the company of his clarinet & **self-portraits**.
*7 Sheldon J. **Plankton**, Mr. Krab's nemesis, was not always an aspiring criminal. In grade school he & Krabs were besties. But despite being the most intelligent guy in Bikini Bottom (his catch phrase: *I went to college!*), adult Plankton's commercial failure combined w/his diminutive physical status results in a Napoleon complex. *See also* **incel**.
*8 **Karen Plankton**, Sheldon's sidekick, best friend & **WIFE** (Wired Integrated Female Electroencephalograph) is also his invention, constructed of a mess of wires & a calculator before her creator broke bad. Karen supports Sheldon's schemes w/superior intellect, focus & nagging. Her heists succeed, before hubby fumbles the ball. The **Plankton marriage**, the only real **romance** in the series, has been comically critiqued for glorifying techno**sexuality**.

helmet... from old English *helm*,[350] (*helm-et*, not *hell-met*) to protect the **spongey** executive especially in combat,[351] impact sports or other risky occupations. *See also* construction, **space flight** & riot control (but not **rodeo**). Sometimes designed to evoke animals, **gods**, alter egos, or to indicate allegiance &/or rank w/other **heraldry**.[352] *See also* God helmet.[353]

tin foil[354] *hat*...a provisional shield to thwart electromagnetic fields, mind control, aliens. Shorthand for paranoid. Nobody's really listening. Nobody's watching. Nobody's making suggestions. Nobody. Nobody. Nobody. Except **Gemini** who would love to write your email, contract, essay, sermon...[355] Feel like a baked potato? *See also* Wade Tillman[356] of *Watchmen*.[357]

---

350 From the Proto-Indo-European root *kel*, to cover, conceal, save. Attaching concealment to survival.

351 *See* Boar Tusk. Lobster-tailed Pot. Cobra Plus. Disc & Stud. Galea. Frog-mouth. Adrian. Turban. Qing Parade. Brodie. Corinthian. Black Mongolian. M33. Type 90. Great Helm. Close Helm. Ottoman Zischägge. BK3. SSh-40. Dragoon. Sallet. Hounskull. Bascinet. Kettle hat. Zhou Dynasty. F2 SPECTRA. M1PASGT. Roman Legion. Lippman. Tarleton. ACH. SSh-68. Morion. Burgonet. Kevlar. Conical. EXFIL ballistic. Spangenhelm. Horned. Kegelhelm, Kabuto. Safavid. Barbute. Enhanced Combat. MARTE. Stahlhelm. Zuckerman.

352 The design, display & study of emblematic armory. A visual language evolved from the need to distinguish ally from enemy in battle. As opposed to **anonymity**. The fields of *achievement* where *achievement* refers to a **coded** shield & coat of arms; achievement may also include a helm, crest, coronet, or other accoutrements. *See also* motto. A medieval symbolism w/elaborate regulations, necessitating professional jurisdiction (*see* herald, **king** of arms), wherein every shape, image & choice of material conveys meaning: Azure or Purpure; Or or Argent; **Weasel** or Red Squirrel. *See also* rules of tincture, ordinaries, variations & divisions of field. *See* blazoning.* Marshalling may be signified via impalement or quartering. *See* **medieval tournaments** (*see also* **rodeo**: the **pageantry**, the **peacocking**). In the dusk of tournaments, freed of utility, heraldry re**doubled** its lavish artistry. *The handmaid of history*. For modern usage *see* Society for Creative Anachronism, modern academia, professional associations, guilds, secret societies, the military, institutional religion, government & their subdivisions. *See* the **hierophant** of tarot.

353 Originally called the Koren **helmet**, after co-creator Stanley Koren (nowhere found) in collaboration w/neuroscientist Michael Persinger.** An experimental headdress used to study creativity, religious experience & the effects of temporal lobe stimulation. *See also* parapsychology. *See also* **magic**. Intended to test the theory that the hemispheres of the human brain house separate components of the self.*** Test subjects are placed in a soundproof **Faraday cage** & fitted w/(shit you not) a snowmobile **helmet** modified w/ solenoids at the temporal lobes to create "weak but complex" magnetic fields in fluctuating patterns.

Persinger claimed 80% of subjects sensed presences they took to be angels, God, the dead, or other metaphysical entities, but attempts to independently replicate failed. Researchers who report participants w/similar experiences observed the same likelihood of a "presence" in the control group (wearing "sham" helmets), attributing the **God** experience to pre-existing beliefs & general suggestibility. Participating subject & atheist **Richard Dawkins** reported sensations of dizziness, limb tingling & changes in breathing, but no "presence," whereas paranormal researcher & experimental psychologist, Susan Blackmore, reported "the most extraordinary experiences I've ever had..."

354 Misnomer for the foil now made of aluminum. In related story, *hang up* the phone.

355 **Gemini*****...Google's 2024 **AI** scribe, named for the **twins**, Castor & Pollux.***** Like you times two, the better to do what you want to do...say what you want to say...what's that you say? No, of course it won't make you impotent.

356 Aka **Looking Glass**, a traumatized, paranoid police officer who specializes in interrogation.

357 An 1980s DC **Comic Book** Series & 2020s **HBO** sequel series satirizing **superhero** culture & political corruption. In HBO's series set in the alt reality of 21st America, militant hate groups formerly underground surge to power in backlash to the liberal policies of former President Robert Redford.

---

* Blazon: to describe arms in accordance w/the formal language of **heraldry** via established syntax & semantics.
** 1945-2018 w/an MA in physiological psychology from the U of Tenn, 1969. University of Manitoba, PhD, 1971. Director of Laurentian University's Consciousness Research Laboratory. Specialized in Neurotheology. Dude had tenure.
*** Which Persinger claims are normally integrated but in special circumstances lead to split selves.
**** Mutable air sign, intellectual & flighty, ruled by the messenger, **Mercury**.
***** **Twin** sons of Leda...one fathered by the **king** of the **gods**, one by the mortal **king** made cuckold. How's that for instant rivalry? Still, somehow, bros. Protectors of athletes & sailors. See also **Argonauts**, **astronauts**, St. Elmo's Fire.

faraday cage...an enclosure to prevent electromagnetic penetration, named for its architect, Michael Faraday,[358] 1836. May keep waves *in* (booster bags, microwaves, elevators) or *out* (airplanes, MRI, linemen suits). Gene Hackman's *Enemy of the State* (1988) hideout. Nobody *is* listening. Nobody *is* watching. *Is* Geolocating. Hungry? Here's a coupon for Applebee's.

ultrasound...Waves we cannot hear,[359] through which we see. A subtle treatment[360] & sound diagnostic for myriad pathologies.[361] May detect objects, movement, distance...integrity...

grail...by way of *graal, gréal, grazal, gresal*...by way of *gradalis* via *cratalis* via *cratus* by way of *krater*, an Ancient Greek container for mixing wine. A cup or bowl of earth, wood, metal...*metal* for *mortal*...vessel for vessel...stuff of miracles...water to wine[362]...wine to blood[363]...blood to **paradise**[364]...given a sip... the Old French slip... of the pen... of the tongue...*san gréal* becomes *sang réal*...*holy cup* to *royal bloodline*[365]...O consummate womb.....you thought that was Dan Brown's invention? It's a gothic transfusion...it's medieval...a high middle **meme**...far cry from the lance & chalice of a **Fisher King** w/E.D. [366]....O **Wasteland**[367]...O **hero blundering** into **wonder**...afraid to speak...to be seen...afraid to ask the question[368]...afraid to receive.

70 **OK King Me.**[369]

An erasure...of **Barry Chudakov**'s "Consciousness In the **Mirror**: A Hopscotch History of Replacing the World" 2020, in which Chudakov traces the integrated evolutions of tech & consciousness to arrive at the current precipice of alt reality...in which **virtual** realms duplicate & threaten to eclipse the "real".

---

358 Self-made physicist & chemist, 1791-1867, who established the concept of electromagnetic fields. Proved magnetic influence on light. Proposed the laws of electrolysis. Made the first electronic generator. Whose obsessive work ethic prompted a nervous breakdown, 6 years to recover. Saw the universe in terms of force. Whose **portrait** hung w/ **Newton**'s in **Einstein**'s* study.

359 Greater than 20 kilohertz, the threshold of the human ear. Perfectly sensible to **cats**, **dogs**, moths, toothed **whales**, **bats** & porpoises. Not to be confused w/**supersonic**.

360 *See* chemical processing, acoustic tweezers, dental hygiene & metallurgical harmonizing. An anti-inflammatory.

361 *See* sonic imaging, acoustic microscopy & pregnancy **spyware**.

362 In celebration of **matrimony**, in Christian theology, His first **miracle**.

363 *See* Last Supper, first Communion, transubstantiation. *See* eucharist. Not by bread alone.

364 Alchemy of **sacrifice**.

365 First transmutation by John Hardyng, followed by Thomas Malory, 15th century. In the 1980s, a band of brothers argued the **grail** was not a cup but a secret bloodline, the love consequence of Christ & Mary Magdalene (*see* **sex**). Their "scholarship" *The Holy Blood & the Holy **Grail*** inspired Dan Brown's *Da Vinci **Code*** & subsequent film.

366 The last **grail** guardian, a **wasteland** custodian, spends his days **fish**ing. For shirking responsibilities, rendered impotent, unable to access the healing powers of the treasure he's sworn to protect. In Terry Gilliam & Richard LaGravenese's** contemporary retelling, the knight, an asshole shock jock à la Howard Stern, shits on a desperate **incel** caller, who in turn shoots up a bar in a NYC **fantasy wasteland**.

367 *See* T.S Eliot's *The **Wasteland***, trumpet of industrial alienation, voiced in part by an abject, post-**romantic Fisher King**. Like F. Scott Fitzgerald & **Kurt Cobain**, the disillusioned voice of his generation. *See also* The Who's 1971 "Baba O'Riley."

368 In Chrétien de Troyes' unfinished 12th century poem & fan fic magnet, Perceval fails the **grail quest** after overcoming many perils. When at last he gains access to the bewitched **King**—indifferent or fearing to speak—the **hero** says nothing of the **wonders** he's given to witness. How different The End had he asked the question (O, Reader—), *whom does the **grail** serve?****

369 Upon reaching the far side, a checkers imperative: to be crowned w/the dead & thereby empowered.

---

* Theoretical physicist, real genius. Violinist. Who, perceiving relational universal music, translated. Resisted quantum entanglement but made strides toward unification. *See also Einstein* as barb: short for **brainiac** or conversely, dolt.
** *See* a tormented Robin Williams soar in *The **Fisher King*** (1991). *See also Monty Python & the Holy **Grail*** (1975).
*** *See also* **Tribe Called Quest.**

*the **mirror** logic*...cognitive processing subsequent to a representational shift from the world depicted via alphabets & static images to one of **mirror** reflections & simulations. *See also* simulacra & panopticon. The systemic sense we make of the digitized world.[370]

Al/ice...if a **mirror** replaces our concept of self, what happens when the **glass** shatters. *See* Picasso's ***Girl Before a Mirror****. See* **Chudakov**. *See* **Lewis Carroll**.

to crowdsource/friends...no more *phone a friend* for advice on what to wear. Just check the friendly **algorithm**.

replacing self   *w/plate*...**self-portrait** as mustard crusted rack of lamb. Self-portrait as poached yam. Mango smoothie. Self-portrait as cookie. Scratch biscotti. Dirty martini. **Amuse bouche**.

we/ Kaczynski...O lost Teddy. Lonesome **incel**. Oh manmade monster. Peerless grade-skipper dropped in a thicket of **bullies**. Whose brain swell outpaced the pumping muscle aerobic. Truth-seeking, academic prodigy,[371] friendless.[372] Brutalized by MK-Ultra.[373] Sought solace in wilderness. In the freedom of self-sufficiency.[374] Until his refuge was mowed for roadway, then revenge.[375] Abhorred Nazis, socialists, feminists, liberals, conservatives, ecofascists & activists for disability/LGBTQ/animals/the environment. Viewed replication as violation. Gave thanks to Grandfather **Rabbit** for the hares by which he survived Montana winters.[376] Tik Tok **icon**.[377]

---

370   Imagine some fab shades (or a biological interface) by which everything seen is scanned for **data** tags to be accessed instantaneously AND imagine traveling **virtually** anywhere because all (known) reality has been digitally replicated full scale, a **hyperreal** map. *See* Kevin Kelly. *See* **Jorge Borges**. *See* **Lewis Carroll**.

371   Harvard graduate at 16. PhD at University of Michigan by 24. Associate Professor at UC Berkley by 25.

372   Until he reached prison & infamy where his people found him.

373   In the late 1950s Harvard Professor Henry Murray recruited Ted, a 17-year-old sophomore, for research Murray began in the CIA during **WWII**. For three years, Murray subjected the already **bullied** young man to extreme psychological stress & mind manipulation the CIA would later describe as "ethically indefensible".

374   But not self-sufficient. When he traded academia for homesteading, his family helped support him. And in the end, they recognized him.*

375   In his manifesto, "Industrial Society and Its Future" TK (referring to himself as FC/"Freedom Club") claims the demands placed on industrialized humans are unnatural. Claims we are regulated as cogs to keep trains running on schedule...a complaint not too different from one unspooled by **hero, Ross Gay**,** though the method of resistance (& most everything else) radically differs. Would that Gay might be as influential.

376   Hand to mouth. Meanwhile, the FBI spent 18 years, hundreds of crew & 50 million dollars to find him. But let us not waste tax dollars on mental health.

377   *See* #tedpilled, anti civ CHADs ironically deploy the Chinese splinter-mind machine to champion the cause of Uncle Ted. Justice warriors idolizing a murderer to undermine the digital **Wasteland** of their childhood, their own digital footprint notwithstanding. Cringe? Sure, but not lost on them...they're jousting w/**shadow**bans... **coding** their dance to attract mates & evade **surveillance**, all the while scrolling the drain. Maybe not so different from **Gen X nihilism***** & Boomers' non-productive free love & *screw the man*.

---

* His brother's **wife** was the first to suspect his alt identity; his brother, painfully, turned him in.
** *See* students as "bundled units" in "Dispatch from the Ruins: School, the Eleventh Incitement" ***Inciting Joy***, 2022.
*** In "The **Nihilism** of **Gen**eration **X** is an Artifact of Privilege" Millennial writer, Shane Burley, critiques "90s **nihilism**" as the domain of privileged White kids, **bullied** in part by an economic comparison of the world American Xers inherited vs the hand-me-downs left to Millennials. He's not the only mil waxing holier than thou. **WG**, who lives w/her adult Gen Z kids in her Silent Gen mother-in-law's house thinks, yes, it's true economic disparity has radically increased over the last 3 decades. It's also true subsequent generations enjoy many privileges 90s adolescents did not, for example destigmatization of mental healthcare, increased inclusion of diverse **sexualities**, ethnicities, neurodivergence, body positivity... Moreover, when **Kurt Cobain** channeled "angst"—perhaps fueled by depression, **heroin** addiction, a broken family, **Ronald Reagan**, undiagnosed GI ailments & rampant **AIDS**—into his music, he wasn't thinking about how hard it would be to buy a house 20 yrs later. Nor, ahem, was **nihilism** limited to white folks. *See* Tupac. *See* B.I.G. *See* LA riots (1992). Also, when folks whatevs on **repeat**, when they lean into it, Sugarplum, they're talljacking, hummer stunting, flojjing, supper's ready, don't be stumb, U know U know it's front.

target/ tech?...but **Kaczynski**'s threats went beyond tech workers. Responsible for 3 unrecognizable corpses & 23 brutally wounded,[378] the bomber terrorized countless postal carriers, airline workers, scientists & ordinary citizens.

king *re placement*...How beautiful he is as someone else. A handsome doll propped on a hotel bed. Invisibly visible. Symmetrically asymmetrical. Déjà vu in a room w/a view; replete w/ **mirror**, shades, wig, polyester jumper—none of it *his*. A self over self draped & left to drip. Like time from twigs. Skin walking. You can make a living as the dead. You can make a living as a **King**. A person impersonator.[379] The **king** is dead long live the **king**.[380] The screen. Stunt **double**...but safer.[381] And let's face it, lots of people make out[382] as someone they're not. Call it conventional.[383] Nothing to confess when you've been so clearly framed.

mirror portraits *con*[384] *& vex*...despite biologist assertions, no one is symmetrical, a fact realized via social media facial-symmetry filters that use a bisected face & **AI** to simulate perfect **symmetry**. The yield is two perfect strangers. And much hysteria.

73   **OK Know Me.**

the sermon/on washing feet...a quick engine search reveals several readily available sermons on the practice, aka maundy.[385] **Gemini** & other **AI** would also be *happy* to write you a "new" one...

spilling wine/into the mouths to deliver us from ourselves...The Christian ritual of **communion**. Some believe the bread & wine symbolic, others in transubstantiation. Both partake to embody an exchange of reality: bread & wine for the body & blood[386] of **Christ**, sinner for clean slate. *See* **alchemy**.

---

378 Among the wounded, **David Gelernter**, author of ***Mirror*** *Worlds or The Day Software Puts the Universe in a Shoebox—How It Will Happen and What It Will Mean*, 1991. Gelernter lost hearing in one ear, use of his right hand & 3-D perspective. Nearly died of blood loss. A Yale professor known for advancements in parallel computation, Gelernter in 1991 predicted digital reality as we know it & what's down the pipeline. Reported shock in being personally targeted, not because he was so beloved, but because he was so obscure. Known also for rejection of evolution, feminism & climate crisis. Profiled as a potential science advisor to **Trump** in 2017. No shit. No saint.

379 The profession of **Elvis** Tribute Artists, aka ETAs, began in the **King**'s reign, w/ETA's occasionally performing alongside the original sauce. Some performers, like Andy Kaufman* & Jeremy Spencer** of Fleetwood Mac, integrate ET into their acts. It's not true that Elvis entered an Elvis lookalike contest & took 3rd place but the story*** bears repeating. Impersonators may look-alike, sound-alike or both. May even, like **AI**, look, sound & "write" Elvis-ish songs. *See* David Daniel, the Great Pretender.****

380 A proclamation of sovereign continuity generally inapplicable to **rockstars**. *See* Don McClean's "**American Pie.**"

381 Though **doubles** of **Rodney**, **MLK** or even **B.B.** might beg to differ.

382 Acting the part, their ship comes in, they make out like a bandit, they're steaming the windows of a parked car.

383 The popularity of **Elvis** impersonation has yielded contests, conventions & other events, often involving Elvis derivatives (Greek Elvii, Lady Elvis, El Vez, the Mexican Elvis), often w/elaborate **pageantry**, impersonation satire &/or evangelism. Some believe *Elvis chose them* to carry on His message.

384 Though they may reveal something true.

385 Practiced in Hindi, Islamic, Judaic, Seik & Christian cultures. An ancient hospitality among many sandal wearing people, in which hosts offer water & sometimes a servant. In the Christian gospels, **Jesus** washes his disciples' feet after the last supper, disrobing & girding himself in the linen by which he also dries them.

386 Today blood banks mean salvation, but only after blood's screened & scrubbed, otherwise it's biohazard, Trojan **horse**, a minister for pathogens. Menstrual blood dubs women unclean since...history. On hands indicates guilt. *See also* blood diamonds, blood in the water, blood on the carpet, in buckets, blood from a stone...We got it bad—blood! Thus & nevertheless, in many houses of worship the faithful drink from a common cup...

---

* **Elvis**' alleged fav, who's act included hilariously awkward failed attempts before sudden perfection.
** Who also played at **Buddy Holly.**
*** Charlie Chaplin *did* enter a lookalike contest as himself, though no one knows whether he won or lost.
**** One wonders if **Elvis** considered himself, as a White musician, a tribute artist...though he only ever used his own name. *See also* **C.D. Wright**'s "Remarks on Color".

a dusty/ sandalled traveler...Christian scriptures chronicle **Jesus'** many ministry transits, his sandaled feet exposed to human, animal, earth & atmospheric excrement.

the last of her precious oils...two women wash Christ's feet according to the Gospels.[387] In **Luke 7**, a *sinful* woman (read *whore*[388]) approaches **Jesus** at the home of Simon, the Pharisee.[389] She falls to Jesus' feet, washes them w/her tears, dries them w/her hair, kisses & anoints them w/oil.[390] Simon thinks Jesus cannot be a man of **God** or he would not, by her, be touched.

The 2nd occurs in His last days at the home of Mary,[391] Martha, & the re-animated Lazarus. After supper, as **John** tells it, Mary opens a jar of nard, worth a year's wages, pours the whole over the savior's feet & wipes w/her hair,[392] the house, a fragrance. Judas, also present, criticizes the woman for wasting what might have been sold to feed the poor.[393]

this man w/the sponge...the first **sponges**, of course, were nicked from the sea. Metazoan phylum porifera, or *pore bearer*. Ancient submissive bound to the seabed.[394] In **Homer's** day, the creatures bathed **Olympians** in oils & scrubbed the tables after **Penelope** entertained her suitors.

asking/to be whipped...So much tendered to deconstruct this.[395] Do your research.

his own shadow...Plato says **shadows** mislead us; Pliny the elder that they're art's first seizure;[396] Hades rules them; **Dante** talks w/them; St. Peter's heals the sick; **Peter Pan** loses his; the **romantics** make silhouette cut-outs; Jekyll

---

387 First books of the New Testament: Matthew, Mark, **Luke & John**, which chronicle the life of Christ + events immediately fore & aft, thought by some to have been written by the aforenamed disciples, others not.

388 Read: woman who survives by giving men pleasure, for which most **shame** her.

389 Experts in Judaic law, oft depicted as self-righteous grammarians. *See also* cancel culture.

390 Who can deny the eroticism &/or awkwardness of this image.

391 Not to be confused w/Magdalene.

392 Again, w/the hair.

393 After sending **Jesus** up the river for 30 pieces of silver & the subsequent crucifixion, Judas attempts to ditch the earnings at the Temple. Wanting none of his blood money, the priests purchase Potter's Field,* where Judas purportedly hangs himself.

394 Free from autonomy. No nervous, digestive, or circulatory systems to disagree. Dependent on waves to deliver & to take away. Ward of the sea.

395 **WG** belatedly recalls reviewing Eric Berkowitz 2012, *Sex & Punishment: Four Thousand Years of Judging Desire* & renews her recommendation. Or consider a prostitute's wisdom from Pietro Artino's 16th century *Dialoghe*, one of numerous nether world infamies Berkowitz uplifts,

> You with your 'rope in the ring,' your 'obelisk in the Coliseum,' your 'leek in the garden,' your 'key in the lock,' your 'bolt in the door,' your 'pestle in the mortar' ... why don't you say yes when you mean yes and no when you mean no, or else keep it to yourself.

396 He describes a woman, anticipating longing, tracing her beloved's **shadow** to darken her wall after he's gone.**

---

* Aka *Akeldama—field of blood*. The field thereafter used to bury non-Jews, the destitute & strangers/anonymous. Prior to the purchase, the field supplied clay for earthen vessels. *See also* the housing development owned by the **villainous** banker Henry Potter in Frank Capra's *It's A Wonderful Life*, **star**ring Jimmy Stewart as a forthright man who gives up his **dreams** to save his father's *Savings & Loan* & the **American Dream** from the clutches of Potter. *See* **hero**. *See* **sacrifice**.
** *See also* the novel *As a Friend*, by **Forrest Gander**, which makes a **mirror** world of **IRL** love triangles involving his late **wife**, the poet **C.D. Wright** & the late poet, **Frank Stanford**.

hides Hyde; Jung deconstructs them; early photographers *fix* them; The **Shadow** knows...early cinema commits murder by them; we hope the groundhog won't see his; **Warhol** got obsessive;[397] Burke said substantiating them is poetry, *lending existence to nothing...*

missionary style[398]...a coitus position the French refer to as *classical*, the Tuscans as angelic, known in Arabic as *the manner of serpents*. Aka *matrimonial* & *male superior*. Variations include the anvil, riding high, Weiner Auster/ Viennese oyster & butterfly. Makes for easy kissing. Makes for **mirroring**. Me see|see you?[399]

74   **OK Life Still.**[400]

View-Master™...O proto VR goggle of Bakelite plastic, O woosh ding promise of mechanical advancement, spinning 7-slide cartridges for armchair globetrotting going back to the Greatest Generation.[401] In 1939, William Gruber sold the rights to **Mattel**™, eclipsing the 80-year-old invention of Oliver Wendell Holmes,[402] whose cheap & easily reproducible stereoscope—darling of 1860s Victorians, pre-tv, pre-radio—he patently refused to patent.[403] Not to be confused w/a view*finder*.[404]

who/in the slantwise...sometimes the **View-Master**™ cartridge, like a record, or a trick heart, skips,[405] an elevator ajar between floors, impromptu ***Choose-Your-Own Adventure***™.[406] Will you panic, pick one, attempt to shimmy through—or stay put & relish the split, second view?

---

397   102 iterations of a single, **anonymous shadow,*** rendered in black & neons via **sponge** mop. Warhol was 50. **WG** was fingerpainting.

398   The oldest record of "**missionary position**" appears in Alfred Kinsey's ***Sexual Behavior in the Human Male***, 1948 in which the American **sex**ologist/biologist, mistakenly attributes the phrase to Polish anthropologist, Bronislaw Malinowski: an origin story that doesn't seem incredible: derived from indigenous ridicule of White copulation.

399   In hetero illustration accompanying the wiki description, we see the white of a woman's teeth but not her eyes. She may or may not be smiling. He hovers above, bare backside, to us, faceless. Through the window between them her left nipple, palpable.

Homo**sexual** pairs further down the page also relate ventro-ventral, one partner w/teeth, one faceless. All White.

400   In the hierarchy of genres** which accords status relative to subject, still lifes lie low. From the Dutch *stilleven*, meaning "quiet life"; Fatalist Italians opt for *natura morta*. Painters, if you want status, skip it; try history, mythology, **Christ**...unless you're an impressionist or post-impressionist, in which case throw subject out the window & paint the splat. *See* Van Gogh's self-**portrait** (sans ears) *Still Life with Drawing Board and Onions*. Speaking of **mirrors**, ancient Egyptians believed fruit drawn on the walls of their tombs would appear in the sweet flesh after.

401   By the time little **WG** was cycling the reels, the backlit pics worked like **comic book** panels in proto **virtual reality** goggles, or old school picture books, telling stories.

402   American Supreme Court Judge, 1902-1932, appointed by **Teddy Roosevelt.** The Great Dissenter. Authored the "clear and present danger" test to narrow exceptions of free speech. Flawed **progressive:** *see Buck v Bell.*

403   As early as the 1830s illusionists created 3-D impressions via 2-D images by subjecting viewers to two distinct images simultaneously. Illusions advanced w/**double** lens **cameras**, a stereographer godsend & photo journalists documented the world over. That each view divided, once reunited—might bring the far corners to you.

404   That transparent bit whose name suggests the spectacle might be hiding, as opposed to the **keyhole** by which we aim the recorder's ocular.

405   **WG**'s sometimes clunks.

406   *See* ***Choose Your Own Adventure***™ books by poet Katherine Factor: ***Spies: Harry Houdini***; ***Spies: Mata Hari: & Spy for Cleopatra*** & discover 24 possible endings!

---

* "Far from replicas, each **Shadow** corresponds to a form that reveals its space with precision and self-awareness... By focusing on the shadow to devise light as sparks of color, **Warhol** returns to the quintessential problem of art: perception." Donnie de Salvo, DIA Art Foundation

** Of the European Academies 1563 to 1800...O Academy...patron of zero-sum prestige.

unfiltered unphotoshopped[407] *light*...light actual, infinitely variable, by which she might in her momentary flesh be momentarily seen seeing what she sees...

who....would think her happiness a ruse?...See the philandering doctor,[408] **WCW**,[409] twirling the house in his birthday suit while his otherwise Otherwise **wife** & boy toddler slumber. *See* him ravishing—**loneliness** relishing—bodily strange & sumptuous & free.[410] Oh, revelatory! As if he were not already (O fallacious fellatio!) the body autonomy.[411]

77   **Sans allure?**

tuna industry...populations have decreased by 90% since the 1970s. In the last decade, owing to collaborative international efforts, populations are rising, but slowly. *See* Greenpeace International's red list.[412] Speaking of industry, Atlantic Blue Fins (topping 1500lbs) migrate thousands of miles for optimum location (Location! Location! Location!) to make love.[413]

poor man's lobster aka ugly fish...Once a *trash fish* sold cheap to men of the cloth, **monkfish** now fetch a pretty penny.[414] Gloriously ugly. Seriously, you seen one? Picture a snarl-toothed visage of half-set Jello™ masquerading as lumpy ocean floor, luring prey to its gaping mow w/a fleshy **fishing** rod. Jaw snap so fast, needs specialized tech for film to catch. Body elastic. Will stretch to swallow swimmers twice its size,[415] to wit, catch one & there might be a prince inside.

---

407   A brick & mortar chemical lab before it was an app. A light tight closet. A black box. Before that—a mind?

408   Back then they made house calls.

409   **William Carlos Williams**—you know the one about the red wheelbarrow?

410   TBH, despite deep & abiding love for **WCW** since **WG** was a kid, **Danse Russe** pisses her off. For 30 years she's wanted to punch him. Like they were **married.**

411   Consider **Michael Pollan**'s *A Place of My Own: The Education of an Amateur Builder* a memoir of his 1990s efforts at the advent of his first child to build a backyard writing studio to get away from it all. A best-selling author, but not so much a carpenter, Pollan devotes many pages to romanticizing the skills of professional builders. As a professional builder, **WG**'s nonbuilder, Pollan-fan friends frequently recommend; she lowkey hates it. First, for the **romance**, which, despite self-deprecating claims, reads as sycophantic, reinforcment of disparities oft espoused by academics regarding *the trades*. Second, again despite self-aware airs, Pollan breezes over **Woolf**'s *A Room of One's Own*, to which his title alludes,* nary a word about his luck—a proper house! w/land & money to augment the domain which—**wife** & kid or not—he historically masters.

412   Confession: **WG** regularly consumes canned **tuna**. She says it's because there is so little prepared food she can safely eat & this is true, but also because it's delicious, nutritious & convenient. *See* **complicit.**

413   To the Mediterranean Sea in the east & the Gulf of Mexico in the west. Spawning involves the expulsion of millions of eggs from each female, gobs of **sperm** from each male. The subsequent plumes of **tuna sex**, visible from aircraft, likewise attract hungry **fish**erman. Tuna trauma seems not to overrule homing instinct. Take the Deepwater Horizon spill amid the 2010 spawn, undeterred tuna annually return to the scene of the **crime.**

414   If we make ourselves scarce, imagine the price we'll fetch.

415   Exaggeration. But a 40lb **monk** has swallowed a 50lb **cod.** And a femme will swallow her mate if he doesn't expedite removal post-coital. Femmes have also taken **fish**ermen's limbs *after* boarding the ship.

---

* But note the difference in possessives: **Woolf**'s both universal & hypothetical vs **Pollan**'s of self singular.

the Geek Squad™...A tech service subsidiary of Best Buy,[416] as opposed to *The Mod Squad*.[417]

four eyes...an insult. *See* **glasses**. *See* disability. *See* **brainiac**.[418]

licked & licked &...to be beaten, brutalized, knocked out, dunzo, to have taken a **licking**, an animal to wounds, mammalian ma to unsack newborns or free the toddling from parasitic tagalongs. Also to groom. *See* **cowlick**. Bootlicker. **Lickety** split. Slice of the **whip**. To reiterate.[419] Would you lick someone when they're down? Where? A salt stick to lure deer. Let's get licked. How many to get to the center[420]...one, two....finger licking bliss. Ice cream annihilation.[421] **Sexual** stimulation. String strumming. Cuplicking.[422] *See also* a spotlit trumpet wail over a syncopated **double-bass**.

---

416 Founded independently in 1994 by "Chief Inspector" Robert Stevens. Geek Squad™ **branding** comically suggests the tech side of government **spy** agencies; employees are referred to as "agents," e.g. CIA (Counter Intelligence agent), DAC (**Double** Agent-Covert). They carry badges & wear uniforms that reinforce the nerd* stereotypes (clip-on ties, etc.) associated w/secret agent & criminal science support staff.**

417 An American crime drama, 1968-1973, produced by Aaron Spelling (*see also Beverly Hills 90210*), following three hip, young, disaffected dropouts*** turned undercover cops. In perhaps the first mainstream **Hollywood** effort to address youth counterculture, *The Mod Squad* explored issues like abortion, racism, **the Vietnam War**, slum lords, police brutality, illegal immigration, **sex** education, euthanasia, PTSD, domestic violence...

418 *See also* insult. Among **Superman**'s most popular antagonists, variously reiterated as a superintelligent android/cyborg/scientist obsessed w/collecting knowledge. Favorite weapon? A shrink ray gun that reduces cities to fit in handy specimen bottles. Favorite specimen? Super's **Krypton**. A **villain** of endless narrative, easily reiterated because, as **AI**, his consciousness is infinitely transferrable.

419 In "Masscult & Midcult," **Dwight Macdonald** describes this as invariably demeaning...to the book. *Against the American Grain*, 1952.

420 of the Tootsie Roll pop...a quandary plaguing consumers since Detroit ad man David Demuth conceived the cosmic **quest** in 1968. Then, too, the world in flames...**Vietnam**, Kent State, Robert Kennedy, **MLK**... Numerous **licking** machines have been constructed & countless human-tongued **surveys** dispensed since lolly popped the question—Results vary. Conclusion: we love **suckers**.

421 *See also* **Superman** ice cream, whose color scheme means to call up the American **hero** but which **WG** thinks more nearly resembles the colors of anti-war-hippies (& finds the hippies more appetizing).

422 In *The Book of Delights*, see "Cuplicking", which begins "Today I found myself (I adore that construction for its **Whitmanian** assertion of multitudinousness) **licking** the little remnants, little stains, from the coffee dribbling down the rim of the cup." **Ross Gay**, 2019.

---

* Irony: that the favorite uniform of the agent presently in charge w/dismantling the government, the public **face** of D.O.G.E, nothing covert about it, is a black T advertising TECH SUPPORT. *See* **Musk**.

** Ironically, the nerd/**brainiac** trope of criminal forensic science frequently depicts such characters as singularly quirky deviants**** relative to their uniformed peers, a nonconformity tolerated & sometimes beloved as the inevitable side-effect (as in defect) of intellectual prowess.

*** "a black one, a white one, a blonde one" each w/undeniable **sex** appeal, *not* **square**.

**** **IRL**, numerous Geek Squad agents have been caught copying **porno**graphic content from their clients' devices, w/evidence suggesting the work is not that of rogue outliers, but shared w/& encouraged by management.

end time footnotes...The problem w/footnotes to an apocalypse is where to put them. Much depends[424] on how the end goes, how the end goes...whether whimper,[425] brimstone[426] or echo...the tale caravaned via **cloud**, tablet,[427] **conquistadors**[428] or **troubadours**.[429] *See also* **Mr. Burns**.[430]

a shortfall amusement... e.g. **meme**coin,[431] shitcoin, $**Sponge**, $DOGE, $**Trump**, $Melania, $Fart...by various **villains** endorsed...shortfall to landfall.

it's not despicable...The same year SpaceX launched, orbited & recovered Dragon 1,[432] Universal Pictures launched *Despicable Me*, that devilish face that would launch a thousand ships:[433] 3 sequels, 3 prequels (not including *Minions*[434]) & endless merch—as of January 2025—12.3 billion gross & counting...

---

423   *See also* Oedipus. *See* **Tyrannosaurus**.* *See* Tyranny.

424   ...upon// a red wheel/barrow...an end may be just what the doctor ordered.

425   As supposed by the old ex-pat a century ago, *this is the way the world ends/this is the way the world ends/this is the way the world ends***...who put his **wife** in a box & threw away the key... *The eyes are not here/There are no eyes here***

In 1958, after the bomb, the poet claimed (*not with a bang, but a wimper...*) if he had the ear worm to write again, he wouldn't.

426   *See* **Tyrannosaurus**. *See* sinners. *See Sinners.*

427   As carried, broken, in the ark of covenant over which...pillar of **cloud** by day, by night, fire.

428   *See also* **Billionaire Space Wars. Bone Wars.** Colonists. **Manifest Destiny.**

429   Medieval poet-musicians of knightly rank. Traveling performers/messengers who entertained w/tales of **courtly love**. Also a nightclub in West **Hollywood.**

430   A "post-electric" play by Anne Washburne centered on a band of **troubadours** who recreate "live-action" episodes of the Simpsons after a 21st century apocalypse. The play tracks the evolution of a particular episode, "**Cape Feare**"*** as amalgamation of memory over 80+ years. In late evolutions, **Sideshow Bob**, the serial killing **clown** & Bart's nemesis, is conflated w/**Mr. Burns**, the maniacal boss at the nuclear power plant where Bart's father **Homer** (*see* ***Iliad***, *see* ***Odyssey***) works. Staged first in Washington DC, (2012), later in NYC, London, Traverse City, MI**** & elsewhere.

431   A **crypto**currency, like all, unregulated, **hyperreal**, in resurgence since the 2024 U.S. presidential election.

432   The first privately developed & operating spacecraft to launch & be successfully recovered from orbit.

433   Retail relation*ships*. *See* Marlow's***** ***Doctor Faustus***, whose Elizabethan devils drove some viewers mad.

434   Aka *henchman*. In the Universal franchise, the small, **pill**-shaped **Minions** evolve from single-celled organisms, biologically driven to locate & bolster **villains**. Whose aid proves ruinous. In their first spinoff (2015), the creatures precipitate the fall of **Tyrannosaurus Rex**, Count Dracula & Napoleon.

---

* Like us, bi-pedal, flightless. Famous & infamous. Big head. Carnivore. Hand-to-mouth. Believed to be both **predator** & scavenger. Charismatic **villain** featured in numerous films, books, stamps, advertisements, plastic figurines. Little boy darling. Brought down by the asteroid &/or **minions.**

** *The Hollow Men*, 1925. *See also* "such deliberate disguises."

*** Whose *Cape Fear* parody (1957 novel turned **Hollywood**, first in 1962, again in 1991) is an **infinity mirror** of allusion & reiteration. As in the parent story, Bart is stalked by **Sideshow Bob**, a sociopathic killer he helped put away, now out on parole. In "Cape Feare" Bart thwarts the evil genius of high culture, once a kiddie show sidekick, by asking Bob to sing the Gilbert & Sullivan operetta, *HMS Pinafore*.*6 The clown, voiced by Kelsey Grammer, *Frasier*'s stuffy psychiatrist **protagonist**, obliges. **WG**'s fav.

**** Witnessed in 2017 by a mesmerized **WG.**

***** The Bard's pal, Christopher, aka Kit. Among the first English wrights to convey the nether realm as **mirror**. To wit, the line spoken by **Dr. Faustus**, "Was this the face that launched a thousand ships" oft taken out of context as testament to Helen's beauty, but spoken in disappointment to a demon attempting & failing to capture her guise.

*6 Performed in Traverse City, 2016 w/**WG**'s son as baffooning Captain Corcoran, to her everlasting delight.

The *Despicable* movies follow **supervillain Felonious Gru** whose ego is bruised when his evil rival steals the Pyramid of Giza. Not to be outdone, Gru, w/the help of **a shrink ray gun**,[435] steals the Moon.[436]

in late descent...might refer to the final stage of an aircraft's landing. Or capitalism. Or democracy.[437]

*yellow **pills** so sweet*...they might be Percocet, Endocet, Diazepam, Naproxen, Cyclobenzaprine, Meloxicam, Clonazepam, Clonidine, Gabapentin, Sertraline, Tadalafil, Zolpidem, Concerta, Mirtazapine...

so they attempted to steal the moon—big deal!/they failed...Though numerous space flight companies formed in the wake of commercial deregulation,[438] have failed, the burgeoning industry of **NewSpace**[439] appears wildly[440] successful.

---

435   In the film **Gru** pilfers the gun from the son of his nemesis, the gun's inventor. In the meta world that authors **superhero/villainy**, the shrink-ray was first weaponized by **Superman**'s nemesis,* hence, like great art, stolen.

436   **Gru** gives up the moon when the three orphan girls aiding his scheme, who he accidentally comes to love, are kidnapped. If only present **villains** had a soft spot for children.

437   In "The Way Home: Space Migration & Disorientation," **Debra Benita Shaw** describes the convergence of bootstrap capitalism & cosmism, the later expressed as "a belief in human destiny as plotted on an inevitable upward trajectory and inextricable from both colonialism and continual technological development."

In other words, as capitalist tech titans see the bottom of our planet's well, a new conquest is necessary to continue "progress." Reenter **manifest destiny!** O righteous necessity! And it better be necessary. For off-worlding will surely expedite Earth's ruin & most of us aren't suicidal, are we? We won't submit to massive wealth redistribution on the backs of masses—the masses dying by war/disease/famine—**nevermind** accelerated mass extinction—just so an elite few can jerk off into space, pull a **rabbit** from another planet—unless it's true—this one's through—will we? We won't give up the berth unless it's beyond hope, truly dying**... no possibility of resuscitating***...surely we wouldn't, surely not, surely—

438   Though space exploration was limited to the military complex for decades, potential for capitalist expansion in the U.S. was built into the mandate w/the US Communications Satellite Act of 1962 under **Kennedy**. **Ronald Reagan** upped the ante w/ the Commercial Space Launch Act of 1984, mandating that NASA encourage private space flight. Then 2 years after **Musk** forms SpaceX,**** George W. deregulates... well...everything...including via the Commercial Space Launch Amendment of 2004, FAA regulations for space flight...indefinitely...

439   The market savvy***** portmanteau of a privatized industry expanding above the Kármán Line*6 including but not limited to space tourism, research, **surveillance**, broadband internet, colonization, mining & other resource speculation,*7

440   If capitalist enterprise can be described as **wild**.

---

* **Brainiac**.
** Though many folks endorsing the billionaire titans also deny the Earth is dying...so...?
*** Someone should tell the **Space War Billionaires** that, in the off-off chance that off-worlding fails, preserving Earth as long as possible will extend their Ozymandian legacies w/ a living audience.
**** W/plans to colonize **Mars**, dead for years.
***** According to MIT, NASA, **AI** & others, **NewSpace**'s many benefits to human existence include "disruptive innovation," new business models, a more sustainable future & the capitalization of various investors. Plus jobs. Plus, in the past you had to work for the government to be an **astronaut** & "now you don't—it's utterly democratic!"*8
*6 The so-called boundary of outer space named for Theo von Kármán, who calculated a theoretical limit to terrestrial flight then rounded way up. An arbitrary legal distinction some recognize, but generally non-binding. *See also* **Wild West**.
*7 An asteroid approximately a kilometer in diameter might contain as much as 30 million tons of nickel, 1.5 million tons of cobalt & 7,500 tons of platinum, the latter of which would gross 150 billion dollars. Or there's Shackleton,*9 a prospecting firm, w/plans to harvest lunar water & become the first refueling base on the moon.
*8 Utterly democratic....as opposed to...our government? Oh, right.
*9 Brave, marooned, Antarctic explorer whose crew is not said to have resorted to cannibalism.

*the swan dive…*Term origin—though, undoubtedly American—unclear. Oxford puts earliest use at 1912, etymology.com says 1898 & Sue Butler, *lexicographer at large*, speculates the source may be an 1886 issue of *LIFE*, a perfect specimen[441] caught in black & white, midflight, his brawny wingspan & back-bowed breast soaring off 5 meter platform[442] o'er a bank of summer bathers—an ariel attributed to one Jamie Swan.

*huntsman's orange fleece…*In deer hunting…any late fall amble…one aims not to get shot. Cue orange. Neon yellow. Siren red. An obnoxious florescence against decomposing neutralities. A scream at visibility, recognition, lest we be prey. Alas, people hunting people's a different **game**; wear gray.

81   **Woman Wonders[443] into a Bakery.**

who'd cut his own legs out/from under…not really. Not on purpose, but it happens. And changes the field of the vision. Think of **Christopher Reeves**[444] post-accident. Dependence realized. Quantum entangled. An upward trajectory reduced. Still, life caught on film. He once said, *flying happens in the eyes.*

---

441   Think da Vinci's Vitruvian Man. Human ideal. Perfectly symmetrical. Muscular. Male. **Olympian** conscribed to tech breakthrough—the wheel. Whose dimensions determine architecture & automobile. Whose iteration is stitched to NASA suits & the first flag on the moon.

442   An estimate. But probably not too far off given the community pool & diving tank where **WG** grew up, where **Olympians** trained, including Scott, who babysat her kid sibs while **WG** crushed. Oh to be Leda w/*that* Swan.

443   If you wonder, as **WG** did, which came first **Wonder Woman**™* or **Wonder Bread**™, it's the pre-sliced goodie** marvel of 20th century ingenuity (builds strong bodies 12 ways!). About the time Otto Fredrick Rohwedder's slicing invention was getting the commercial treatment (circa 1930), **comic books** hit the scene depicting wondrous violence, often **sexual**. By 1940 the industry lambasted w/complaints called in a consultant, Harvard over-educated psychologist/lawyer/professor **William Moulton Marston**,*** who'd already written & consulted for Universal Studios. A liberal progressive & covert **polyamorist** cohabitating w/his **wife** (a practicing lawer) & another woman (his former student),**** Marston suggested that since comics critics focused **superhero** disdain on the "blood-curdling masculinity," why not counter w/a female culprit.

Marston's creation was an Amazonian justice warrior descended from women who'd freed themselves from ancient Greek enslavement, whose self-empowerment produced profound strength, skill & intelligence. The crusades of his feminist American **hero**, clad as **dominatrix**, oft led to capture & **bondage** via elaborate chains,*⁶ that she might reenact over & over the struggle for **freedom**.*⁷ Also giving a heap of pleasure to men who fetishized bondage, as evidenced by explicit fan letters.

444   **Star** of the 1980s **Superman** cinema franchise who, in the 1990s, thrown from his **horse** in an equestrian competition, went from the "face" of **superhero** invincibility to a paraplegic champion for accessibility.

---

* **WG**'s girlhood **hero**. Exhibit 1: **Wonder Woman** Underoos™. When worn under her 4 year-old digs, & despite spinning round & around, confounded **WG** never turned into her **hero**. Still spinning. Maybe non-Amazonians take longer.

** The advent of commercial bread in 1925 led to an uptick in bread consumption, which led to an uptick in bread production, which led to changes in wheat production, which re**double**d disease. E.g. in **WG**, whose family has farmed wheat since before sliced bread, developed late onset celiacs.

*** Also credited w/inventing the human lie detector test. Also, as a **polyamorous** man in early 20th century NYC, living w/two romantic partners & 4 children, half of whom did not "know" he was their father, a good **liar**.

**** Niece of the feminist **rockstar, Margaret Sanger***⁷ & their children's primary caregiver.

***** Though some objected to the frequent use of chains & encouraged alternate forms of restraint, chains echoed feminist iconography of the era, by design. Ropes, like chains, appear in 20th century suffrage propaganda, a tool transformed in WW's iconography to a lasso by which she captured **villains** & compelled truth-telling.

*⁶ A petition w/her endorsement sent to President Woodrow Wilson reads, "While men stand proudly and face the sun, boasting that they have quenched the wickedness of slavery, what chains of slavery are, have been or ever could be so intimate a horror as the shackles on every limb—on every thought–on the very soul of an unwilling pregnant woman?"

*⁷ *See* **George Michael** deconstruct his image as a straight man in "Freedom! '90". *See* the **icon** flex, refusing to appear in his own video, mocking beauty as **MTV** currency, filling the screen w/ warehoused **super models** lip syncing: *See I don't belong to you and you don't belong to me yeah yeah.*

*he's got...no plans to vacate...*neither as off world vay-cay, nor **Mars pilgrim**. Besides, even in this desolate landscape,[445] there's so much good tv—courtesy of the ever-expanding satellite constellations[446] &—in the not-so-distant future— a vacuum tube[447] to suck him off to the big city.

*New Worlding...*Think **Conquistadors, pilgrims**[448] or, if you want to go there, refugees.[449] Like contemporary homesteaders[450] but more out there. For example, unless you read sci-fi, dystopia, or post-apocalyptic fiction,[451] all the survival manuals are unwritten.

***Krypton's** asylum...*Is "America" the intended ejection destination of **Kal-El**? Do his folks mean to land him in the New World,[452] where he may be mistaken for other immigrants?

*plenty hostile planet here...*e.g. the poles, deserts, jungles, swamps...the deep sea...mountain tops...we might call our dear mother passive aggressive, but who could blame her...when folks defile us we call it **rape**. Still, proponents of **panspermia**[453] say, as a girl, she was receptive.

---

445 **Nevermind** the highway.

446 As of July 2024,* Harvard-Smithsonian astronomer, **Jonathan McDowell**, estimates there are upwards of 10K active satellites orbiting Earth, a number that's quadrupled over the last 5 years. Adding to the metal aviary: 3,300 inactive satellites & 25,000 other pieces of *cataloged*** space junk. Approximately 60% of the active **birds** belong to **Musk's** internet provider **Star**link w/another 36K fowl slated for release in the near future. Not to be undone, Jeffrey **Bezos'** Project Kuiper (*see also* **Billionaire Space Wars**) will soon envelope the Earth w/fewer but larger **birds** that talk to each other.*** Each clutch snares the Earth in a mesh sleeve, a knit bag, a slip knot, the internet turned outernet, the whole of life as we know it caught in a world wide web.

447 *See Hyperloop,* **Musk's** would-be train tube. Hurling payloads 700 mph, it's the next best thing to teleporting.

448 Read *colonists*. Similarily, the righteous fervor w/which the pursuant address their mission is often religious.

449 A misleading flippancy. Refugees don't *go there*, they flee.

450 The trials of whom you can, on numerous platforms, stream.

451 **Terraform, cyber**space, gaslight: terms from fiction science realized, or tries. Like **Tinkerbell**, may require belief. O **hyperreal hyperstition**. *Welcome,* says Morpheus, *to the desert of the real.* O **mirror world**, O virtuous **cloud**, O VR google goggles....
. It's not hard to map. *See* **Carroll's** farewell,**** *see* **Borges** micro,***** *see* maps overtake their subjects; *see* Baudrillard's *information devouring its own contents*; *see* social media FOMO trumping **IRL** dance parties.

452 *See* **NewSpace**, New Glenn, New Armstrong, New Shepard.

453 The scientific theory that life on Earth originated elsewhere & was carried here, like seeds on galactic winds, so much flotsam & jetsam, spores that piggy backed on asteroids or by alien **birds** intending (or not) to return, stuff left by purpose or accident...from whom, from which, as from Earth's womb, we are descended.

Or, as *directed* **panspermia**[*6] advocates have it, the theory that organic matter necessary for generating life was left by some intelligence hoping for progeny, a theory which, incidentally, supports an Earth womb exodus as a pre-destined reunion w/our father.[*7]

---

* **WG at 50**. Whereas estimates place a mere 128 satellites in orbit the day of her birth, not including the moon in Libra.
** Current estimates place the pieces of orbiting, *un-cataloged* debris at 170 million, any one of which, improperly intercepted, could launch a cascade of explosions, generating a satellite-nullifying smog w/inestimable effects. Despite potentially cataclysmic circumstances a *Forbes* journalist notes, "Good news!" It's in **Musk's** interest to keep the worst from happening!
*** *See also* Bubo, a mechanical owl made by Hephaestus & gifted to Perseus in the 1981 **fantasy** *Clash of the Titans.*
**** *Sylvie and Bruno Concluded*, the second volume of **Carroll's** last novel, 1893.
***** "**On Exactitude in Science**" a single paragraph short story of an elaborate, abandoned, full scale map, 1946, inspired by Carroll.
*6 Though *directed panspermia* is considered a fringe theory, *pseudo panspermia*, the notion that an influx of diverse organic & inorganic materials seeded the Earth via asteroids & comets after its geological formation, is widely entertained by evolutionary scientists, reinforced by the discovery of microbes in extraplanetary substances in the 1970s. **Panspermia**, in its modern iteration was first proposed by Swedish scientist Svante Arrheius (1908), in answer to the evolutionary question not explicitly addressed by **Darwin**, where did organic matter come from?
*7 How's that for **eternal return**. *What happened before will happen again.* Then will we deposit our own **sperm** on future planets? *See* **Starbuck**. *See* **Nietzsche**. *See* ***Battlestar Galactica**. See* Fascism. *See* the 2024 election. *See* revolution?

terraform[454]...a method of renovating **Mars**[455] might include offloading our greenhouse gasses...win win! Or outfitting it w/**mirrors** to catch more rays...provisioning the already crimson planet w/a tanning bed.[456]

But the big problem is the iron planet, once shrouded in its own cuddly atmospheric blanket, lost its dynamo. No magnetism? No atmosphere. No atmosphere? No air. No air? No happy human lair.

*to farm/what makes none sick...***WG** wonders what miracles of innovation, what mastermind genius, will yield humanoid health on **terraformed** planets when what we grow on this one—the one that grew *us*—now industrialized, genetically modified, processed w/exponentially advancing efficiency to prolong shelf life *en masse*, makes **Earthlings** sick.

*bodies suited...*if the human body is a suit outfitted to Earth, it makes sense, another planet might just require a good tailor. *See* the Borg.[457] *See* NeuraLink.[458] *See* **WALL-E**.[459]

*red velvet cake...*Bakers who deploy beets for its hue may think it a red velvet fundament. In truth, the old root's new. The namesake tint was first caused by a chemical reaction between acid & cocoa, till red food coloring upped the ante. Amid **WWII** when superfluous red dye got nixed folks growing Victory gardens discovered the dirty **Earthling**'s lusciousness.

---

454 Another entry under **hyperreal**, **terraform**, first appears in a 1942 sci-fi short story, "Collision Orbit," by Jack Williamson & is later adopted by scientists w/designs on extending human habitat through planetary re-engineering. Among terraforming's earliest apostles, **Carl Sagan** had eyes on **Venus**, but ditched the goddess of love in favor of **Mars**. For all its problems—lack of atmosphere, frigidity, etc.—the war **god** was just more reasonable. Typical.

In 1972 chemist **James Lovelock** & microbiologist Lynn Margulis published the Gaia Hypothesis, proposing that living organisms interact w/their inorganic surroundings to form synergistic, self-regulating systems that co-create environment. **Lovelock** then applied his thesis to Martian **terraforming** in a 1984 book co-authored w/Michael Allaby, *The Greening of Mars*, describing how adding chlorofluorocarbons to its scant atmosphere might trigger a strong greenhouse effect. Trouble is, w/o magnetic attraction operating at its core, a cozy atmospheric blanket, however aggressively knit will be subject to galactic winds...*See* **"You've Lost that Loving Feelin,"** by The Righteous Brothers, 1964.

455 Thought to have been once lush in water & atmosphere, scientists posit **Mars** took the brunt of the **Late Heavy Bombardment**, a cataclysmic comet & asteroid shower—a compound trauma globally exhausting.

456 *Stop me if you've heard this one before**, matter is neither created nor destroyed. So whence the velvet to make **Mars** some new drapes? *See also How Stella Got Her Groove Back*, 1998.

457 **Alien** species of the *Star Trek* fantasy, evil, cybernetic, all consuming, linked via *hive mind*. Hive mind!—O Earthly honeys notwithstanding**—stuff of nightmares. Hive mind! The ubiquitous social media salutation, communal resourcefulness notwithstanding, incites **WG** grimace.***

458 **Musk's****** neurotech attempt to capitalize human-computer interfaces.*****

459 A dystopian sci-fi **romance** from Disney Pixar™, in which a sentient robot left to sort waste on vacated Earth, stows away to an off-world human colony to find his sweetheart. A visually arresting charmer of minimal dialog; a dystopian **fantasy** of narcoticized civilization, 2008, sadly eclipsed by global recession.

---

* *See* The Smiths, 1987 single...before the anti-pop **idol** went solo. But not before claiming celibacy. O **mono**nymous Morrissey, who neither threads nor buries the needle. Troubling, **rockstar.**
** Whose sweet fill cups—holy honeycomb—masterclass in architecture—
*** & yet! delights in the anarchies of the **hacker** group **ANONYMOUS!**
**** Asked to donate to World Food Programme & other such, **Musk**, wealthiest man in the universe, declines. For cause cites a species-persevering preference in colonizing **Mars**. **Bezos** follows suit.
***** **Musk** bought the company name from Pedram Moseni & Randolf Nudo, neuroscientists working on an implant to help those w/traumatic brain injury. Preliminary testing was promising but, unable to secure additional funding, they were dead in the water. So when offered tens of thousands for their name from an **anonymous** buyer, Moseni & Nudo agreed.

a fool... in occult **Tarot**, the shoeless, singing **protagonist**, little **dog** at his side, approaching a drop-off. Harbinger of possibility, **dreaming** impossible beauty.[461] Perpetually optimistic/naïve.[462] *See also* divine madness, sacred **fool**.[463] *See* **clowns**, creepy! The bedeviled servant of **Faustus**. Poltergeist. **Sideshow Bob**. Pennywise.

*He...O helium...*atomic number 2, first of the noble gasses.[464] Colorless, odorless, inert, nontoxic. 2nd lightest, 2nd most abundant element in the observable universe. Child of fusion & decay. Big bang progeny, whence pair-bonded helium-4, w/its *doubly magic*[465] nucleus primordial. Perpetual voyager drawn to the expanse beyond. Named for the sun, whence its discovery in the solar eclipse of 1868. Will buoy your blue balloon,[466] but given free reign, will take it from you. Made new in the nuclear fusion of **stars**.

trash of radical radio action \[467]...what helium remains on Earth is mostly of radioactive decay,[468] the primordial pair-bonds of yore, long since run away.

*were he in/strument...***WG** thinks his balloon tethers suggest a **double bass**.

*kaleid/oscope...*from the Greek *skopeō* (to look, to examine), *kalos* (beauty) & eidos (that unseen). An optical instrument of **wonder**,[469] constructed of interfacing **mirrors** that perpetuate a transitory image in radial **symmetry**. A whole made of fragment. The unfixing of stained **glass**. A mercurial mandala.

---

460 **"Send in the Clowns"**...Not a call for more egomaniacal jesters...but a song from **Stephen Sondheim's** *A Little Night Music*,* recorded by Judy Collins for *Judith,* 1975.** A melancholy reflection of missed **romantic** opportunity, sung by the **heroine** in Act Two, an actress who, after refusing his many proposals realizes she loves a man now married. The title? Theatrical shorthand—if the show is going poorly, *send in the clowns...*or resort to jokes.

461 *Only **fools**/go on tending/roses without gloves. See **A Wake with Nine Shades**,* 2019. *See* the limited edition, ***Infernal Spits***, an according book housed in a makeshift matchbox, *for matches not made in heaven.*

462 Pet slur of early **Superman villains**, especially the scientists. As in, "Beware—you **fools**!...Total destruction will come to those who laughed at me and failed to heed my warnings!" **Fleisher's** *Superman* "The Mad Scientist."

463 ***Paradise*** *is less plausible than hell but it is surely no less real.* **Charles Baxter**, "Rhyming Action."

464 When **WG** completes a close draft of **"Send in the Clowns"** the morning of her twenty-fifth **wedding** anniversary & reads it to her **husband** he first asks *are you sure it's a noble gas, then, did you know when helium is released it isn't bound by gravity or atmosphere....it lifts off & just keeps going.* She was & didn't. Indeed, love, indeed.

465 ***Magic*** when the number of individuals bound together, in this case 2,*** make the bond stable.

466 & inhaled will temporarily freeze your vocal chords, raising the timbre an octave or two. *See also* **Chipmunk**.

467   The backslash (\) they say is useless unless
         you're a computer or a computer
         programmer in need of an escape
         character to differentiate between characters
         that is   to articulate sets   make separate beds
         like how the heart has four monsoon balloons
         that doctors need sometimes to stop
         talking lest the whole thing pop.

468 W/limited deposits caught in the Earth's crust entangled w/others.

469 Intended as "rational" amusement by Scottish inventor David Brewster who patented his invention in 1817 after witnessing too many people ogling deficient copies. *See also* ***A Treatise on the Kaleidoscope***, w/diagrams.

---

* A 1973 musical inspired by Ingmar Bergman's 1955 film *Smiles of a Summer Night,* which also inspired **Woody Allen's** *Midsummer Night's* **Sex** *Comedy*, 1982.
** Which **WG's** parents (55 years **married**) let sometimes spin.
*** Other spell bindings—for **polys** & folks who play the lottery—occur at 8, 20, 28, 50, 82 & 126...

*that **god** all/seeing by whose/light we play at/oath k e e p i n g*...Helium's namesake, **Helios**, divine chariot driver, who draws the primordial fire across the sky[470] & because he's got the **overview**/topsight, because he's all-seeing[471] (providing there's light to see by),[472] a good guy to swear by.[473]

***chipmunk** tunes*...music of the platinum, grammy-winning band of virtual rodents, striped, known variously as **The Chipmunks**, Alvin & the Chipmunks & **Alvin, Simon & Theodore**. Brainchild & tech innovation of **Ross Bagdasarian**, creator of the 1958 "**Witch Doctor**."[474] The revolutionary technique— recording his voice at half speed then playing it back at full, an octave higher, is now mimicked by many, e.g. **Kanye West**[475] (*see* chipmunk soul).

In the early 60s, CBS ran an animated series of the 'munks[476] anthropomorphized antics in primetime. Though initial ratings stank they soared in syndication & after **Bagdasarian**'s death in 1972, Ross B. Jr. took up the mantle. *See also* **double** take.[477]

impervious isolationist...given free reign, both singles & pair bonds, gallop off into the sunset.

*wannabe **Beaver Cleaver** families*...ah, ***Leave It to Beaver**,*[478] or rather, leave it to white-collar **Ward**[479] & apron-adorned **June**,[480] model parents teleported from the 50s to populate 80s childhoods in syndication. A *shining beacon*

---

470 **WG** has a vague memory of *Chariots of Fire*—was it good? Were there chariots? (It was not *Ben Hur*.) A man ran along a shore; an **epic** theme song dubbed him **hero**.

471 *See also* satellite **surveillance**, *see* broad band internet.

472 But also when there's no light, like when we need an MRI, helium cools the magnets so we don't combust. Essential to producing the semiconductors essential to computers, tablets, TVs, phones... *See also* **mirror worlds**.

473 Not so much a 'good guy' as well poised to see & strike down whosoever reneges & dishonors him. Of course many vows are broken by dead of night, cover of night, in one-night stands, by midnight oil, ships passing in the night, a long kiss goodnight, wearing nighties, thieves in the night, while the night is still young, as creatures of night, going bump in the night, when all **cats** are gray, the easier to fly, how then do we keep faith, do we not rue the night, how sleep, or is this why, nighty night, we try & sometimes fail to sleep at night?

474 A duet between himself & himself bewitched, topped billboard charts for 3 weeks.

475 No comment.

476 Inspired by a real rodent interposing his car as he cruised Sequoia National Park (*see* big meet small), the musician created the twitchy personas, now w/their own **Hollywood Star**. *See* hyperreal.

477 The Chipmunk discography includes over 55 albums & counting, not including re-releases. Their albums are comprised almost entirely of covers.*

478 A tv sit-com (1958-1963) chronicling the **blunders** of "Beaver"** (**Theodore**) **Cleaver**, a schoolboy who lives in small town America w/his parents & elder brother.*** Perpetually trustful & naïve (*see also* ***SpongeBob***), Beave is often led astray, as when his friends convince him to break into the principal's office to assess a fantastical spanking machine.**** Alas, the sleuth gets trapped in the sanctum after hours, disgraced when escape necessitates the Fire Department.

479 What did he do? Nobody knows! But his going & coming made the world possible; success evidenced by the work's invisibility (**nevermind** the man behind the curtain).

480 Ever the spring air, w/her string of pearls & high heels—the former to hide a scar & the latter for authorial stature over the child actors.*****

---

* E.g. "**romantic** goofball," **Kurt Cobain**, owned 4 sealed copies of *The Chipmunks Sing the Beatles*. Presumably a fifth copy was opened & played.

** The origin of **Beave**'s nickname remains a mystery until the series finale, when we discover it's the evolution of mispronouncement by young **Wally** addressing his baby brother: *Theodore* turned *Tweeter*, thence *Beaver*.

*** Handsome & good at everything (multiple sports, dating), **Wally** is a benevolent child-parent go-between w/a considerable fan base, but—though he sometimes comes to the rescue—is not our **hero**.

**** O to tender the tragedy as pseudo-**sex**ual comedy!—who among us hasn't found trouble looking for what isn't there.

***** Though authority garnered by height is undermined in script, "just wait until your father gets home." O sweet moral instruction bequeathed father to son, privilege of two parent home w/o which—*a generation of men raised by women*—we devolve to **Fight Club**?

for that first generation of broken families.[481] Oh cleaving **Cleavers!** O (thermal) nuclear![482] O conservative ideal inciting clinging & punk anarchy.[483] Truth is, despite its White picket fence,[484] *Leave It* was about a kid—the befuddled boy of **wonder bread**—for whom the world—despite post-war boom economy, super power semi-stability & pre-adolescent simplicity—was oft confusing & disappointing, as evidenced by his scuff-kneed catch phrase, *gee Wally.*

spontaneous combustion…when heat generated cannot escape, as w/materials given to insulate, e.g. hay put up wet—woosh—gone, etc.. May also apply to coal, cotton, peat, nitrate film, compost, oil rags, seed oils, the dried flesh of coconuts, manure, pistachio nuts, humans.[485]

---

481 In its 6-season run, ***Leave It to Beaver*** never made top 30, yet beloved (& scorned) in memory…& **syndication**. A made-for-TV reunion in 1983 revised the nuclear binding, w/**the Beave** a divorced father of sons living w/his widowed mother. A spin-off series followed.

482 A metaphor for the family unit coined in the early 20th century, as extended family bonds weakened & scientists split the atom.

483 *See cleave*, a contronym.**

484 *See also* the **American Dream**.

485 The case for our own sudden & brilliant end, stuff of much myth, but only anecdotal evidence…

---

* Ancient beavers—reports **WG**'s eldest on his 25th birthday—were industrious **terraformers**, disrupting water ways to create lush ponds & fertile bottomlands. Their lodge & bank den communities changed the landscapes of North America & Europe, prolific families dwelling in harmony w/ their neighbors via the clearly demarcated territories of *dear enemies*…

The species nearly but not quite hunted to extinction…

** *See* see saw. *See* saw. See.

BOYS BEHIND GLASS:

THE ORIGIN STORY

I met Jenny Walton at Vermont Studio Center, a wondrous artist residency tucked in a rural valley, attuned, nevertheless, to tidal shifts. That was in January, 2017. Obamas decamped; Trump lurched; pussyhats marched; Me Too amassed. In other news my marriage was on the rocks. I buried myself in multiple projects, including the artifact that became *Her Read, A Graphic Poem*.

Jenny and I presented at the same artist talk and admired each other's work. She had recently completed *Match/Enemy*, a series documenting her experience on OK Cupid, and I was intrigued by the way her watercolor gallery of algorithmically matched men became a kaleidoscopic self-portrait. On closer examination, what the self-selected images revealed about the men, intentionally or not, was fascinating. And though, in theory, the men seeking romance had submitted themselves to female inspection, many portraits seemed to project their own gaze back on the female surveyor. Curiouser and curiouser, I approached Walton about a poetic response to her images and she agreed.

Over the next eight years, I drafted my response. I thought I'd write boxy prose poems to mirror the square portraits, but what came were sonnets. Duh. A fair form for romantic inquiry by a woman struggling in a marriage older than online dating, my little songs hypothesizing a third person. I imagined a woman imagining men, their possible futures w/wonderment.

Not only did third person match my voyeuristic relationship to the work, but it offered a "topsight" view of the double gaze which I began to see as an intimacy infinity mirror. Through the sonnets I attempted to see beyond 2-D projections, what aspects of selves, male & female, surveyor or surveilled, audience or performer, tried to hide off screen.

Over the years as themes emerged, I began to envision a meta-text to illuminate cultural and scientific allusions, particularly those that offered commentary on intimacy and masculinity. As has been noted elsewhere, the men that "appear" in the 200+ images of Walton's *Match/Enemy* deploy anonymity to varying degrees; of further note: the vast majority appear to be White. Walton shared that as a resident of Washington DC, the lack of racial diversity conveyed herein is atypical of her matches, which, given that what distinguishes this subset is portrait anonymity, suggests White men are more reluctant to subject themselves to the gaze. Or perhaps feel more entitled to refusal.

I began to think of the accompanying text, "The Speculum", as kin to "murder boards" by which detectives track suspects, motives, timelines, theories. The murder board analogy appeared late in my thinking, just after the U.S. 2024 election, the maximalist glossary expanding to something less bulletin board and more the cold case papered study of a beaten detective (single or divorced, of course), obsessed w/the one that got away.

The title *Boys Behind Glass* also came to me late. In my mind "behind glass" refers to the ways we reduce ourselves and others to images in screens, cameras, mirrors, and the way men in the public eye broadcast control. Conversely it nods, at "behind bars" and the "glass ceiling," prisons of hierarchy. "Boys" calls to my mind, "boys will be boys" & bro-culture, but also the innocence of adolescence, the giddiness of new romance, and the vulnerability of the child self.

I live in a swing state, home of the Michigan Militia. I have spent my life in intimate relationship with many boys and men: decades in the male-dominated industry of construction, twenty-five years of marriage, I am mother of two men in their 20s and a daughter & sister. As an educator and literary citizen, in so far as I am able, I have endeavored to light othered voices and in the years of this project's development, amid so much else, the undertaking sometimes seemed trivial. But in 2025, returning to the inaugural ground on which, for me, the investigation begun, I feel newly compelled to shine a light down populous rabbit holes, for hurt places in the dim warrens beneath the stronghold.

MATCH/ENEMY:

THE ARTIST'S NOTES & REFLECTION

Match/Enemy developed out of Singles Faire, a series of paintings in watercolor I did that looked at the nonverbal communication of attraction and rejection of singles through awkward postures of physical therapy diagrams. *Match/Enemy* is about the judgment and personal taste that we make in digital glances through dating apps.

Match/Enemy shows a small sampling of men in my dating pool from the OkCupid app from 2014 to 2016. It reveals how each chose to portray himself through a profile picture that obscured, altered, hid, or used alternate images to represent themselves. These paintings integrate narrative and portraiture through a reflective lens turned toward the social and personal habits of single men. It magnifies the way people present themselves to potential mates online, how they communicate through body language, and how they choose to feather themselves in the mating rituals of modern singles (or not-so single looking for something on the side). Interestingly, most dating apps now require users to be identifiable in their profile pictures.

As the project developed, I started looking at the female power structure and how a woman has more choices, options, and leverage. Dating sites can be seen as fantasy shopping. How do we respond to the unintentional or intentional branding, advertising, and fantasy play that potential mates utilize in their profile pictures? How are those ideas conveyed through environment, gaze, cropping, focus, and mathematical algorithms developed by programmers for dating sites? These are some of the questions that I explored through these portraits.

Painting images allowed both myself and the viewer to get to know these individuals better through their choice of image. Each portrayal was painted in roughly the time it would take for a first date (sometimes I invested too much time on them, an apt metaphor for dating).

Online dating is like speed dating or playing twenty questions—not enough time to explore through conversation or physical chemistry. Through a series of questions and preferences the OKCupid users answer, we are algorithmically sorted and assigned a percentage of how much we Match and also how much we would be Enemies. How do the percentages of Match and Enemy influence the way that I view a picture? What emotions does a picture evoke when thinking of that person as a mate?

Utilizing the critique of the female gaze allowed me to deconstruct meaning within these images as I took them apart and puzzled them back together in paint. Whether a profile pic started to convey a fun time, potential danger, illusions of fantasy, or romance book covers, the power of choice was mine to control the connection with these individuals.

These works are in watercolor on 9 x 12" paper with a 7 x 8" image, approximately four times the size of the dating app photos on my iPhone screen, where most of my "shopping" research occurred.

These paintings were displayed in a grid of 200 works split in two sets. The paintings were placed according to OkCupid's percentage of match from 100% to 0% or mismatch (Enemy) from 0% to 100%. The Match set went numerically from best to worst match and the Enemy set least to worst enemy. This made a 6 x 35' wall installation that offered a broad look at contemporary masculinity. These portraits offer promises, intrigue, fantasy, passion, beauty, and a chance to explore desire. In the end, all of these, because they lacked clear identification through a recognizable face, were a no: I wouldn't date any of them.

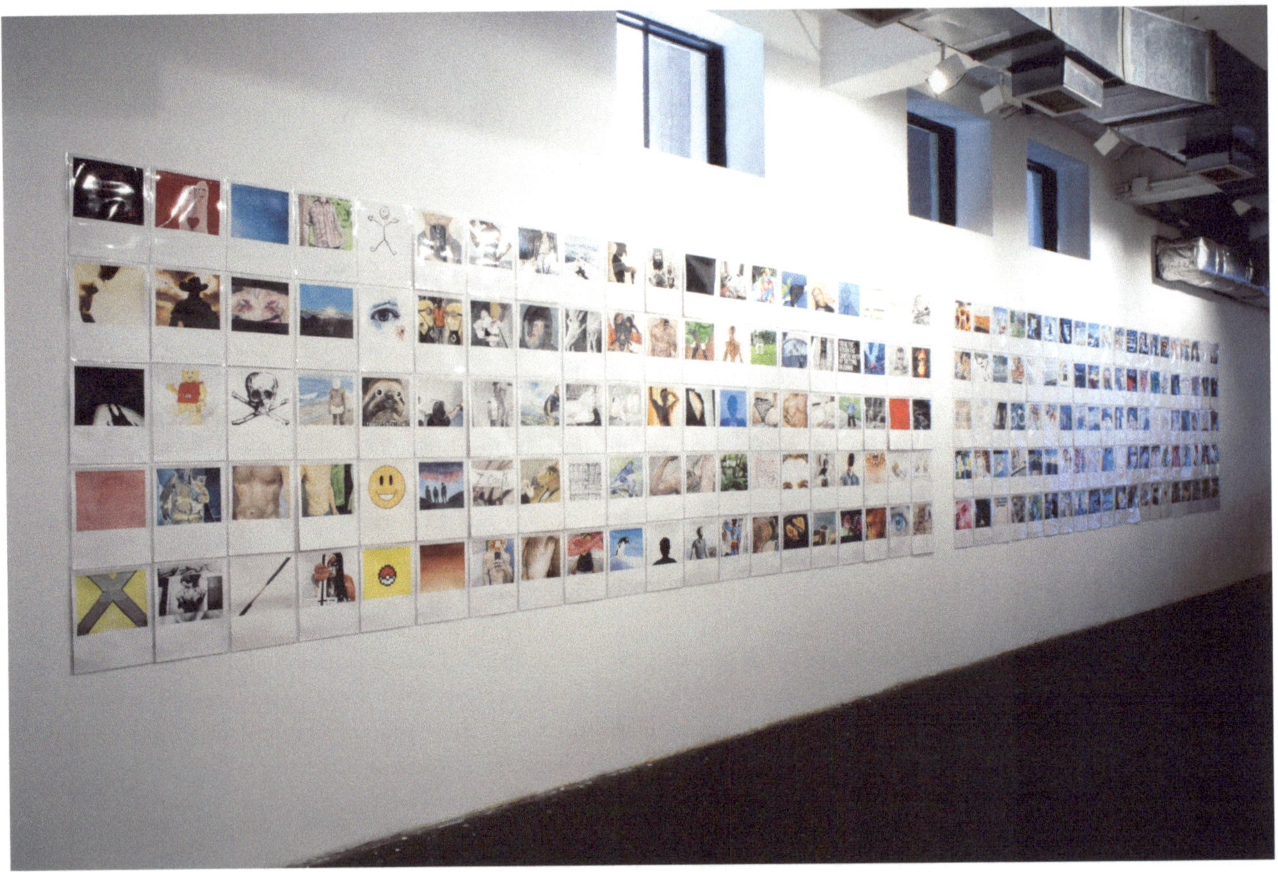

85/9   COVER A well-shaved head…a balding progression or an advertisement for other clean things?

97/5   It was interesting that this was the highest match I received even outside the confines of this project. It exemplified the culture of masculinity in which I grew up in Eastern Washington, that of a rural lifestyle, hard work, farm life. There is a casualness to his posture, an unhurried waiting, exuding confidence, strength & a hint of cockiness that I was drawn to.

58/31   There was something about the arresting portrait, specifically in the eyes & their shine that drew me. The pensive look & cropped composition of the photo were small clues to the trouble lurking behind them.

92/0   I questioned whether this portrait was a suggestion, like many others. Was this a once-in-a-lifetime trip or a regular hobby that would require a new wardrobe suitable to a yeti. And who took the photo? A buddy? A family member? A significant other? This image reminded me of the Cascades at the height of ski season. I was particularly happy with the background as I was able to retain the feeling of brightly crisp & cold alpine landscapes.

47/22   This was such an intimate photograph with recent evidence of another's mark. Not my preference, but maybe for the next person.

Technically, I got the freckles right. I never thought I would paint butt hair, but there you have it.

00/91   I am a risk-averse person, gambling—as the first impression— makes it a solid NO. The potential bonfire this alludes to put it in the "enemy" camp for me, even without the 00 Match percentage.

14/46   It was a disappointment that someone who loved this floofer was such a poor match. I'd take the dog though.

06/39   Who doesn't like a gooey grilled cheese? I love them. These looked like sandwiches to be proud of, good bread, solid amount of melty cheese, maybe a few too many sesame seeds, but that can be overlooked. Nicely browned & one for each of us. There would be crumbs.

03/66   Hands behind his back, chains on nipples, waiting for them to be pulled, yanked? Also why was his skin so orange? Belly protruding below the chain resting on it. No hair to get caught.

He couldn't have taken this photo, unless timers were used. It found it strange, while painting the work in Match/Enemy, all the photographs from the vantage of an intimate participant, advertising for a new one.

87/20   The question for me was, is the intent of this image more to proselytize or to convey self-realization. The posture of relaxed arrogance also caught my curiosity. What I assume are chakras in this image are something that I had seen previously in illustrations rather than imposed over photographs of people.

I knew this image would be hard to paint and waited until midway through the project to tackle it. In watercolor is notoriously difficult to keep the luminosity, opposite of traditional oil or acrylic painting. Light and light colors are the first layers in watercolor, then one progressively gets darker and more opaque with the paint, rather than adding them on top of layers as in oils. So, figuring out how to make someone glow with Chakras, keep the vegetation highlighted behind, and obscure a lot of the background in darkness was a learning process for me.

00/96   I used to work with a film festival that would screen movies at the Navy Memorial in Washington, D.C. In the underground museum, they display a diving suit very similar to this. It might even be the same one. I selected thinking though we'd been in the same place, had vastly different ideas according to the algorithm.

78/24   The bright pink satin of what looks to be a corset drew me in. It's practically fluorescent. The flesh around the tattoos seemed raw, freshly inked or recently hit, sensitive and vulnerable. The birds seemed sweet in contrast. I used Opera Pink throughout, in the corset & the flesh, to mimic the fluorescence.

45/83   This was a hard one to paint. The words in their profile made it clear they wanted to be demeaned while cleaning. Emotionally, it was hard to reconcile the shame they were seeking, it was heart wrenching. I tried to paint this one as quickly as possible and leave it in the pile.

47/45   I thought a lot about including this one. To me it was far more about power - more about exercises & excesses that religion has enacted upon women to control, contain & keep them, dogmas built by men.

51/44   These are the only two pieces in Match/Enemy that I planned to be side by side. It was a visual representation of the sacred & profane: two opposites that encompassed much of the project.

46/37, 37/39, 38/56 O! the many bare chests! — There were sooooo many more that it was often hard to pick which ones to paint. The telling clues in the background, objects held, postures & gestures helped me choose. It became a great technical challenge to paint chest hair (hairy bodies in general) and water droplets.

07/59, 00/50, 45/47 Similar to the torsos there were plenty of crotch shots to choose from. Some subtle, some not so subtle. My challenges in all were the topography and perspective. Often I felt the images were more about looking at oneself than attracting my gaze.

33/38   Horse's head, marijuana pipe, Carhartt jacket, undistinguishable background that looks like a derelict garage. Seems like a bad college comedy.

76/23   Stormy skies at the beach, a couple in silhouette, shadows of themselves, walking along...away...toward...? Who knows, but it didn't give me the romantic feeling that I think was intended. I was interested in how to paint the atmosphere around them. Certainly it's a precursor to my current work.

89/19   There were quite a few non-objective fields of color. Some black, some in other colors. I picked each of them as a resting space from the visual circus that would appear around them in the final presentation.

Technically, it was challenging to create a matte field of even color with little variance. To paint them required a slow build of darkness, eliminating luminosity and light. Creating nothingness.

45/38   This was a hard one to paint. The words in their profile made it clear they wanted to be demeaned while cleaning. Emotionally, it was hard to reconcile the shame they were seeking, it was heart wrenching. I tried to paint this one as quickly as possible and leave it in the pile.

94/06   I chose this more for the water than anything else. I painted it with a strong sense of being under it. Of being under the anonymous diver, looking up as they obscure the light.

27/55   No. Clearly a black-and-white cartoon advertisement. Just no.

56/35   To me, this image is about white-collar masculinity & power—strong hands that have built empires. With the black, white, and gray tones, it screams of marketing, fantasy, glossy luxury ads. The hands also reminded me of the muscled and weathered hands of the blue-collar men I grew up with.

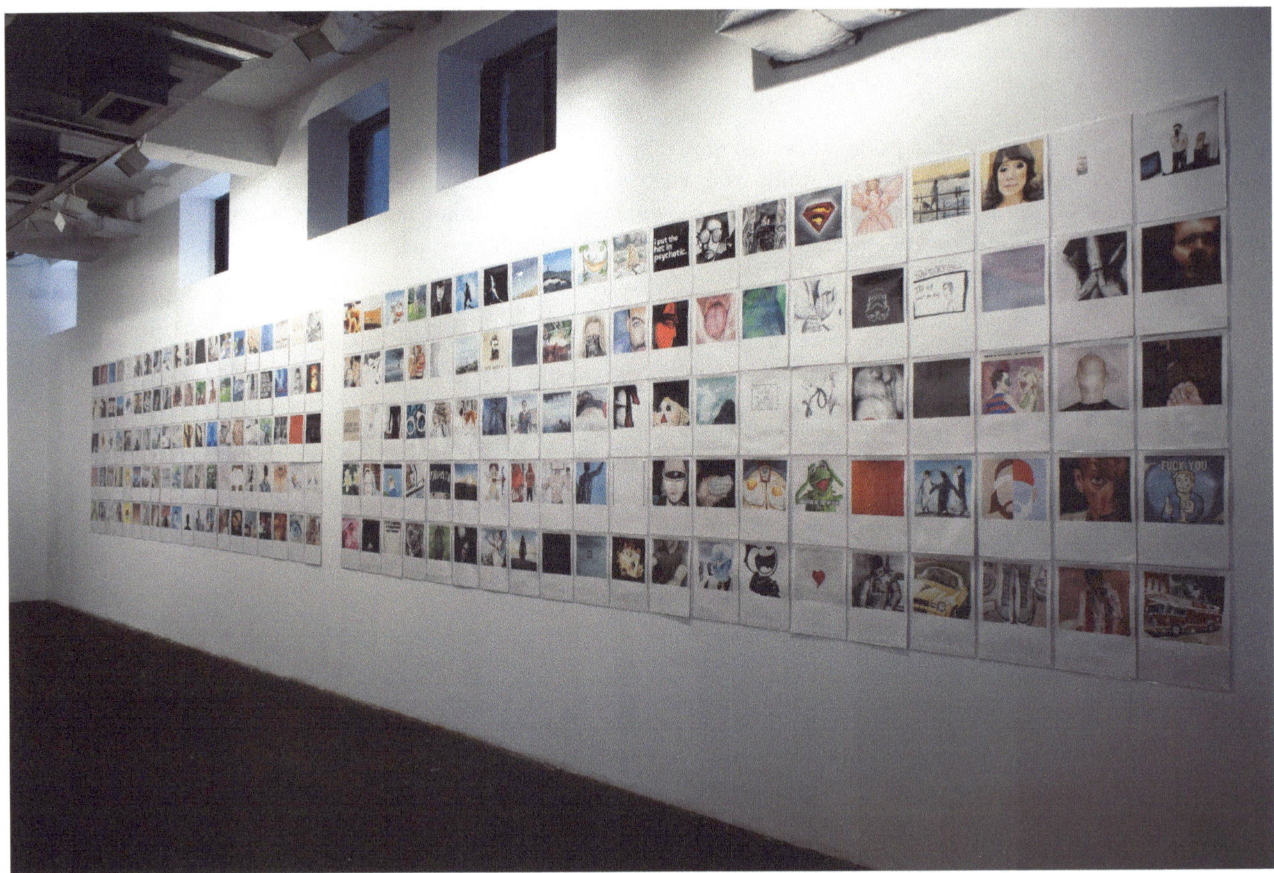

The image played along with romance novels I listened to while painting Match/Enemy. Many were period romances by writers like Julia Quinn, Eloisa James, Lisa Kleypas, and Sarah McLean. I was drawn to dynamic female characters that had strong opinions and weren't afraid of voicing them.

76/22   Blue eye, bloody red heart bruise —I saw heartache and potential for violence. I read the red as a cut on the cheekbone as from a punch to the face.

26/43   Eyes looking skyward, a very small hint of blue, overexposed forehead of pure white paper. No middle ground in this piece. It felt empty rather than hopeful.

02/43   There were a lot of close-up eyeballs to choose from. Like chests, erections, supermen & cowboys, this was another tropes in the advertisements. I chose to paint the ones that created variety within the monotony.

53/25   This reminded me of driving through a white-out, no definition, just hoping that you get there safely.
58/48, 08/50, 0/0E   Some Supermen seemed to be Halloween costumes, some projecting, some hopeful embodiment or idolization, some superhero comic book nerdiness. The one that drew the most empathy and understanding from me appears later.

91/10, 63/29, 79/20 I have a special place in my heart for cowboys. I grew up in the west, where there were bull riders, wannabe bull riders, farmers, and cowboys coming together for rodeos often in the late summer. The County Fair and Rodeo was a special time of year that was perfect before school started, when the days seemed longer and everyone showed off the best of their labor. The images I selected out of the many were more about the iconography of nostalgia than yearning for reality.

25/47   This image was among a handful of others that were hard for me to include. This is such an intimate showcasing of desire suggesting a need to be understood and accepted for who this person is in private versus in public. It was clearly a home photo shoot. I felt it was an asking rather than a demand.

00/90   This was such a lonely and desolate image to me. A lack of warming light, the old-school square clock reading 9:37 a.m.? Or p.m.? It's hard to tell. It seemed endless rather than timeless.
21/87, 29/47 This image of Cupid reminded me of the saccharine colors and narratives of French rococo painting. Fragonard's swing paintings and Boucher's coupled tableaus are references in my head with their coded underpinnings in idyllic forested settings. The leering mischievous look this Cupid gives is alluding to narratives, yet untold, that could very well be nested in one of those paintings.

In contrast, in a very outward gesture, this gentleman, whose identity is obscured while standing in a forested landscape, does not hide his message through subtle narratives or suggestive looks like the rococo painters. Whether his gesture is a "get outta here" or a "come over here" is left to the viewer's interpretation.

73/13   There was a mystery to this man in a long unused form of protection, a knight's helmet. Is it a regular costume for a reenactor or a one-off for Halloween? Is this someone with a thirst for the brutal violence, chivalry, the romanticism of the past? What is he looking at, bracing for, hoping to gain?

00/99   Including this image was a no brainer. An Elvis, particularly a late stage representation of the bygone icon made sense, portraying someone so much more than the man hiding behind a glittery costume.

45/38   This was a hard one to paint. The words in their profile made it clear they wanted to be demeaned while cleaning. Emotionally, it was hard to reconcile the shame they were seeking, it was heart wrenching. I tried to paint this one as quickly as possible and leave it in the pile.

68/18   It's the little toilet paper robot that could. It's such an adorable, nerdy thing. Particularly the whisk hanging out in the back says this guy is making plans. Pancakes in the morning maybe?

56/37   The irony that this cartoon is their first impression. It leads me to many questions like: Is it self-deprecating? An attack on the competition? And how old is this person? Is it an awkward pimply teenager or someone soliciting pity or empathy?

75/13   The Minions did it. But how does this guy fit into the caper? Is this just a quick photo op or a request to tag along on the next misadventure?

75-8   A comic dude in the landscape of nothingness. I grew up in a similar barren landscape. He was awkwardly placed in the landscape like an unwitting tourist on the dating scene. But if Henry Cavill were really on here, then, well, I guess I missed out.

56/42   Google, balloons, Pixar, nerdiness, smart, savvy, tech life. Squirrel!

Jenny Walton, 2025

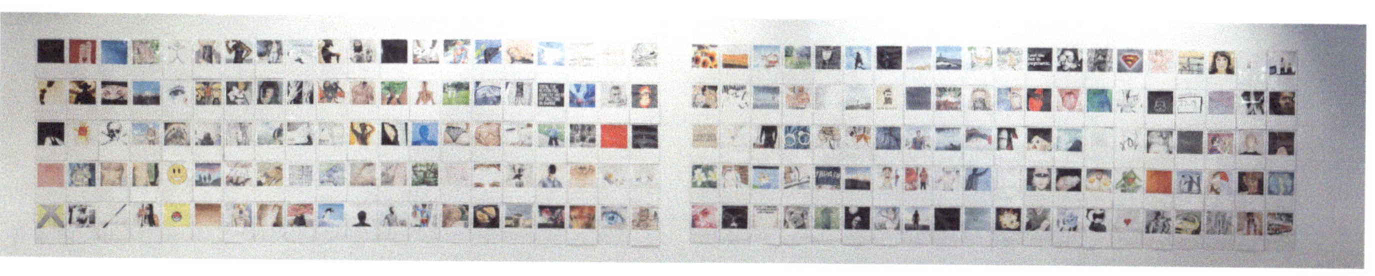

ANIMALS, IDEAS, OBJECTS, LOCALES

CHARACTERS, GODS, PEOPLE

Curtis, Ian, 120
Dante, 41, 87, 101-2, 104, 109, 119, 123-6, 144
Darling, Wendy, 135
Darwin, Charles, 62, 91, 118, 120, 134, 151
Day, Dorris, 13, 95, 100
Dent, Harvey, 90
    See also Two Face
Dickinson, Emily, 110, 122
Earthling, 124, 126, 152
Eliot, T. S., 91
Eros, 91, 137
    See also Cupid
Faustus, Doctor, 148, 153
Fincher, David, 93, 98
Fisher King, The, 98, 109, 141
Fitzgerald, Ella, 100, 106
Flynn, Errol, 108
Fonda, Jane, 94
Fool, the , 82, 85, 92, 153
    See also Clown, Joker
Ford, Harrison, 130
Garner, James, 95
Gay, Ross, 93, 142
Gelernter, David, 91, 143
General Lee, The, 101
God, gods, goddesses, 25, 29, 82, 85, 88, 90-3, 97, 104, 106,
121-3, 128, 139-140, 144, 152, 154
Grant, Cary, 95, 127
Gray, Dorian, 89, 124, 135
Gru, Felonius, 149
Gyllenhaal, Jake, 97
Hacker, 87, 128, 152
Hawkins, Yusuf, 100
Hays, Will H, 100, 126-7, 132
Helios, 154
Hintnaus, Tom, 105
Hitchcock, Alfred, 127
Holly, Buddy, 106, 124, 143
Homer, 123, 125, 138, 148,
Hook, Captain James, 135
    See also Pirate
Hope, Bob, 127
Hoyle, Edmund, 10, 92
Hudson, Rock, 95
Humbert, Humbert, 110
Husband, 90, 95-98, 104, 123, 129, 153
Huxley, Thomas Henry, 41, 120
Jason, 119
Jeans, James, 120
Jeffries, Michael, 105
Jennings, Waylon, 101, 124, 133
Jesus, 143-4
    See also Christ
Johnson, Lyndon B, 97, 137
Joker, The, 92, 107
Kaczynski, Ted, 70, 91, 142-3
Karen, 126
    See also Plankton
Kelly, Gene, 100
Kennedy, John F., 106, 108, 137, 147, 149
King, *ix*, *xiii*, 70, 96, 108, 120, 137, 139-41, 143

B.B.---, 106; ---Ahab, ---Arthur, 106; ---Lear, 139,
The Lion ---, 129; Martin Luther ---, Jr., 137, 143, 147; Nat ---
Cole, 106; Robert --- Merton, 138; Rodney --- , 137
    See also The Fisher King
Landseer, Edwin, 94
Lane, Lois, *vii*, 90, 124
Lazarsfeld, Paul Felix, 138
Ledger, Heath, 92
Lee, Spike, 100
Lennox, Annie, 88
Lonely Hearts Killers, 135
Lonely Island, The, 133
Lonos, 97
Lost Boys, 136
Love, Courtney, 106. 109, 121
Lovelock, James, 152
Luther, Lex, 128
Macedo, José Anibal, 112-4, 118
Macgyver, 53, 125
Major Tom, 92
Manson, Charles, 95
Marston, William Moulton, 150
McDonald, Dwight, 95
McDowell, Jonathan, 151
Melville, Herman, 129, 139
Mike the Headless Chicken , 89, 104
Minions, 78, 96, 101, 148, 161,
Monroe, Marilyn, 95, 106
Mulvey, Laura, 125, 139, 147
Musk, Elon, 98, 106, 119, 147, 152
Nabokov, Vladimir, 110
Narcissus, 91, 139
Narcissist, narcissist-, 110
Nelson, Horatio, 94
Nelson, Willie, 131, 133
Neo, 130
Newton, Isaac, 128
Nietzsche, Friedrich, 90, 100, 151
Nijinsky, Vaslav, 88
Nixon, Richard, 97, 100, 128, 137
Nothing, The, 101, 120
Nussbaum, Karen, 94
Oberon, aka Big O, 108
Pan, *ix*, 123
Parker, Dorothy, 124
Penelope, 123, 144
Persephone, 105
Peter Pan, 136, 144
Phoenix, Joaquin, 92
Pilgrim, 92, 151
Pitt, Brad, 98
Plankton, (Sheldon, Karen), 139
    See also WIFE
    See also Plankton (marine life)
Pollan, Michael, 146
Polonius, 120, 124
Porter, Darwin, 95
Protagonist, 98, 124-5, 148
    See also Hero
Proud Boys, 98
Puck, *ix*, 108, 137

ARTS & MEDIA

(SOME) TEXTS DIGESTED

"Abyss." *Google Books ngrams viewer.* https://books.google.com/ngrams/graph?content=abyss&year start=1900&year_end=2019&corpus=en-2019&smoothing=7&case_insensitive=false, last accessed Jun 18, 2025.

Acosta, Nicole. "Match Made in Hell: How the 'Lonely Hearts' Killers Seduced Their Prey with Newspaper Ads During Murderous Spree." *People,* 4, Jan 2025, https://people.com/lonely-hearts-killers-raymond-fernandez-martha-beck-match-made-hell-8767599, accessed Jan 11, 2025.

Adams, Lee. "True Romance Evolved Out of the Same Project as Natural Born Killers & Pulp Fiction." *SlashFilm.com,* Feb 25, 2023. https://www.slashfilm.com/1205004/true-romance-evolved-out-of-the-same-project-as-natural-born-killers-and-pulp-fiction/, last accessed, Jun 18, 2025.

Amsallem, Yaëlle. "Why Surfing Is the Antidote to the Relentless March of Capitalism." *The Conversation,* Sept 14, 2021. https://theconversation.com/why-surfing-is-an-antidote-to-the-relentless-march-of-capitalism-165147, last accessed Jun 16, 2025.

Andre, Brandon. "Male Model Posing Guide: 35 Poses to Help You Pose Like a Pro." By Brandon Andre, Aug 31, 2024, https://www.brandonandrephoto.com/blog/male-model-posing-guide, last accessed May 17, 2025.

"Andy Warhol. Shadows." *Guggenheim-bilbao.eus,* Feb 26, 2016. https://www.guggenheim-bilbao.eus/en/exhibitions/andy-warhol-shadow, last accessed Jun 18, 2025.

"Animal Attraction: The Many Forms of Monogamy in the Animal Kingdom." *NSF.gov,* Feb 13, 2013. https://www.nsf.gov/news/animal-attraction-many-forms-monogamy-animal#:~:text=Scientists%20now%20estimate%20that%20only,bird%20species%20were%20truly%20monogamous. last accessed Jun 18, 2025.

Areias J, Gato J, Moura-Ramos M. Motivations and Attitudes of Men Towards Sperm Donation: Whom to Donate and Why? *Sex Res Social Policy.* 2022;19(1):147-158. doi: 10.1007/s13178-020-00531-0. Epub 2021 Jan 27. PMID: 33527001; PMCID: PMC7838658.

Argun, Erin. "Ten Facts About Andy Warhol's Shadows." *MyArtBroker.com,* Aug 30, 2024. https://www.myartbroker.com/artist-andy-warhol/10-facts/10-facts-andy-warhol-shadows, last accessed Jun 16, 2025.

Baker, Peter. "The Men Who Still Love *Fight Club.*" *The New Yorker,* Nov 4, 2019, https://www.newyorker.com/culture/cultural-comment/the-men-who-still-love-fight-club, accessed Dec 1, 2024.

Baltimore Sun, The.

Barossa, Julia and Caroline Rooney. "Suffering, transience and immortal longings Salome between Nietzsche and Freud." *Journal of European Studies* (Vol. 33, Issue 3-4), Dec 2003, https://journals.sagepub.com/doi/abs/10.1177/0047244103040419, last accessed May 17, 2025.

Baxter, Charles. "Rhyming Action" *Michigan Quarterly Review,* Vol 35, issue 4, 1996.

Beccia, Carlyn. "A Ballsy History of Dick Pics: from Ancient Greece to today we can understand sexuality through penis art." *Conversations with Carlyn,* July 22, 2022, https://carlynbeccia.substack.com/p/a-ballsy-history-of-dick-pics, last accessed Feb 2, 2025.

Bell, Anna Lena Phillips. " 'This resonant, strange, vaulting roof': Contemporary Sonnets beyond Iambic Pentameter." *An Anthology of Poems and Essays,* edited by Dora Malech and Laura Smith. Iowa City: University of Iowa Press, 2023.

Berger, John. *Ways of Seeing.* Penguin, 1972.

Bimm, Jordan. "Rethinking the Overview Effect." *Quest: the History of Spaceflight.* Volume 21:1, 2014. https://gwern.net/doc/psychology/2014-bimm.pdf

Blanks, Tim. "History of the Male Supermodel." *VMan9*, Fall/Winter 2007, https://vmagazine.com/article/history-of-the-male-supermodel-2/, last accessed Feb 1, 2025.

Bloom, Harold. *The Anxiety of Influence: A Theory of Poetry*. New York: Oxford University Press, 1973.

Borges, Jorge Luis. "On Exactitude in Science." *Collected Fictions*, translated by Andrew Hurley. New York: Random House, 1998.

—. "The Library of Babel." *Ficciones*, trans by Emecé Editores. New York: Grove Press, 1962.

Boruch, Marianne. "Diagnosis, Poetry, and the Burden of Mystery." *New England Review*, 2015, Vol. 36. No. 2 (2015), pp. 23-36. https://www.jstor.org/stable/24772589, last accessed Dec 8, 2024.

Bueno, Antoinette. "5 Things You Didn't Know About Doris Day." *Y!Entertainment*, last updated May 19, 2019, https://www.yahoo.com/entertainment/5-things-didn-apos-t-165255256.html?guccounter=1, last accessed May 18, 2025.

Burley, Shane. "The Nihilism of Generation X is an Artifact of Privilige." *Medium*, April, 11 2020, https://medium.com/arc-digital/the-nihilism-of-generation-x-is-an-artifact-of-privilege-be897abd1db0, last accessed May 17, 2025

Butler, Judith. *Gender Trouble*, 1990.

Cable news networks.

Carroll, Michael P. "Praying the Rosary: The Anal-Erotic Origins of a Popular Catholic Devotion." *Journal for the Scientific Study of Religion*, vol. 26, no. 4, 1987, pp. 486–98. JSTOR, https://doi.org/10.2307/1387099. Accessed 8 Dec 2024.

"Cat Eye Lake Clocks and Ojibwe Metaphors." *Mii Dash Geget: Ojibwe, Algonquian languages, historical linguistics, and randomness*. April 20, 2021, updated July, 1, 2023. https://miidashgeget.wordpress.com/2021/04/20/cat-eye-lake-clocks-metaphors/, last accessed May 17, 2025.

Chudakov, Barry. "Consciousness in the Mirror: A Hopscotch History of Replacing the World." *Medium*, April 21, 2020, https://bchudakov.medium.com/consciousness-in-the-mirror-a-hopscotch-history-of-replacing-the-world-94e7bc94f122, last accessed Dec 17, 2024.

Christy, Kathrine. "Ulysses in Hell" *The Scarlett Review*, https://scarletreview.camden.rutgers.edu/archive/2017edition/ulyssesinhell.html. Last accessed Jun 17, 2025.

Clark, Tiana. "New Ways of Surviving: Writing Through A Global Pandemic." *Poets & Writers Magazine*, March/April 2021.

Crawford, Pippa. "Nijinsky on Nijinsky: the Rise and Fall of Ballet Russe." *Pushkin House*, March 3, 2020. https://pushkin-house.squarespace.com/blog/2020/3/1/nijinsky-on-nijinsky-decline-and-fall-of-the-ballet-russes, last accessed Jun 15, 2025.

Crum, Maddie. "*Fight Club* Author Reflects on Violence and Masculinity 20 Years Later." *Huffington Post*, Dec 6, 2016. https://www.huffpost.com/entry/fight-club-2-chuck-palahniuk_n_5845c35ae4b028b32338a632, last accessed Jun 18, 2025.

Conrad, Peter. "Nijinsky: A Life by Lucy Moore--review." *The Guardian*, May 5, 2013, https://www.theguardian.com/books/2013/may/05/nijinsky-lucy-moore-review

Corbett, Rachel. "From You Must Change Your Life: The Story of Rainer Maria Rilke and Auguste Rodin." *PoetryFoundation.org*, Aug 31, 2016. https://www.poetryfoundation.org/poetrymagazine/articles/90278/from-you-must-change-your-life-the-story-of-rainer-maria-rilke-and-auguste-rodin, last accessed Jun 18, 2025.

Cunha, Darlens. "Red pills and dog whistles: It is more than 'just the internet.'" *Aljazeera*, Sep. 6, 2020, https://www.aljazeera.com/opinions/2020/9/6/red-pills-and-dog-whistles-it-is-more-than-just-the-internet, accessed May 18, 2025.

Dahlin, Britt. "Peacock Courtship." *Lake Forest College News*, Feb 28, 2018, https://www.lakeforest.edu/news/peacock-courtship, last accessed May 17, 2025.

Dante.

The Darwin Correspondence Project. Keyword: peacock. https://www.darwinproject.ac.uk/search?keyword=peacock&tab=

"David Bowie made androgyny cool, and it was about time." *PBS News*, Jan 11, 2016. https://www.pbs.org/newshour/arts/david-bowie-made-androgyny-cool-and-it-was-about-time, last accessed May 17, 2025.

Dawkins, Richard, ed. *The Oxford Book of Modern Science Writing*. Oxford University Press, 2008.

"Deified as the voice of his generation Kurt Cobain lives" *Manila Bulletin*, 4 April, 2019. Gale In Context: Opposing Viewpoints, link.gale.com/apps/doc/A587239715/OVIC?u=umuser&sid=bookmark-OVIC&xid=4ef21f46. Accessed 24, January, 2025.

DeLuca, Leo. "Before Folding 30 Years Ago, the Sears' Catalog Sold Some Surprising Things." *The Smithsonian*, Jan 26, 2023. https://www.smithsonianmag.com/innovation/before-folding-30-years-ago-the-sears-catalog-sold-some-surprising-products-180981504/

Dent, Mark. "Why you never see "attractive" people on your OKCupid page: founder reveals dating sites secrets during Philly visit" *BillyPenn.com*, Feb 10, 2015, https://billypenn.com/2015/02/10/why-you-never-see-attractive-people-on-your-okcupid-page-founder-reveals-dating-sites-secrets-during-philly-visit/

Dumanis, Michael. "Subverting the Tradition in The Tradition." *An Anthology of Poems and Essays*, edited by Dora Malech and Laura Smith. Iowa City: University of Iowa Press, 2023.

Ebbs, Tommy. "How David Bowie Inspired DC's Joker and Two Other Powerful Comic Book Devils" *CBR.com*, Jan 16, 2022. https://www.cbr.com/david-bowie-joker-inspiration/, last accessed Jun 18, 2025.

Edwards, Elisabeth. "Bizarre Facts about Errol Flynn Almost Too Bizarre to Be True." *TheVintageNews.com*, Nov 25, 2022, https://www.thevintagenews.com/2022/11/25/bizarre-facts-errol-flynn/ last accessed June 15, 2025.

Elicia, Jane. "Single Father Households Do Vastly Better Than Single Mother—Here's the Real Reason Why." *Medium*, April 8, 2023. https://medium.com/the-knowledge-of-freedom/single-father-households-do-vastly-better-than-single-mother-heres-the-real-reason-why-8a7fd7c5611d, last accessed May 17, 2025.

Eliot, T.S.

Elkind, David. "Freud, Jung, and the Collective Unconscious." *New York Times*, Oct 4, 1970. https://www.nytimes.com/1970/10/04/archives/freud-jung-and-the-collective-unconscious-jungs-has-been-the-only.html, Jun 18, 2025.

"Epitaph for Generation X: appreciation – Kurt Cobain." *The Guardian* [London, England], 12 Apr. 1994, p. 19. Gale In Context: U.S. History, link.gale.com/apps/doc/A170745038/UHIC?u=umuser&sid=bookmark-UHIC&xid=00932555. Accessed 24 Jan. 2025.

Ernulf, K.E., Innala, S.M. Sexual bondage: A review and unobtrusive investigation. *Arch Sex Behav* 24, 631–654 (1995). https://doi.org/10.1007/BF01542185

"The Extremist's Medicine Cabinet: A Guide to Online 'Pills'." *The Anti-Defamation League*, Nov 6, 2019, https://www.adl.org/resources/article/extremist-medicine-cabinet-guide-online-pills, last accessed Dec 1, 2024.

Falvo, Joseph. "The Irony of Deception in Malebolge: Inferno XXI-XXII" a lecture delivered at the University of Virginia, March 28, 1988. www.brown.edu/Departments/Italian_Studies/LD/numbers/02/falvo.html. Accessed 22 Dec, 2024.

Fink, Josh. "Fun Facts About the General E. Lee." *Herbertstandc.com*, Sept 25, 2020. https://www.hebertstandc.com/fun-facts-about-the-general-lee/#:~:text=The%20General%20Lee%20was%20a,from%20the%20vehicle%20during%20filming, last accessed Jun 18, 2025.

"Five Ways the New Space Economy Can Improve Human Life on Earth." *MIT Professional Programs* https://professionalprograms.mit.edu/blog/technology/what-is-new-space-economy/, last accessed Jun 16, 2025.

Fleischer, Dave. "Superman." Fleisher Studios, 1941.

Foust, Rebecca. "Freedom in Form: Tricking Ourselves into Delight and Play." *Denver Quarterly Review*, Fall 2022, https://www.dmqreview.com/foustfall22, last accessed May 17, 2025.

Frank, Rebecca Morgan. "Standing in One Place to Move: The Repeated-Line Sonnet." *An Anthology of Poems and Essays,* edited by Dora Malech and Laura Smith. Iowa City: University of Iowa Press, 2023.

Garelick, Rhonda. "When Did We Become So Obsessed with Being 'Symmetrical'?" *The New York Times*, August 23, 2022. https://www.nytimes.com/2022/08/23/style/is-your-face-symmetrical.html, last accessed May 17, 2025.

Gelernter, David, *Mirror Worlds: Or: The Day Software Puts the Universe in a Shoebox...How It Will Happen and What It Will Mean* (NY, 1991; online edn, Oxford Academic, 12 Nov. 2020), https://doi.org/10.1093/oso/9780195068122.001.0001, accessed 4 June 2025.

Goethel, Ellen. "Monkfish: 'The poor man's lobster' that's now a delicacy for the rich". *SeaCoastOnline.com*, Sept 2, 2022, https://www.seacoastonline.com/story/news/2022/09/02/monkfish-the-poor-mans-lobster-thats-now-delicacy-rich/7954043001/, last accessed 17 May 2025.

Gogola, Tom. "Generation why." *The Nation*, vol. 258, no. 17, 2 May 1994, p. 581. Gale In Context: Opposing Viewpoints, link.gale.com/apps/doc/A15203213/OVIC?u=umuser&sid=summon&xid=a25854c2. Accessed 24 Jan. 2025.

Goldsztajn, Iris. "10 Mind-Blowing Facts About Justin Timberlake's Sexy Back." *Cosmopolitan*, July 18, 2016. https://www.cosmopolitan.com/entertainment/music/a61376/justin-timberlake-sexyback-facts-trivia/, last accessed Jun 17, 2025.

Gordon, Mary. "Mysteriously Woman: A Feminist View of the Rosary." *The Furrow*, vol. 55, no. 5, 2004, pp. 259–72. JSTOR, http://www.jstor.org/stable/27664955, last accessed 15 May 2025.

Gresko, Brian. "Craft Therapy: A Profile of Melissa Febos." *Poets & Writers Magazine*, March/April 2021.

Grierson, Tim. "When Did Everyone Agree Keanu Reeves Was Actually Good at Acting?" *Mel Magazine,* 2022(?) https://melmagazine.com/en-us/story/young-keanu-reeves, last accessed Jun 18, 2025.

Griffiths, Jay. "The Fisher King: Sacrificing the oceans in pursuit of an unholy grail". *Orion*, November/December 2012. October 24, 2012, https://orionmagazine.org/article/the-fisher-king/, last accessed May 17, 2025.

Gross, D J. "The role of symmetry in fundamental physics." *Proceedings of the National Academy of Sciences of the United States of America* vol. 93,25 (1996): 14256-9. doi:10.1073/pnas.93.25.14256

Grossi, Joseph. "Dante, Peacemaker of the Lunigiana." *Dante Studies*, vol. 139, 2021, p. 58-93. Project MUSE, https://dx.doi.org/10.1353/das.2021.0002.

"Grunge icon and reluctant voice of a generation." *The Independent* [London, England], 14 Apr. 2019, p 37. Gale In Context: Opposing Viewpoints, link.gal.com/apps/doc/A582237270/OVIC?u+umuser&sid=bookmark-OVIC&xid=2c035840. Accessed 24 Jan. 2025.

Harmetz, Aljean. "Doris Day, Movie Star Who Charmed America Dies at 97." *New York Times*, May 13, 2019. https://www.nytimes.com/2019/05/13/obituaries/doris-day-death.html, last accessed, Jun 18, 2025.

Harris, Aisha. "The Central Park Five: 'We Were Just Baby Boys'". *New York Times*, May 30 2019. https://www.nytimes.com/2019/05/30/arts/television/when-they-see-us.html

"Helium's Role for Semiconductor Production in the Digital Age." *Rockymountainair.com*, https://rockymountainair.com/blog/heliums-role-for-semiconductor-production-in-the-digital-age/, last accessed, June 15, 2025.

Heller, Jason. "How 'Ashes to Ashes' Put the First Act of David Bowie's Career to Rest" *The Record, NPR*, Oct 6 2017, https://www.npr.org/sections/therecord/2017/10/06/555850186/how-ashes-to-ashes-put-the-first-act-of-david-bowies-career-to-rest, last accessed May 18, 2025.

"The History of Sing Sing Prison, by the Half Moon Press." *Hudsonriver.com* May 2000. https://web.archive.org/web/20010124104200/http:/www.hudsonriver.com/halfmoonpress/stories/0500sing.htm, last accessed May 17, 2025.

Holt, Macon. "Hyperstitional Theory-Fiction." *Full Stop Quarterly,* Oct 21, 2020, https://www.full-stop.net/2020/10/21/features/essays/macon-holt/hyperstitional-theory-fiction/, last accessed May 18, 2025.

Honderich, Holly. "How Mike Jeffries used shirtless models to sell Abercrombie." *BBC.com*, October 2, 2023. https://www.bbc.com/news/world-us-canada-66957726

Hooten, Christopher. "Photo developers share the weirdest things they've seen on customers cameras." *The Independent,* August 11, 2015. https://www.the-independent.com/arts-entertainment/tv/news/photo-developers-share-the-weirdest-thing-they-ve-seen-on-a-customer-s-camera-10449761.html, last accessed June 5, 2025.

Horwitz, Rainey. "Vaginal Speculum (after 1800)." *Arizona State University Embryo Project Encyclopedia*, Oct 31, 2019, https://embryo.asu.edu/pages/vaginal-speculum-after-1800

Huang-Tiller, Gillian. "E. E. Cummings: The Iconic Metasonnet and the Cultural Emblem of the American "i/Eye." *The American Sonnet: An Anthology of Poems and Essays*, edited by Dora Malech and Laura Smith. Iowa City: University of Iowa Press, 2023.

"Hubble Space Telescope." Science.*NASA.gov*, https://science.nasa.gov/mission/hubble/, last accessed Jun 18, 2025.

Hughes, Brian and Cynthia Miller-Idriss. "Uniting for Total Collapse: The January 6 Boost to Accelerationism." *CTC Sentinel* April/May 2021. Combating Terrorism Center at West Point: https://ctc.westpoint.edu/uniting-for-total-collapse-the-january-6-boost-to-accelerationism/, last accessed May 17, 2025.

Hunt, Elle. "The peacock's tail: How Darwin arrived at his theory of sexual selection." *The Guardian*, May 1n, 2017. https://www.theguardian.com/science/2017/may/19/a-peacocks-tail-how-darwin-arrived-at-his-theory-of-sexual-selection, last accessed Jun 18, 2025.

Jackson, Lauren Michele. "The Invention of the Male Gaze." *The New Yorker*, July 14, 2023.

Jaffe, Larry. "The Gender Politics of David Bowie." *Women Across Frontiers*, Feb 29, 2016.   https://wafmag.org/2016/02/gender-politics-david-bowie/, last accessed Jun 16, 2025.

Jane, Elicia. "Single Father Households Do Vastly Better Than Single Mother Households—Here's the Real Reason Why." *Medium.com* https://medium.com/the-knowledge-of-freedom/single-father-households-do-vastly-better-than-single-mother-heres-the-real-reason-why-8a7fd7c5611d Last accessed June 5, 2025.

Javadiszadeh, Kamran. "Can Rilke Change Your Life?". *The New Yorker*, May 26, 2021, https://www.newyorker.com/books/under-review/can-rilke-change-your-life, accessed 10 Dec, 2024.

Jerome Robbins Dance Division, The New York Public Library. "The search for Nijinsky's Rite of spring" *The New York Public Library Digital Collections*. 1989. https://digitalcollections.nypl.org/items/d3a1b050-ef93-0133-\fff5-60f81dd2b63c

Jones, Andrew Zimmerman and Alessandro Sfondrini. "String Theory for Dummies Cheat Sheet." *Dummies.com*, June 30, 2022, https://www.dummies.com/article/academics-the-arts/science/physics/string-theory-for-dummies-cheat-sheet-209405/

Kantor, Jodi. "Tarantino on Weinstein: 'I Knew Enough to Do More than I Did.'" *The New York Times*, Oct 19, 2017. https://www.nytimes.com/2017/10/19/movies/tarantino-weinstein.html, last accessed Jun 18, 2025.

Katz, Jonathan Ned and Tavia Nyong'o. "The 'Man-Monster'" *OutHistory*, first published in 2011. https://outhistory.org/exhibits/show/sewally-jones/man-monster, last accessed 11 Jan. 2025.

Kaye, Danielle. "Former Abercrombie C.E.O. Is Charged With Running Sex-Trafficking Ring" *The New York Times*, Oct 22, 2024. https://www.nytimes.com/2024/10/22/business/mike-jeffries-arrested-sex-trafficking-abercrombie.html

Kelly, Kevin. "AR Will Spark the Next Big Tech Platform—Call it Mirrorworld." *Wired Magazine*, Feb 12 2019, https://www.wired.com/story/mirrorworld-ar-next-big-tech-platform/, last accessed May 17, 2025.

Kertscher, Tom. "Many More Criminal Indictments Under Trump, Reagan, and Nixon than under Obama, Clinton and Carter." *Politifact.com*, Jan 9, 2020. https://www.politifact.com/factchecks/2020/jan/09/facebook-posts/many-more-criminal-indictments-under-trump-reagan-/, last accessed Jun 18, 2025.

Kilgannon, Corey. "Man convicted in 1989 Killing of Black Teen Will Present New Evidence." *The New York Times*, Nov 14, 2024. https://www.nytimes.com/2024/11/14/nyregion/yusuf-hawkins-murder-hearing.html#:~:text=It%20was%20one%20of%20the,off%20months%20of%20furious%20protests.

Kneitel, Seymor. "The Underground World" based on *Superman* by Jerry Siegel and Joe Shuster. Famous Studios, 1943

Kotula, Bonnie Crawford. "This Is Why I'm Single." *Bmoreart.com*, March 7, 2016. https://bmoreart.com/2016/03/thisiswhyimsingle.html, last accessed Jun 15, 2025.

Kurgan, Laura et al. "Homophily: The Urban History of an Algorythm." *E-flux Architecture*, October 2019, https://www.e-flux.com/architecture/are-friends-electric/289193/homophily-the-urban-history-of-an-algorithm/, last accessed May 17, 2025.

Kuta, Sarah. "Chimpanzees Could Never Type the Complete Works of Shakespeare, Study Finds." *The Smithsonian Magazine*, Nov 8, 2024. https://www.smithsonianmag.com/smart-news/chimpanzees-could-never-randomly-type-the-complete-works-of-shakespeare-study-finds-180985394/, last accessed Jun 18, 2025.

Kuttner, Robert. "Tales from the Crypt." *The American Prospect: Ideas, Politics & Power*, November 1, 2024. https://prospect.org/blogs-and-newsletters/tap/2024-11-01-tales-from-the-crypt/

Kyriazis, Stefan. "Doris Day 100: Star had an affair with 'oversexed' Ronald Reagan 'He wanted to Propose.'" *Express.com*, April 7, 2022. https://www.express.co.uk/entertainment/films/1592860/Doris-Day-100-birthday-Hollywood-affair-with-Ronald-Reagan-wife, last accessed Jun 18, 2025.

Laing, Olivia. "Joseph Cornell: how the reclusive artist conquered the art world—from his mum's basement." *The Guardian*, July 25, 2015, Last accessed Jan 1, 2025.

Lamont, Tom. "'I want to get as much done as I can': Keanu Reeves on poetry, grief, and making the most of every minute." *The Guardian*, Dec 19, 2021. https://www.theguardian.com/film/2021/dec/19/i-want-to-get-as-much-done-as-i-can-keanu-reeves-on-poetry-and-grief, last accessed Jun 18, 2025.

Leca, Diana. "Kay Ryan's Miniature Sonnets." *An Anthology of Poems and Essays*, edited by Dora Malech and Laura Smith. Iowa City: University of Iowa Press, 2023.

Leith, Sam. "'I wanted to do pulpy, hyper-violent action': Keanu Reeves on his novel with China Miéville and the afterlife of The Matrix." *The Guardian*, July 20, 2024. https://www.theguardian.com/books/article/2024/jul/20/i-wanted-to-do-pulpy-hyper-violent-action-keanu-reeves-on-his-novel-with-china-mieville-and-the-afterlife-of-the-matrix, last accessed May 17, 2025.

Lepore, Jill. "The Surprising Origins of Wonder Woman." *The Smithsonian Magazine*, October 2014. https://www.smithsonianmag.com/arts-culture/origin-story-wonder-woman-180952710/#:~:text=Wonder%20Woman%20made%20her%20debut,%2Dhigh%2C%20red%20leather%20boots.

Lerher, Bryan. "A Rosary for the Anthropocene." *BryanLeher.com*, Aug 29, 2019. https://www.bryanlehrer.com/entries/anthrosary/, last accessed Jun 18, 2025.

Leslie, Kreiner W. "Mae West, She Done Him Wrong, and the Code." *Americana : The Journal of American Popular Culture, 1900 to Present*, vol. 16, no. 2, 2017. *ProQuest*, https://proxy.lib.umich.edu/login?url=https://www.proquest.com/scholarly-journals/mae-west-she-done-him-wrong-code/docview/2062663417/se-2.

Levy, Lisa. "Dwight MacDonald Takes a Machete to the Culture of the 1950s." *Medium.com*, Oct 1, 2011. https://medium.com/dead-critics/dwight-macdonald-takes-a-machete-to-the-culture-of-the-1950s-8b1dedf80521, last accessed Jun 18, 2025.

Lim, Dennis. " 'Fight Club' Fight Goes On." *The New York Times*, Nov 6, 2009, https://www.nytimes.com/2009/11/08/movies/homevideo/08lim.html, last accessed Dec 1, 2024.

Licitra Rosa, Carmelo et al. "From the Imaginary to Theory of the Gaze in Lacan." *Frontiers in psychology* vol. 12 578277. 30 Mar. 2021, doi:10.3389/fpsyg.2021.578277

Locklear, Mallory. "5 Icky Animal Odors that are Prized by Perfumers." *Discover Magazine*, Oct 12, 2014, updated May 17, 2020. https://www.discovermagazine.com/mind/5-icky-animal-odors-that-are-prized-by-perfumers, last accessed Jun 18, 2025.

"The Lonely Hearts Killers are executed." *History*. https://www.history.com/this-day-in-history/the-lonely-hearts-killers-are-executed accessed Jan. 11, 2025.

Lott, Eric. "All the King's Men: Elvis Impersonators and White Working-Class Masculinity." *Race and the Subject of Masculinities*, ed by Harilaos Stecopoulos and Michael Uebel, Duke University Press, 1997. *ProQuest Ebook Central*, http://ebookcentral.proquest.com/lib/umichigan/detail.action?docID=3008126

Lowder, Stephanie. "The History of Mirror: Through a Glass Darkly." *Bienenstock Furniture Library*, https://www.furniturelibrary.com/mirror-glass-darkly/ last accessed June5, 2025.

Lowry, Rich. "Our hero, heroin." *National Review*, vol. 48, no. 20, 28 Oct. 1996, pp. 75+. *Gale In Context: U.S. History*, link.gale.com/apps/doc/A18819153/UHIC?u=umuser&sid=summon&xid=ff7ff96e. Accessed 24 Jan. 2025.

Lucks, Daniel. "How Ronald Reagan's Time at General Electric Pushed Him to Conservatism." *LitHub.com*, Aug 25, 2020. https://lithub.com/how-ronald-reagans-time-at-general-electric-pushed-him-to-conservatism/, last accessed Jun 18, 2025.

MacDonald, Dwight. "A Theory of Mass Culture." *Diogenes*, No 3, Summer 1953, pp1-17. https://doi.org/10.1177/039219215300100301, last accessed May 17, 2025.

—. *"Masscult and Midcult." Essays* Against the American Grain. New York: Random House, 1965, pp 3-41.

Mack, Eric. "There are 10,000 Active Satellites in Orbit. Most of Them Belong to Elon Musk." *Forbes*, Jul 19, 2024. https://www.forbes.com/sites/ericmack/2024/07/19/theres-now-10000-active-satellites-in-orbit-most-belong-to-elon-musk/, last accessed Jun 16, 2025.

Macnab, Geoffry. "Incels, Trump and neo-Nazis: why do men keep misunderstanding *Fight Club*?" *The Independent*, February 16, 2024, https://www.the-independent.com/arts-entertainment/films/features/fight-club-men-masculinity-brad-pitt-trump-b2496587.html, last accessed Dec 1, 2014.

Manuel, Jessica Schad. "Hyperreality: Tracing the Evolution with Jean Baudrillard." https://bookoblivion.com/2019/02/26/hyperreality/, last accessed Jun 16, 2025.

Marche, Stephen. "Swallowing the Red Pill: a journey to the heart of modern misogyny." *The Guardian*, April 14, 2016, https://www.theguardian.com/technology/2016/apr/14/the-red-pill-reddit-modern-misogyny-manosphere-men, last accessed Dec 1, 2024.

—. "The Unexamined Brutality of the Male Libido." *The New York Times*, Nov 25, 2017. https://www.nytimes.com/2017/11/25/opinion/sunday/harassment-men-libido-masculinity.html, last accessed Jun 18, 2025.

Martino, Ariel. " 'From the you to me': Interpersonal Exchange in Margaret Walker's *For My People* Sonnet Sequence." The American Sonnet: An Anthology of Poems and Essays, edited by Dora Malech and Laura Smith. Iowa City: University of Iowa Press, 2023.

McDaniel, Spencer. "Did the Ancient Greeks and Romans Practice BDSM?" *TalesofTimesForgotten.com*, Sept 19, 2021. https://talesoftimesforgotten.com/2021/09/19/did-the-ancient-greeks-and-romans-practice-bdsm/, last accessed Jun 18, 2025.

McNamee, David. "When did sampling become so non-threatening?" *The Guardian*, Feb 16, 2008, https://www.theguardian.com/music/musicblog/2008/feb/16/whendidsamplingbecamesono, last accessed May 17, 2025.

Meiers, Allison C. "15 Old Fashioned Ways of Keeping Time." *Mental Floss*, Nov 14, 2016. https://www.mentalfloss.com/article/88484/15-old-fashioned-ways-keeping-time, last accessed, Jun 16, 2025.

"Michael Faraday." Science History Institute. https://www.sciencehistory.org/education/scientific-biographies/michael-faraday/ Last accessed June 5, 2025.

Mickelson, Nate. "Sonnets and/as Boxes: Ken Taylor, Joseph Cornell, and the New Lyric Studies." *The American Sonnet: An Anthology of Poems and Essays*, edited by Dora Malech and Laura Smith. Iowa City: University of Iowa Press, 2023.

"Modern Wheat Issues." *GrainstormHeritageBaking.com*, https://grainstorm.com/pages/modern-wheat?srsltid=AfmBOoqAIEbBp_7HcTGd9YlweHwz9HI9idI00OInxIGzSLaz7JWLFHlz, late accessed Jun 16, 2024.

Montgomery, Blake. "TechScape: Elon Musk's global political goals." *The Guardian*, 22 Oct. 2024. https://www.theguardian.com/global/2024/oct/21/elon-musk-global-political-goals, last accessed May 17, 2025.

Moore, Lisa L. "The Sonnet Is Not a Luxury." *An Anthology of Poems and Essays*, edited by Dora Malech and Laura Smith. Iowa City: University of Iowa Press, 2023.

Moore, Lucinda. "Showtime at the Apollo." *Smithsonianmag.com*, November 2010. https://www.smithsonianmag.com/arts-culture/show-time-at-the-apollo-64658902/, last accessed, Jun 15, 2025.

Moser, Maurice. "Handcuffs" *Policehistory.com* Irish Police History, first published in The Strand, Jan 1894. https://www.policehistory.com/handcuffs.htm#:~:text=Having%20established%20this%20remote%20and,been%20held%20ready%20in%20confident

Munoz, Christopher. "'Space is the Wild West': Expert Says International Action Needed to Avoid Growing Debris Problem." *Syracruse News University*, Oct 17, 2023. https://news.syr.edu/blog/2023/10/17/space-is-the-wild-west-expert-says-international-action-needed-to-address-growing-space-debris-problem/, Jun 17, 2025.

Nadelson, Reggie. "The Theatre Where Ella Fitzgerald Got Her Start." *The New York Times Style Magazine*, June 25, 2020. https://www.nytimes.com/2020/06/25/t-magazine/harlem-apollo-theater-ella-fitzgerald.html

Negussie, Tesfeye. "Brooklyn man convicted of 1989 murder of Yusuf Hawkins will try to prove his innocence." *Abcnews.com*, Nov 21, 2024, https://abcnews.go.com/US/brooklyn-man-convicted-1989-murder-yusuf-hawkins-prove/story?id=115875493

"NewSpace: The Emerging Commercial Space Industry, ISU MSS 2017." *NASA.gov*, Feb 22, 2017, https://ntrs.nasa.gov/citations/20170001766, last accessed May 17, 2025.

Nodelman, Perry. "Neverland and Our Land: Imagining Indigenous Peoples in the World of Peter Pan" *PerryNodelman.com*, 2020. https://perrynodelman.com/neverland-and-our-land/, last accessed June 15, 2025.

Nureyev dancing Apollo via *youtube.com*.

Oswald, Flora et al. "I'll Show You Mine so You'll Show Me Yours: Motivations and Personality Variables in Photographic Exhibitionism." *The Journal of Sex Research*, 57(5), 597-609, 2020, https://www.tandfonline.com/doi/full/10.1080/00224499.2019.1639036, last accessed May 17, 2025.

Palmer, Sherry. "Fatherless Single Mother Home Statistics." *Fixfamilycourts.com*. March 20, 2017, modified July 19, 2023, https://www.fixfamilycourts.com/divorce-child-custody-blog/single-mother-home-statistics/ Last accessed June 5, 2025.

Panneton, Daniel. "How Extremist Gun Culture is Trying to Co-opt the Rosary." *The Atlantic*, Aug 14, 2022.

"Panspermia." *ScienceDirect.com*. https://www.sciencedirect.com/topics/physics-and-astronomy/panspermia#:~:text=Panspermia%20is%20the%20concept%20that,or%20even%20advanced%20extraterrestrial%20beings. Last accessed, Jun 18, 2025.

Phelan, Kevin. "The Joker's 'Boner' Comic is Crazier Than You Think." *ScreenRant.com*, May 9, 2020. https://screenrant.com/joker-boner-comic-meme/, last accessed Jun 18, 2025.

Plum, Hilary. *Hole Studies*. Portland: Fonograf Editions, 2022

Pollock, Sean. "Is Donnie Darko a Tale for Our Times?" October 21, 2024. https://www.pollocksean.com/blog/is-donnie-darko-a-tale-for-our-times. Accessed 26 January 2025.

Popova, Maria. "Gertrude Stein on Writing and Belonging." *The Marginalian.org*. https://www.themarginalian.org/2021/03/30/gertrude-stein-country/, last accessed Jun 18, 2025.

Porter, Katherine. "Dominique Pelicot and 50 Others Guilty in Rape Trial That Shook France." *The New York Times*, Dec 19, 2024, updated May 9, 2025. https://www.nytimes.com/live/2024/12/19/world/france-rape-verdict-pelicot?campaign_id=60&emc=edit_na_20241219&instance_id=142649&nl=breaking-news®i_id=90015591&segment_id=186126&user_id=5ea76af29fbe4f348dcaa602bdde2aeb, last accessed Jun 18, 2025.

Potts, Kevin. "A Decade of Noise and Nihilism." *Medium.com*, March 1, 2016. https://medium.com/9-for-the-90s/a-decade-of-noise-and-nihilism-c62ef56b8034

"Portrait of an unknowable artist; Remembering Kurt Cobain as a sweetly childlike, achingly opaque creative force." *Spectator* [Hamilton, Ontario], 5 Apr. 2019, p. GA. *Gale in Context: Opposing Viewpoints*, link.gale.com/apps/doc/A581310547/OVIC?u=umuser&sid=bookmark-OVIC&xid=ed1528d9, accessed Jan. 24, 2025.

Prodanovich, Todd. "Now's the Time for Surfers to Prove We Really Are Anti-Establishment." *Surfer*, Jul 18, 2024. https://www.surfer.com/news/opinion-surfing-and-racial-justice-counterculture, last accessed Jun 16, 2025.

Pruitt, Sarah. "When Sears Sold Everything from Houses to Hubcaps." *History.com*, Oct 16, 2018, updated May 25, 2025. https://www.history.com/articles/sears-catalog-houses-hubcaps, last accessed, Jun 18, 2025.

Raftery, Brian. "How The Matrix Built a Bullet-Proof Legacy." *Wired.com*, Mar 29, 2019. https://www.wired.com/story/the-matrix-legacy-book-excerpt/, last accessed Jun 18, 2025.

Regan, Stephen. "Broken Hearts and Broken Homes: The Desolation of the American Sonnet." *An Anthology of Poems and Essays*, edited by Dora Malech and Laura Smith. Iowa City: University of Iowa Press, 2023.

Rilke, Rainer Maria.

Robbins, Ira. "When pop music's fascination with Nazis went way over the line." *Forward*, Jan 31, 2022. https://forward.com/culture/music/481040/punk-nazi-symbols-third-reich-sex-pistols-joy-division-damned-dead/ Last accessed, June 5, 2025.

Rodgers, Daniel. "Soft porn, white supremacy, and Epstein: Abercrombie & Fitch's sordid past." *Dazeddigital.com*, April 14, 2022, https://www.dazeddigital.com/fashion/article/55905/1/abercrombie-fitch-netflix-documentary-sexual-exploitation-racism-bruce-weber, last accessed June 5, 2025.

Romano, Aja. "Reddit's TheRedPill, notorious for its misogyny, was founded by a New Hampshire state legislator." *Vox*, Apr 28, 2017, https://www.vox.com/culture/2017/4/28/15434770/red-pill-founded-by-robert-fisher-new-hampshire, last accessed May 17, 2025.

Rosa, Carmelo Licitra et al. "From the Imaginary to Theory of the Gaze in Lacan." *Frontiers in Psychology*, 20 Mar. 2021, https://www.frontiersin.org/journals/psychology/articles/10.3389/fpsyg.2021.578277/full, last accessed Dec. 1, 2025.

Rose, Steve. "The sad, stupid rise of the sigma male: how toxic masculinity took over social media." *The Guardian*, June 12, 2024, https://www.theguardian.com/society/article/2024/jun/12/the-sad-stupid-rise-of-the-sigma-male-how-toxic-masculinity-took-over-social-media, last accessed May 17, 2025.

—. "Who doesn't think they're an outsider? David Fincher on hitmen, 'incels' and spiderman's 'dumb' origin story." *The Guardian*, Oct 27, 2023, https://www.theguardian.com/film/2023/oct/27/david-fincher-on-hitmen-incels-and-spider-mans-dumb-origin-story, accessed Nov. 23, 2024.

Sassatelli, Rebecca. "Interview with Laura Mulvey: Gender, Gaze & Technology in Film Culture" *Theory, Culture & Society*, 2011 (SAGE, Los Angeles, London, New Delhi, and Singapore), Vol. 28(5): p. 123-143. https://doi.org/10.1177/0263276411398278, last accessed 31 Dec, 2024.

Satariano, Adam and Roser Toll Pifarré. "An Algorithm Told Police She Was Safe. Then Her Husband Killed Her." *The New York Times*, July 18, 2024, https://www.nytimes.com/interactive/2024/07/18/technology/spain-domestic-violence-viogen-algorithm.html?algo=combo_clicks_decay_6_lda_unique_80_diversified&block=3&campaign_id=142&emc=edit_fory_20240720&fellback=false&imp_id=121607687509615&instance_id=129327&nl=for-you&nlid=90015591&pool=channel-replacement-ls&rank=1®i_id=90015591&req_id=5559714229820917&segment_id=172715&surface=for-you-email-channelless&te=1&user_id=5ea76af29fbe4f348dcaa602bdde2aeb&variant=0_channel_translated_pool_popularity_pers

Saunders, Fr. William. "The History of the Rosary." *EWTM.com*, first published Oct 6, 1994 in *Arlington Catholic Herald*. https://www.ewtn.com/catholicism/library/history-of-the-rosary-1142, last accessed Jun 18, 2025.

Scarry, Elain. *The Body in Pain*. Oxford University Press, 1985.

Schambelan, Elizabeth. "League of Men: Suddenly this seducer appears." *N+1 Magazine*, Issue 28, Spring 2017.

"Sears Catalog, A History." *Searsarchives.com*, http://www.searsarchives.com/catalogs/history.htm, last accessed Nov 1, 2024.

Segal, Corinne. "David Bowie Made Androgyny Cool and It Was about Time." *PBSNews.com*, Jan 11, 2016. https://www.pbs.org/newshour/arts/david-bowie-made-androgyny-cool-and-it-was-about-time, last accessed Jun 18, 2025.

Semley, John & Edward Millar. "Influencer Society and Its Future: Swallow the Ted pill on Unabomber stan TikTok". *The Baffler*. September 27, 2021. https://thebaffler.com/latest/influencer-society-and-its-future-semley-millar

Shakespeare, William. All, esp, *Hamlet* & *A Midsummer Night's Dream*. *Opensourceshakespeare. com* & elsewhere, eg: https://www.opensourceshakespeare.org/views/plays/play_view.php?WorkID=midsummer&Act=3&Scene=1&Scope=scene, last accessed Jun 18, 2025.

Sharpe, William Chapman. "What's Going On with the Shadows: A Visual Arts Timeline." *Oxford University Press, OUPblog.com*, Nov 9, 2017. https://blog.oup.com/2017/11/shadows-visual-arts-timeline/, last accessed Jun 16, 2025.

Shaw, Debra Benita. "The Way Home: Space Migration and Disorientation." *new formations: a journal of culture/theory/ politics,* vol. 107, 2022, p. 118-138. Project MUSE, https://muse.jhu.edu/article/881496, last accessed May 18, 2025.

Shaw, Jonathan and Jennifer Carling. "Eye on the Universe." *Harvard Magazine*, July-Aug 2008, updated Sept 8, 2017. https://www.harvardmagazine.com/2008/07/eye-on-the-universe-html, last accessed Jun 18, 2025.

Simula, Brandy L., 'Introduction: Understanding BDSM', in Brandy Simula, Robin Bauer, and Liam Wignall (eds), *The Power of BDSM: Play, Communities, and Consent in the 21st Century* (New York, 2023; online edn, Oxford Academic, 18 May 2023), https://doi.org/10.1093/oso/9780197658598.003.0001, accessed 11 Dec 2024.

Singh, Akanksha. "From ancient Egypt to Taylor Swift: The historic roots of 'the cat lady.'" *BBC*, Aug 2024, first published 2022, https://www.bbc.com/culture/article/20220225-the-batman-the-ancient-roots-of-catwoman, last accessed May 18, 2025.

Sommerlad, Joe. "OJ Simpson Got into a White Bronco 30 Years Ago Today." *The Independent*, Jun 17, 2024. https://www.independent.co.uk/news/world/americas/oj-simpson-bronco-chase-anniversary-b2564077.html, last accessed Jun 18, 2025.

Sontag, Susan. *On Photography*. New York: Farrar, Straus & Giroux, 1973.

Spahr, Juliana M. "Postmodernism, Readers, and Theresa Hak Kyung Cha's 'Dictee.'" *College Literature*, vol. 23, no. 3, 1996, pp. 23–43. JSTOR, http://www.jstor.org/stable/25112272. Accessed 8 June 2025.

Sparks, Brandon et al. "Involuntary Celibacy: A Review of Incel Ideology and Experiences with Dating, Rejection, and Associated Mental Health and Emotional Sequelae." *National Institute of Medicine*, Nov 17, 2022, https://pmc.ncbi.nlm.nih.gov/articles/PMC9780135/, last accessed Jan 3, 2025.

Spencer, Russ. "Sherman Alexie on Writing and Kurt Cobain." *Utne Reader*, October 30, 2007, https://www.utne.com/arts/shermans-march/, last accessed May 17, 2025.

Starr, Marlo. "Restaging the American "Freakshow" in *Olio*: Tyehimba Jess's Syncopated Sonnets." *An Anthology of Poems and Essays*, edited by Dora Malech and Laura Smith. Iowa City: University of Iowa Press, 2023.

Stevens, Aaron. "Nihilistic Nirvana" April 23, 1997. https://people.bu.edu/azs/portfolio/nirvana.html, last accessed Jun 18, 2025.

Swanson, Barrett. "The Anxiety of Influencers: Educating the Tik Tok generation." *Harper's Magazine*, September 2020.

Taylor, Ariette and Rebe. "Nijinski misrepresented." *Dance Australia*, July 21, 2023, https://www.danceaustralia.com.au/artists/nijinsky-misrepresented#comments, last accessed June 5, 2025.

Taylor, Tess. "But Could a Dream: Form and Freedom in Gwendolyn Brooks's Domestic Sonnets." *An Anthology of Poems and Essays*, edited by Dora Malech and Laura Smith. Iowa City: University of Iowa Press, 2023.

Theune, Michael. "Strange Voltas." An Anthology of Poems and Essays, edited by Dora Malech and Laura Smith. Iowa City: University of Iowa Press, 2023.

Tinline, Phil. "*Fight Club* in the manosphere." *The New Statesman*, Oct 9, 2024, https://www.newstatesman.com/culture/film/2024/10/fight-club-in-the-manosphere, last accessed May 17, 2025.

Tobias, Scott. "The New Cult Canon: *Donnie Darko*." *AVClub.com*, Feb 22, 2008. https://www.avclub.com/the-new-cult-canon-donnie-darko-1798213361, last accessed Jun 18, 2025.

Traub, Alex. "Ted Kaczynski, 'Unabomber' Who Attacked Modern Life, Dies at 81." *The New York Times*, Jun 10, 2023. https://www.nytimes.com/2023/06/10/us/ted-kaczynski-dead.html last accessed, Jun 16, 2025.

"T.S. Eliot, the Poet, is Dead in London at 76." *The New York Times*, Tuesday, January 5, 1965, https://archive.nytimes.com/www.nytimes.com/books/97/04/20/reviews/eliot-obit.html, last accessed Jan 1, 2025.

Turner, Christopher. "A Short History of the Shadow: An Interview with Victor Stoichita: from Plato's cave to Duchamp's widow." *Cabinet*, Issue 24, Shadows, Winter 2006-2007, https://www.cabinetmagazine.org/issues/24/turner_stoichita.php, last accessed May 17, 2025.

"The Ultimate Satellite Internet Showdown: Kuiper vs Starlink." *AnalyticsIndiaMag.Com*, Dec 20, 2023. https://analyticsindiamag.com/ai-features/the-ultimate-satellite-internet-showdown-kuiper-vs-starlink/, last accessed Jun 16, 2024.

"Understanding Andy Warhol's Shadow Paintings." *LVHArt.com*, Sept 7, 2020. https://lvhart.com/journal/understanding-andy-warhols-shadow-paintings/#:~:text=The%20canvases%2C%20which%20were%20primed,bright%20hues%20with%20cheerful%20excess, last accessed, Jun 16, 2025.

Venema, Vibeke. "Revenge of the Secretaries: The Protest Movement that Inspired the Film 9 to 5." *BBC*, Dec 10 2020, https://www.bbc.com/news/stories-55089013, last accessed, May 17, 2025.

Wade, Francesca. "Revisiting Diane Wakoski's "Complete Motorcycle Betrayal Poems." *Harvard Review Online*, May 3, 2024. https://www.harvardreview.org/content/revisiting-diane-wakoskis-complete-motorcycle-betrayal-poems/, last accessed, Jun 16, 2025.

Weinberg, Thomas S., 'Research in BDSM: 40 Years Along', in Brandy Simula, Robin Bauer, and Liam Wignall (eds), *The Power of BDSM: Play, Communities, and Consent in the 21st Century* (New York, 2023; online edn, Oxford Academic, 18 May 2023), https://doi.org/10.1093/oso/9780197658598.003.0002, accessed 4 June 2025.

Werner, Debra. "The Big Question: Is It Time to Regulate Space Flight." *Aerospace America*, Sept 1, 2024. https://aerospaceamerica.aiaa.org/features/the-big-question-is-it-time-to-regulate-commercial-human-spaceflight/, last accessed, Jun 16, 2025.

West-Knights, Imogen. "The Hunks are All Right." *Slate.com*, May 26, 2021. https://slate.com/human-interest/2021/05/abercrombie-fitch-hunks-shirtless-where-are-they-now.html, last accessed, Jun 18, 2025.

Wexler, Anna. "The Ethical Implications of Elon Musk's Unorthodox Approach to Medical Science." *STAT*, July 8, 2024, https://www.statnews.com/2024/07/08/neuralink-elon-musk-scientific-ethics-brain-computer-interface/, last accessed June 15, 2025.

"What Are Plankton?" *National Ocean Service. NOAA*. https://oceanservice.noaa.gov/facts/plankton.html#:~:text=The%20word%20%E2%80%9Cplankton%E2%80%9D%20comes%20from,for%20their%20entire%20life%20cycle. Last accessed June 5, 2025.

Wheeler, Lesley. "Partial Visibility: Short-Lined Sonnets." *An Anthology of Poems and Essays*, edited by Dora Malech and Laura Smith. Iowa City: University of Iowa Press, 2023.

Wilde, Oscar. *The Picture of Dorian Gray*. Penguin, 2003.

Williams, A. (2020). Black Memes Matter: #LivingWhileBlack With Becky and Karen. *Social Media + Society*, 6(4). https://doi.org/10.1177/2056305120981047 (Original work published 2020)

Wikipedia rabbit holes, partial:
Alvin and the Chipmunks, Annie Oakley, Apex predator, Aphantasia, Apollo, Apollo (disambiguation), Apollo Program, Apollo Theatre, Archaic Torso of Apollo, Aretha Franklin, Artemis program, Atlantasaurus, Auguste Rodin, Beaver, Beaver Cleaver, Billionaire Space Race, The Blue Marble, Bone Wars, Brainiac, Buddy Holly, Burlesque, Captain Ahab, Captain Hook, Cary Grant, Choose Your Own Adventure, Copernican revolution, Cosmological Principal, Cowboy, Cybernetics, Dante Alighieri, Dead Kennedys, Delivery Man, Dick in a Box, Dictee, *Doctor Faustus* (play), *Donnie Darko*, Edmund Burke, Edmond Hoyle, Elizabeth Taylor, Elvis Impersonator, Errol Flynn, Eternal return, Eva Marie Saint, Fannie Sperry Steele, Faraday cage, Film Noir, Fisher King, Flying Dutchman, The

Fool, The Fool (tarot card), Fortress of Solitude, Friedrich Nietzsche, Gaia hypothesis, Gaze, Gestalt psychology, George Michael, German Expressionism, Gertrude Stein, Gilded Age, Gold helmet, Guns N' Roses, Hays Code, Helium, Helios, Helmet, Hera, Heraldry, Heroin, History of the camera, History of HIV/AIDS, The Hollow Men, Holy Chalice, Holy Grail, Home on the Range, "Hotel California," Hudson River, Hyperreality, Incel, James Brown, Jean Baudrillard, Jerry Siegel, Jim Morrison, J. M. Barrie, Joe Shuster, Kaleidoscope, Kármán line, Kennedy Space Center, King Arthur, La Vita Nuova, *Leave It to Beaver*, Lewis Carroll, Limbo, *Limbo* (video game), Loser (Beck song),The Lost Boys, *The Lost Boys*, Lou Andreas-Salomé, *Love Is Blind* (TV series), *The NeverEnding Story,* Nomen dubium, Manic Pixie Dream Girl, Manosphere, Meme coin, Mirror symmetry (string theory), Missionary position, *Moby Dick*, MTV, Musk, Network science, Neverland, *New Poems* (Rilke), NewSpace, Object d'art, Oliver Wendell Holmes Jr., The Overview Effect, Outlaw country, Pal Joey (musical), Panspermia, Pareidolia, Paul Lazardsfeld, Peanut butter and jelly sandwich, Pequod, Pequod (*Moby Dick*), *Peter and Wendy*, Peter Pan, *Peter Pan*, Plankton, Plankton and Karen, *Point Break*, Private spaceflight, Punk rock, Rainer Maria Rilke, The Red Headed Stranger, The Revolution Will Not Be Televised, Rite of Spring, Robert K. Merton, Ronald Reagan and AIDS, Sampling (music), Scandals of Ronald Reagan administration, The Seduction of the Innocent, Self-transcendence, Sing Sing, Spaceship Earth, Sperm bank, Spoil tip, Sponge, SpongeBob SquarePants, Spontaneous Combustion, *Squid Game*, Stereoscope, Stevie Wonder, Still life, Superman, Sylvie and Bruno, Ted Kaczynski, Terraforming, Theodore Roosevelt, Thomas Henry Huxley, Timeline of private spaceflight, Tin foil hat, Tinker Bell, Tyrannosaurus, Vaslav Nijinsky, Virgil, Vox in Rama, *The Waste Land,* Whipcracking, White Rabbit (song), Willie Nelson, Wine-dark sea.

Wilkie, Benjamin. "Art and the Virgin Mary in early-modern Florence." *Medium*. https://medium.com/@bvwilkie/sacred-places-religion-and-meaning-in-the-art-music-and-architecture-of-florence-fa8e323dbe5c Accessed 21 Dec 2024.

Williams, A. (2020). Black Memes Matter: #LivingWhileBlack With Becky and Karen. *Social Media + Society*, 6(4). https://doi.org/10.1177/2056305120981047

Williams, Leoma. "What Animals Mate for Life." *BBC Wildlife*, February 14, 2025, https://www.discoverwildlife.com/animal-facts/animals-that-mate-for-life, accessed Feb 21, 2025.

Williamson, Jack. "Salvage in Space." *Project Gutenberg*, https://www.gutenberg.org/files/29283/29283-h/29283-h.htm, last accessed Jan 31, 2025.

Wimsatt, James I. "BEATRICE AS A FIGURE FOR MARY." *Traditio*, vol. 33, 1977, pp. 402–14. JSTOR, http://www.jstor.org/stable/27831035. Accessed 5 June 2025.

Wimsatt, William Upski. "My Generation." *Utne Reader*. Sept 1, 2002. https://www.utne.com/community/mygeneration/print/, accessed 24 Jan. 2025.

Wohan, David. "Not Releasing the Genie: On the Poetry of Stuff vs the Poetry of Knowledge." *The Writer's Chronicle*, May/Summer, 2014.

Wong, Julia Carrie. "The Year of Karen: How a Meme Changed the Way Americans Talked About Racism." *The Guardian*, Dec 17, 2020. https://www.theguardian.com/world/2020/dec/27/karen-race-white-women-black-americans-racism, last accessed, Jun 18, 2025.

Zielin, Lara. "Hey Siri, Are We Cool?" *LSA Magazine*, Spring 2024, https://lsa.umich.edu/lsa/news-events/lsa-magazine/spring-2024/hey-siri-are-we-cool.html, last accessed May 17, 2025.

ACKNOWLEDGMENTS

Sincere gratitude to the journals who featured earlier versions of this work, the sonnet-portrait pairs: in *Hunger Mountain*, OK Buddha, Let's Not Puck & On the Range; in *The Massachusetts Review*, OK Pan to the Heroine, OK Pack a Flashlight, OK Switch, OK Astronaut? OK Sans Allure; in *Pleiades*.....OK Wounded, Don't Look Down, Decorative Arts, OK Grovel, OK Angel Go Fish, Protagonist Rex, Woman Wonders.

Image Credit for gallery images of *Match/Enemy*: Brandon Webster (gallery down the wall shots) and Michael Matason (full gallery install stitch shot)

I would first and foremost like to thank Jennifer Sperry Steinorth for being persistent and taking great care with this project.

To DC Arts Studio mates especially Megan Maher, Leslie Goldman, Dafna Steinberg, and Jordan Wine whose conversations, encouragement, and shared laughter helped me through all the painting.

Thank you to Vermont Studio Center whose support allowed *Match/Enemy* to take its first steps of realization in 2014 and found flight into new realms in 2017.

To the supporters of each of those residencies including the former Corcoran College of Art Faculty Development Grant, kickstarter funders and campaign co-creators whose support was instrumental in this project's success.

To Dafna Steinberg and Jennifer Towner and again to Dafna Steinberg for pushing me through the process of #thisiswhyimsingle at Flashpoint Gallery in Washington, DC, where Match/Enemy premiered along with their work. To Liz Georges, who was prescient enough to know that I would need notes to live by later. Thank you to Jackie Steven, Kimiko Atkins, Jason Horowitz, Ian Jehle, Mark Casale and Rob Parrish for all of the support in getting *Match/Enemy* done. And thanks to Lois Baron for holding my hand and being my accountability buddy.

Jenny Walton

To Jenny Walton for your fierce, fastidious, expansive vision. For generous, ongoing conversations. Trust & patience. For permitting your work to appear here amid subsequent revolutions—

To Vermont Studio Center—the visionary founders, funders, caretakers, then, now, ongoing—

To the many who waded, splashed, swam, plumbed these troubled waters with me, who housed, fed, healed, shared meals, walks, funds, wisdom, courage, made me laugh, look again, argue, sing, wrote words on my behalf, on all of our behalf, stood shining—

Especially my husband— especially my sons— especially Melissa Fournier, Ellen Welker & Carrie Tebeau, who swallowed it whole...& Daisy Fried, Aaron Coleman, Charlotte Pence, Jenny Molberg, Dan O'Brien, Ananda Lima, Keetje Kuipers....especially Kurt & Laura Froese, Lee & Paul, Bill & Connie, Ellen & Roger Stone, Dane Slutzky & Sebastian Merrill, Fleda Brown & Jerry Beasley, Sarah Audsley, Rachel Trousdale, Michael Sharick, Leah Nieboer, Sally Schuiling & Addison Proctor, Patrick Stockwell, Lauren Carlson, Anne-Marie Oomen & David Early, Tim Tebeau, Shelley Whitaker, Zach Welker, Catherine Turnball & Jeff Wescott, Nathan McClain & J. J. Starr, Lesley Ann Finn, Jillian Hickok, Terry Blackhawk, Tommye Blount, Carrie Mar, Octavio Quintanilla, Rachel Brownson, Ryan Vine, Scott Kaukonen, Kate Murr, Kerrin McCadden, Jeremy Chamberlain & Natalie Bakopoulos, Jason Storms, Morris Collins, Steve Stern & Sabrina Jones, Christina Hodsden, Tyler Barton & Erin Dorney, Fay Dillof, Erin Murphy, Kwoya Maples, Alison Swan, Brecht Gander & Geogia & co, Keith Taylor, Teresa Scollon, Philip Metres, Dave Villaverde, Ross Gay, Amanda Peppe, Scott Beal, Jess Smith, Tom Reike, Zeynep & Jazz, Jack & Zach, Terry & Michelle, Steph & Brian, Pam & Sheryl, Petra Kuppers & Stephanie Heit, Jack & Lois Driscoll, Brant & Brian, Brad & Amanda Kik, Sarah McKinstry Brown, Carolyn Hembree, Nandi Comer, Tracy Zeman, Ro Skelton & Nomi Stone, Tracy Anderson, Lida Junghaus, Jennifer Metsker, Joseph Capista, Amanda Newell, Forrest Gander, Lara Egger, Sarah Anderson, Mitzi Rapkin, Jenny Robertson, Maurice Manning, Lauren Russell, Rodney Jones, Alan Williamson, Eleanor Wilner, Michael Mercurio, Pete Muñoz, Amanda & Brad Kik, Peter Gizzi, Chad Pastotnik, Matt Miller, Howard Hinze, Jerry Dennis, Sharon Randolf, Tim Wade, Maria-Eirini Panagiotidou, Megan Gillespie, Joel Turnipseed, Helen E. Mundler, A. Van Jordan, Brenda Hillman, Joseph Lozano, Francine Conley, Alfred Martin, Cindy & Rich Milock, Douglas Kearney, Karen Schubert, Jess Mesman, Karen Brennan, Samantha Deal, Jack & Julie Ridl, Sue Mell, Cynthia Quiñones, Misti Reynolds & Santiago Galvan, Lisa Huffaker, Meg Reynolds, Judy French, Miranda Ramírez, Thomas Lynch, Steven Leyva, Miriam Bird Greenberg, Kylie Gellatly, Elizabeth Hamilton, Chloe Martinez, Karla Van Vliet, Stephanie Burt, Shereen Vernon, Shannon Winston, Julie Babcock & David Ward, Jen Funk, Nikki Fragala Barnes, Iris Dunkle, Martha Rhodes, Gabrielle Calvocoressi, Avra Elliott, Susie Schlesinger, Scott Stubbs—

To the Beinecke folks, Community of Writers & all those making room, unlocking doors, occasioning safe the havens for conversation—

To my students, nimble seers, see also teachers—
To you, dear reader—
To TRP...especially J. Bruce Fuller—
& again to my husband, again to my sons—

my ongoing gratitude, my unrelenting love—

Jen Steinorth

ABOUT THE MAKERS

Jennifer Sperry Steinorth's books include *A Wake with Nine Shades*, a finalist for the Eric Hoffer Prize, & *Her Read, A Graphic Poem*, recipient of the Foreword Reviews Bronze Prize for Poetry & the Fred Whitehead Award from the Texas Institute of Letters. A poet, educator, interdisciplinary artist & scholar, she has received grants from Yale, Vermont Studio Center, the University of Michigan, Sewanee Writers' Conference, Community of Writers & the MFA for Writers at Warren Wilson College. She lectures at the University of Michigan, Ann Arbor & is writing a biography of American poet, C.D. Wright. Steinorth began her artistic life as a dancer, practicing & performing with the Houston Ballet, the School of the Pennsylvania Ballet & Interlochen Arts Academy. For fifteen years she was president & lead designer for a design-build construction company specializing in environmentally-responsible homes; their architectural work has been featured in *Fine Homebuilding* & other national journals. Their visual art has appeared at the Denos Museum, Woman Made Gallery in Chicago & elsewhere. She divides her time between Ann Arbor, Traverse City, Michigan & wherever else the winds carry her. She moonlights as an architectural designer & building consultant when the light falls just so.

Jenny Walton holds a BFA from Central Washington University & an MFA from American University (D.C. & Italy). Walton has shown nationally in New York, Miami, Boston & Seattle & internationally in Italy. She received an Artistic Fellowship from the D.C. Commission on the Arts & Humanities among other grants & residencies including Vermont Studio Center, Pyramid Atlantic Art Center & Hamilton Princess, Bermuda. She has been critically published in several catalogs & articles, & her work is held in several distinguished private & public collections. She lives & works in the Washington D.C. area.

CON[TEXT]UAL

Illuminating the intersection of visual art and text in the context of ideas that deepen our understanding of the contemporary world.

BOOKS IN THIS SERIES:

No. 003 – Jennifer Sperry Steinorth, paintings by Jenny Walton – *Boys Behind Glass*

No. 002 – Octavio Quintanilla – *The Book of Wounded Sparrows*

No. 001 – Jennifer Sperry Steinorth – *Her Read, a Graphic Poem*